PLEASE
STAND
BY

*A Prehistory
of
Television*

MICHAEL RITCHIE

THE OVERLOOK PRESS
WOODSTOCK • NEW YORK

Every reasonable effort has been made to contact copyright holders to secure permission to quote passages from works not in the public domain. Any omissions brought to the publisher's attention will be remedied in subsequent editions.

Grateful acknowledgment is hereby made for permission to reprint excerpts from the following works:

Television, Programming and Production, by Richard Hubbell; reprinted by permission of Holt, Rinehart & Co. Copyright 1945 by Richard Hubbell.

The New Yorker, Teleball article, May 27, 1939 issue; reprinted by permission of *The New Yorker*.

The New Yorker, Instead of Dirigibles, March 25, 1939 issue; reprinted by permission of *The New Yorker*.

Howdy and Me, by Buffalo Bob Smith and Donna McCrohan; reprinted by permission of Penguin Books USA Inc. Copyright 1990 by Buffalo Bob Smith and Donna McCrohan.

The Golden Age of Television, by Max Wilk; reprinted by permission of Moyer Bell. Copyright 1989 by Max Wilk.

The Great Clowns of American Television, by Karin Adir; reprinted by permission of McFarland & Company, Inc. Copyright 1988 by Karin Adir.

Super Spectator and the Electric Lilliputians, by William O. Johnson, Jr.; reprinted by permission of The Wallace Literary Agency. Copyright 1971 William O. Johnson, Jr.

First paperback published in the United States in 1995 by
The Overlook Press
Lewis Hollow Road
Woodstock, New York 12498

Copyright © 1994 Michael Ritchie

Library of Congress Cataloging-in-Publication Data

Ritchie, Michael, 1938–
Please stand by : A prehistory of television / Michael Ritchie
p. cm.
Includes bibliographical references and index.
1. Television—History. 2. Television—Production and direction—History. 3. Television programs—History. I. Title.

TK6637.R58 1994
791.45'09—dc20
Book design by Bernard Schleifer
ISBN: 0-87951-615-1

94–19089
CIP

135798642

*Dedicated with love
to my parents
PATTY and BENBOW*

CONTENTS

PROLOGUE

In the mid-1940s, Moss Hart was president of the New York Dramatists Guild. One afternoon he called together the guild's foremost members to discuss demands and standards for writers in the new medium of TV.

Many viewed the meeting as a joke. One veteran Broadway playwright described what he had seen already on TV as "amateurs playing at home movies."

Hart insisted the members address the problem at hand. "The time will come when stations will be telecasting twelve, perhaps fourteen hours a day," he told them.

A colleague interrupted, "I won't write for television, and I don't know anyone else who will."

Hart pushed on. "The day is coming when a two-hour play will be seen once by millions of people. The network will be looking for writers to supply them with thirty-six full plays—or seventy-two hour-long plays—each week."

The silence was deafening. Finally, the oldest writer in the guild slowly raised his hand.

"Where was it ever decreed that man had to have so much entertainment?"[1]

INTRODUCTION:
THE CHICKEN
OR THE EGG?

Television is something we take for granted. Like Kleenex. Or *TV Guide*. It has always been a part of our lives. But, while it is often as disposable as Kleenex, television certainly has a greater impact on our lives; and its early history, unlike that of facial tissue, is often funny and continually surprising. There's a cottage industry of books about the origins of Milton Berle and *The Texaco Star Theater*, Jackie Gleason and *The Honeymooners* —you name it. Anything remembered from old films and kinescopes ends up in book form on a shelf called "The Golden Age of TV."

This book is about what happened *before* scripts were saved, *before* scripts were even written. This is the "prehistory" of television, because no one has ever written comprehensively about TV programming before 1948, and the history of the haphazard experimental programming in the 1930s is unknown even to many of those who participated at that time. There are a number of good technical books about the development of the science behind television and the hardware of the sets and cameras themselves. But no one thought the earliest television programming was worth studying or preserving.

This book fits in a strange gap between "History" and "Nostalgia." It is "History" because what this book chronicles really happened, and the events it narrates shaped future TV history. But there is no place in this particular history for a larger social context outside of TV. It could be "Nostalgia," but few remember these early programs or their own participation in this "prehistoric" era. There can be no nostalgia for something that is not even remembered.

Through interviews with the original programmers, through oral histories in the Broadcast Pioneers' Library in Washington, D.C., and by connecting many separate biographical memoirs, this book has reconstructed a lost era. The difficult part of the research was that many of the people who participated in the early programs didn't remember they had been on TV before 1947. Dinah Shore and Eddie Albert, for example, had to be reminded with the pictures and diaries of a 1937 NBC soundman. Most pioneers have been interviewed so often about TV post-1948 that, when questioned about pre-1947, they skip haphazardly into post-1948 anecdotes.

It is not widely known that the technologies of early radio and TV were very close to each other. The first radio stations began broadcasting in 1920, and the first TV station was broadcasting in 1927. But most television experiments were conducted in secret, because the companies involved in TV already had a big investment in radio, and they were afraid that the boom in radio sales would be dampened as the public waited for "radio with pictures." Then the Great Depression ruined the sales of everything. After 1933, RCA could not have sold very many TV sets even if they had them. The nation's financial crisis put everything on hold, and during this television delay, radio became the major social influence of the 1930s and 1940s.

Television pioneers came in many different shapes and with different attitudes toward the new medium. Inventors like Philo Farnsworth and Allen DuMont were determined to perfect TV technology, but they thought that putting entertainment programs on their TV sets was a nuisance. At no time did either man talk about the *art* of television. They were both interested in the technology of TV—and TV photo histories show these men smiling only when they're holding up giant TV picture tubes.

David Sarnoff and William Paley, the respective heads of NBC and CBS, had their own personal visions for television. Sarnoff dreamed of an RCA monopoly, while Paley lay awake at night with plans to upstage Sarnoff. There were other businessmen in early TV. Edward J. Noble, the founder of Life Savers candy, was one, and before that a used car dealer, Earl "Madman" Muntz and a jeweler named LeRoy. But none of them could articulate what kept their noses to the television grindstone. Only a tiny and motley band of programmers sensed that television might be at the dawn of a new era in information and entertainment. Gilbert Seldes, author and arts critic, was in charge of programming at the birth of CBS television and said something remarkable in his memoirs: "Everything in the movies exists in the past tense. In radio and television everything is in the present."[1]

This *immediacy* that defined television—sometimes for the worse— was what kept DuMont's Harry Coyle directing sports and CBS's Worthington Miner inventing live TV drama. It speeded KTLA's Stan Chambers to fast-breaking news scenes, and it prompted celebrities to play charades at Paramount with Mike Stokey for free. Most pioneers were like Hugh Downs, who started in television in 1943 in Chicago and thought TV was "just a gimmick." Since the turn of the century, the importance of show business had been defined by the amount of money at stake, and TV in its infancy was poverty stricken. Hugh Downs candidly says that he never contemplated the importance of television until 1955, when he participated in a program budgeted at $500,000. Downs recalled, "I then realized that TV was more important than I had ever thought."[2] Television had grown into something that couldn't be ignored.

All this seems naive in hindsight. Today we are bombarded with new forms of television—from home shopping to interactive. Although public-access cable shows seem like echoes of the primitive TV programming described in this book, today's amateur shenanigans are more akin to ham operators in early radio. The artists you will read about in *Please Stand By* were dedicated professionals usually blundering their way into television history.

Today's American TV picture is not a picture in the "motion picture" sense. Its 525 separate lines per screen are the broadcast result of a continuously scanned, original broadcast image. In Europe, TV pictures are even sharper with the PAL (phase alteration line) standard of 625 lines. Back in 1928, TV images had 48 lines. They formed a picture only because the screens were three inches square. As tubes got bigger the number of lines increased. By 1933, there were 60 lines, the most ever achieved by the early mechanical systems. By 1936, electronic technology had completely replaced that primitive early system, and 276 lines were available. By 1939, RCA had 450 lines, and DuMont, in 1941, had over 600 but failed to set the industry standard.

Two completely different systems—mechanical and electronic—competed for acceptance in the earliest days of television. One was called "mechanical" because it used a perforated metal disk that scanned the broadcast image. The other was called "electronic," and it was the direct precursor of today's television. This book is more focused on the development of electronic TV, without forgetting the shoebox inventors who first broadcast a television image.

In the pages ahead we will meet the pioneers and share their dreams and disasters. We'll see how the "Please Stand By" card was on the air more than the programs were, and see that the first professional football telecast was a simple shot of a toy football game board.

Feature films would have been a natural way to fill airtime, but in TV's infancy, film studios weren't selling, much less giving away, their product. Finally in 1938, NBC telecast *The Return of the Scarlet Pimpernel*, starring Leslie Howard. This triumph was undercut by the W2XBS staff projectionist who played the last reel out of order, ending the film twenty minutes early. After that blunder, no Hollywood films were sold to TV for more than ten years.

Late in television's second experimental decade, commercials were finally allowed. Advertisers were slow to sign up after they watched live television murdering their carefully prepared spots. The very first Ford Motor Company commercial was intended to be shot live through a fish aquarium, but on air, the fish panicked and disappeared.

On the first broadcast of a new TV soap opera telecast from New York City, a terrified actress tried to run away from the live cameras to escape the studio. Before the show could move to the next set, her co-star had to grab her and perform her missing dialogue, as well as his own.

Much of television's prehistory took place in New York, but this account will also introduce small stations in Philadelphia, Schenectady, Seattle, and dozens of other cities including Washington, D.C., where the station manager for W3XWT had a metropolitan map on his office wall with tiny flag pins marking each one of the forty-eight TV sets in town.

Long before the Indian head appeared on the test pattern, it was common to end a broadcast day by playing the National Anthem. Willard Edge, a broadcast technician at W3XWT, had the distinction of being the first disc jockey to play "The Star Spangled Banner" at the wrong speed.

In 1926, the radio editor of the *New York Times*, Orrin Dunlap, described television as "an inventor's will-o'-the-wisp." A few years later, Dunlap tried to imagine what television might be like as far in the future as 1950: "By that time, tap dancers ought to be in demand, and television may be able to do justice to portrayal of the best-dressed girl in radio."[3]

Television pioneers, and the reporters who observed them, believed radio was an entertainment standard that television could never achieve. Tap dancers were, of course, no use on radio, so they would naturally be good on television. But what could replace the immediacy and content of an Edward R. Murrow war report? What on TV could amuse audiences as successfully as a radio comedy with Fanny Brice as an eight-year-old "Baby Snooks" talking to a boxing kangaroo? What stars would be willing to spend long hot hours rehearsing television when they could make a fortune "cold reading" a script into a radio microphone?

The prehistory of television is a story of scientists with vision but no money and businessmen with plenty of money but little vision. It is the continuing saga of newsmen wondering if a five-alarm fire had value as television news and sportscasters who couldn't help inject their personalities into the events they reported. It is the record of a tightwire act of performers who worked nightly without a net, with a tango of intrigue and backstabbing behind the scenes. In short, television before 1948 was a shadow on the cave wall reflecting an invention that in four or five decades would become a dominant influence in the life of every citizen of the world.

1

TOM SWIFT
AND HIS
ELECTRONIC
TELEVISION
MACHINE

The invention of today's TV: 1920–1939

Philo Taylor Farnsworth's first brush with electricity was in 1920, at the age of fourteen, when he wired a Delco battery to run his mother's washing machine. On a farm in Beaver, Utah, this was quite an achievement, and it drew a gawking crowd of local farmers. The teenager wasn't around for compliments; he was up in his room poring through electrical journals.

Philo lived in this Utah town of Beaver because sixty years earlier Brigham Young had commissioned his grandfather to found a town there, even though it was in the middle of nowhere. The newest train track was fifty miles away. As a boy Philo saw a train no more than twice a year, but with such limited observation he could make an accurate model of it just as he could of an airplane. Beaver had no library, so Philo bought himself a popular ten-volume library on electricity, paying for it on an installment plan, a dollar a month for ten months. Since there was no high school in town, he rode on horseback to Rigby High School in nearby Idaho, where, thanks to his home study, the teachers found Freshman Philo qualified for the senior course in chemistry.

Two years later, he described to his science teacher an idea for an electronic television system. To his teacher's amazement, he covered several blackboards with equations to show how the electronic problems might be solved.

Philo Farnsworth as a sophomore at the University of Utah was a bright student, particularly in math and science. He had to drop out of college after his father's death, taking a job as a janitor to provide for the needs of his widowed mother and younger siblings.

Those were the circumstances that led Farnsworth to interview for an office-boy job at the Community Chest office in Salt Lake City. The interviewer, George Everson, was impressed with Farnsworth's school record and asked why he was dropping out. Everson remembered the meeting verbatim in his worshipful biography of Farnsworth:

> "I can't afford school," the boy explained. Then he brightened, "Besides, I need to finance an invention of mine."
>
> "What is your idea?"
>
> "It's a television system."
>
> "A television system. What's that?"
>
> "Oh, it's a way of sending pictures through the air the same as we do sound. I thought of it when I was in high school. I went to Brigham Young University and told a couple of professors about it. They encouraged me to try out some things in the lab, and now I think I've got something that works."[1]

Young Farnsworth needed five thousand dollars to build a model and prove his system. Everson and a San Francisco partner named Leslie Gorrell drew up a contract to help him, since only a working model could fulfill patent requirements.

Los Angeles was the best place to secure all the equipment, and the invention went forward in a rented house with the curtains drawn. This was a suspicious sight in the days of Prohibition. Neighbors called the police, who demanded a full search of the premises. The officers thought they had discovered something even more sinister than an alcohol still, and the brash inventor had to reveal his television invention. The police left in a state of bafflement.

Television consumed Philo Farnsworth; it always had. On his wedding night, according to Emma Farnsworth, Philo confessed to his nineteen-year-old bride, "You know, there's another woman in my life." Emma didn't say anything. She was dumbstruck. Philo dropped the other shoe, "Her name is television, and in order to have enough time together, I want you to work with me. It's going to be exciting, and we'll always be right on the edge of discovery."[2]

Farnsworth's laboratory was full of tools, many of which he had created to solve the problems of his invention. He'd had to learn electrochemistry and metallurgy—even glassblowing. The cathode-ray tube that he used was made from glass hand-blown by Farnsworth himself.

More time and more money were needed. Farnsworth applied to W. W. Crocker, a famous San Francisco banker and investor. To the fastidious Crocker, Farnsworth looked like a hobo. His clothes were so shabby that friend Everson rushed him into a new suit and hat for his meeting with the Crocker people at the Palace Hotel. The meeting, which was only scheduled for lunch, lasted the entire day, and it netted the inventor the twenty-five thousand dollars he needed. The only condition was that he move his laboratory to San Francisco. Philo agreed, quickly packed up, and moved north. Enroute, someone stole his new suit.[3]

The first image Philo ever telecast was one that should go down in history with Eadweard Muybridge's film of a galloping horse. Three decades earlier, that California scientist had used a film strip of sequential photographs to prove that a race horse has moments when all four feet leave the ground. By coincidence, Stanford contributed to the developing science of the motion picture. Philo Farnsworth's own "race horse" was simply a stationary image painted on a piece of glass. One of the Crocker banking people, a man named "Daddy" Fagen, had scoffed, "When are we going to see some dollars in this thing, Farnsworth?" Farnsworth flipped a switch, and his second electronic TV image emerged: a dollar sign.[4]

The first *moving* image, a few days later, was a burning cigarette. The production problem with the "cigarette show" was that the smoker had to stick his face so close to the transmitter tube that he blistered his nose on its hot lights.

Every day Farnsworth tried new images: more figures printed on glass, hands holding a pair of pliers, still photographs, and finally motion picture film, using an old projector and a 16-mm movie of a hockey game. TV's first sports show. At the Green Street building in San Francisco, where Farnsworth had his lab, there is a historical plaque honoring the occasion. Philo Farnsworth was now a mere twenty years old.

The high point of television broadcasting in 1926 was a loop of film bootlegged from the Mary Pickford-Douglas Fairbanks silent movie, *Taming of the Shrew*, in which Pickford combs her hair over and over and over. Day by day, the video image got better, and the detail became finer and clearer as the loop was scanned month after month. TV's first dramatic film.

An invitation to Pickford and Fairbanks to appear on Farnsworth television was a masterstroke in public relations. Fairbanks was a *celebrity* in the sense that we think of celebrities today—in Daniel J. Boorstin's phrase, "known for your well-known-ness." America's sweetheart, Mary Pickford, was modest in the spotlight, whereas Fairbanks relished attention. He was more than a movie star, he was an ideal. His suntan was said to have changed the way Americans viewed suntans. Formerly the mark of the outdoor laborer, after Fairbanks, a tan was a symbol of chic virility and health.

Pickford and Fairbanks were invited to San Francisco for a peek at television. Farnsworth, always sure that he could improve his invention, began overnight to revise it, but the more he "improved" his machine, the more he made it worse! The stars were left cooling their heels at the

Palace Hotel while Farnsworth tried to patch things back together. His demonstration, at the end of a long and nervewracking day, was a distinct disappointment.[5]

Even though Philo Farnsworth was unquestionably television's boy genius, the giant Radio Corporation of America (RCA) was not about to take Farnsworth's technological advances lying down. RCA's attorneys fought Farnsworth's patent application and challenged the originality of his ideas at government proceedings. But platoons of lawyers could not shake Farnsworth, and in August 1930, the twenty-four-year-old got his own television patents. The Farnsworth system was declared technically unique, and RCA knew it could not further develop television without it. Early the next year, General David Sarnoff and RCA's chief inventor, Vladimir Zworykin, visited Farnsworth's laboratory. Both smugly announced to the press that they didn't need anything that Farnsworth had, but quietly, behind the scenes, RCA began talking with the young inventor. The negotiations were difficult, but ultimately Farnsworth was guaranteed royalties for his patents. The RCA attorney was said to have had tears in his eyes when he signed the contract Farnsworth demanded.[6]

In 1930, Farnsworth won further recognition of his patents from the Federal Radio Commission (FRC), a unique concession from a so-called regulatory board that constantly favored the corporate monopolies of Sarnoff and Paley. With his patents secure, Farnsworth was willing to share his technology with Westinghouse and RCA. It made sense to Philo to move his operation to the East Coast to keep pace with fast-changing developments. This was achieved by a licensing agreement with the Philco Laboratories in Philadelphia, where Farnsworth set up actual physical production on a five-thousand-dollar monthly budget.

In England in 1934, Farnsworth demonstrated electronic television technology to a committee of Parliament and focused international attention on Philco. The French, Germans, and even Japanese were interested in the new technology. Thinking that their inventions had no possibility of being exploited in Japan, Farnsworth and his partners gave a tour of the laboratory to a Japanese scientist representing the Mitsui Company. George Everson recalled the visit:

On the second or third day after the visitor had seen the television transmitter and receiver and had spent some time in technical discussion, our engineer inquired of the Japanese regarding the progress of television in his country. He replied 'We already make your receiver set. When I go home we make your transmitter.'[7]

In 1935 throughout the United States, there were fewer than four thousand electronic TV sets. Farnsworth was at last beginning to understand that increased entertainment programming was the only way to get people to buy new television sets. The success of radio networks convinced him that TV needed to plan ahead for the inevitable television networks. Cooperating with A, T&T and the Bell Laboratories, he oversaw the laying of the first coaxial cable between New York and Philadelphia in 1937. The cable was simple enough: a flexible copper tube with a fine wire suspended in the center, with insulating washers every few inches. Simple, but initially very expensive. So expensive that people with a vested interest in radio publicized the costly delays and predicted that TV was "far off" and "years away."

Farnsworth never became as involved in TV programming as he should have been. His partner, Everson, complained, "He seemed unable to recognize full the merits of what he had achieved and was unwilling to apply the skillful and patient engineering to get the maximum practical results from his inventions."[8]

So while his rivals at RCA, General Electric, and DuMont were scrambling to get primitive shows "on the air," Farnsworth Television and Philco focused all their attention on getting bugs out of the system. According to Everson, whenever Farnsworth confronted any problem that lacked a technical solution, he would explode in a fit of temper and proclaim, "this is my laboratory. No one comes in here giving me orders as to what is to be done."

Beyond their goal of perfecting the technology, Farnsworth television had another key aim. It was garnering publicity for television itself, and there was no better publicity stage for the new medium than the 1939 New York World's Fair.

In the spring that year, while frantically preparing exhibits for the fair, Farnsworth began showing the strain of his horrendous work schedule. Looking much older than thirty-three, he went for a medical checkup. Then he went straight to the office of the president of Farnsworth Television and made an announcement: "I'm going fishing."⁹

Farnsworth Television without Farnsworth was unthinkable, and officials of his company scrambled to accommodate him without letting him retire. On a farm in Maine, they set up an extensive laboratory within a stone's throw of Philo's own private lake. It suited Farnsworth just fine, but it was the death knell for Farnsworth Television. Many of his prize patents were soon sold to RCA, even as that company proclaimed the "Birth of Television" at the New York World's Fair. Farnsworth sarcastically joked that "the baby is being born with a full beard."¹⁰

Commercial television was almost a reality fifteen years after Farnsworth had "broadcast" that first dollar sign, and it was only nineteen years since he had invented electronic TV. Perhaps if he had paid more attention to tap dancers, midgets, and ventriloquists, the "Emmy" award might today be called the "Philo."

During the decade that he was perfecting television, Farnsworth's passion for inventions had led him to other new discoveries—electronic microscopes, baby incubators, and a "gastroscope" that viewed the inside of a human's stomach without surgery. Ironically, at the 1939 World's Fair, Farnsworth was more identified with his baby incubator than with television.

He was responsible for another invention that was ahead of its time. In the early 1940s, he demonstrated a machine that transmitted facsimile copies of documents over phone lines. Other systems worked over radio lines, but only Farnsworth's invention could have been used by the general public. Yes, Farnsworth invented the "fax." Unfortunately, in 1940 phone lines were costly and delivery boys were cheap. So much for the "fax."

In 1957, long after Farnsworth's patents had expired, he appeared on *I've Got a Secret* and whispered into host Garry Moore's ear words that appeared on millions of home screens: "I invented television."

Farnsworth won fifty dollars since none of the panelists could guess who he was or what he had done. Depressed and in ill health, Philo T. Farnsworth died in 1970, at the age of sixty-four. Twenty years later, a group of school children from Utah unveiled a statue of Philo Farnsworth in the halls of the United States Congress. The event was, of course, televised.

2

FIRST OUT
OF
THE GATE
Mechanical Television: 1925–1933

The very first television system was a mechanical system, and it was *not* invented by Philo Farnsworth. It was incredibly able to broadcast all the way from New York to Los Angeles. Only the sound could be heard on the West Coast, however, and reception was limited to shortwave sets. A second problem was that there were only 48 scanning lines forming a very fuzzy little picture (compared to today's 525 lines). Reception was bad even in the city of transmission, but it was truly television: live pictures with sound, even though the first synchronized transmission on June 13, 1925, in a Washington, D.C., laboratory was merely a film of a Dutch windmill.[1]

This mechanical process, developed in 1884 by Paul Gottlieb Nipkow, a Russian-German scientist, was a cross between flipping your thumb over a stack of index cards and the original spinning zoetrope with its vertical slits. It was called "mechanical" TV because the transmission used a metal disc that was punched with holes in a spiral pattern. A beam of light shot through the disc, "scanned" the subject, and the scanned information was transformed into electrical impulses.

The major American developer of this mechanical system, Charles Francis Jenkins, was the broadcaster of the Dutch windmill in 1925. Jenkins was a confirmed tinkerer. He designed the first automobile with an engine in front instead of under the seat and introduced the first self-starter, as well as the first sightseeing bus. After developing the first mass-market motion picture projector he founded the Society of Motion Picture Engineers.

"Radio Vision," as he called television, was crudely limited to 48 lines per screen. It would always be a disappointment for someone like Jenkins, who had helped the birth of motion pictures. Comparisons between 35-mm film and the spinning disc were always being made. Nevertheless, Jenkins insisted on a bright future for his "Radio Vision":

> "In due course, folks in California and Maine, and all the way between, will be able to see the inauguration ceremonies of their President, in Washington; the Army and Navy football games at Franklin Field, Philadelphia; and the struggle for supremacy in our national sport, baseball. . . . The new machine will come to the fireside as a fascinating teacher and entertainer . . . with photoplays, the opera, and a direct vision of world activities."[2]

On April 17, 1927, Jenkins broadcast Secretary of Commerce Herbert Hoover speaking in front of a "televisor" in Washington, D.C. Both sound and picture were received in New York City. At the same time this broadcast was also transmitted to New York from the AT&T labs in Whippany, New Jersey. Jenkins had successfully connected a three-city network in only his second year of television!

The show began with General J. J. Carty in Washington, holding a telephone transmitter as he spoke with Walter Gifford, AT&T's president in New York.

"How do you do, General? You are looking well."

"Thank you. You are too."

"We are all ready and waiting here. Mr. Hoover is here."

In the New York City TV reception room, the lights were lowered. In the center of the Radio Vision screen a white glare appeared. It slowly became a large luminous patch, which turned into Herbert Hoover's forehead. The future president was leaning in such a way that his forehead took up too much of the picture, and the telephone he was holding blocked most of his mouth and chin. A technician quickly prodded the secretary into his correct position. Hoover's lips began to move:

> "It is a matter of just pride to have a part in this historic occasion. We have long been familiar with the electrical transmission of sound. Today we have, in a sense, the transmission of sight, for the first time in the world's history."[3]

After Hoover spoke for two minutes, his wife was invited to sit in front of the televisor to talk with Gifford in New York.

"What will you invent next?" she coyly asked. "I hope you won't invent anything that reads our thoughts."

The Hoovers were followed on this historic telecast by a comedian named "A. Dolan" appearing from Whippany, New Jersey, wearing side whiskers and holding a broken pipe in his mouth as he told Irish jokes. Then he disappeared for a quick change, coming back on the screen "black-faced with a new line of jokes in negro dialect."

Bell Telephone Laboratories continued their experiments in mechanical TV. By August 1928, they did their first outdoor telecast, using a tennis player on the roof of the Bell Laboratories, which was clearly seen on a receiver on the seventh floor. By 1929 they were telecasting in *color*. Using the same basic apparatus, they altered the arrangement of the photocells in the transmitter and the glow lamps in the receiver. Suddenly the red, blue, and green filters in front of the lamps, combined with the spinning scanning disc, produced a composite color picture. The first color TV program showed British and American flags, followed by a man picking up a piece of watermelon. The technique was impressive but the applications, because of technical difficulties, were limited. While there are no surviving scripts or copies of Jenkins's efforts, there are letters from enthusiastic viewers who tuned in Jenkins's "movie stories" during 1930. None of them were skilled letter writers, which leads to the conclusion that early television—despite the relatively high receiver costs—was not just an entertainment for the idle rich.

From Goshen, Indiana:

I have received parts of your baseball game, seen Sambo, the little girl bouncing the ball, and parts of many others.[4]

From Baltimore:

That's That seemed to consist of much love at the breakfast table, many embraces, kissing and a good-bye and then the husband going back to the job swining (sic), the pick-ace (sic) and stopping to limber up his muscles and finally streaking for home and more embraces.[5]

Ernst Frederik Werner Alexanderson, General Electric's resident scientific genius at the company's headquarters in Schenectady, had already become America's first television programmer. On January 13, 1928, he sent a telecast into his own home and that of two other GE officials. The picture was a tiny three-inch square, and the TV set itself looked more like a bank vault than a television receiver. It was four-feet high, a yard wide, contained forty tubes, and had a gigantic transformer in the base. The television camera was equally bulky and the operator had to hide under a black blanket at the rear of the instrument, much like a nineteenth-century still photographer.

Alexanderson was an ambitious inventor, under contract to GE, who knew that people wouldn't buy the GE television sets with their

3-by-3-inch screens unless there were programs to see. In 1926, while Philo Farnsworth was busy with dollar signs and burning cigarettes, Alexanderson was broadcasting ukelele performances. If Farnsworth was the ultimate loner, Ernst was the quintessential corporate player, and the company backed him to such an extent that by September 1928, he was televising the world's very first television drama, *The Queen's Messenger* on GE's Schenectady station WGY.[6]

The Queen's Messenger was one of those high-society, European-setting melodramas, with fancy cigarettes, switched suitcases, and heroic sacrifices, which were so popular on the stage at the turn of the century. It had been written in 1899 but the author, J. Hartley Manners, died the year of this historic telecast without ever knowing of the event.

The WGY cast starred Izetta Jewell, a retired stage actress living in Schenectady. The program was directed by Mortimer Stewart, a paranoid perfectionist who locked the studio and began rehearsals at four in the morning on September 11, 1928. The play was to be performed twice: at 1:30 in the afternoon and again at 11:30 at night, in the hope that the waves might go across a greater distance late at night to be received by amateur TV enthusiasts. Two other actors were hired to play the hands of the male and female leads since the cameras were locked down and couldn't pan. It was the first three-camera show, as well as the first drama. One camera was for Miss Jewell, another for her co-star Maurice Randall, and the third for the hand doubles. Orrin Dunlap, radio editor of the *New York Times*, described this all important TV first:

> While the actors play their roles in a locked studio, the audience sees and hears them through a television receiving set in another room in the same building. The pictures are about the size of a postal card and are sometimes blurred and confused. They are not always in the center of the receiving screen. Sometimes they are hard on the eyes because they flicker.

Otherwise, Alexanderson's drama was a triumph. Trade publications raved, and there was a rush of rhetoric from television enthusiasts.

On the Pacific coast, amateurs receiving the audio signal on shortwave triumphantly reported that they had held a signal for a full thirty seconds!

Alexanderson soon demonstrated *portable* cameras on his first remote telecast in 1928. GE's radio station, WGY, one of America's earliest, did a TV simulcast of Governor Al Smith in Albany accepting the Democratic party's presidential nomination. In May of that same year, GE had "regularly scheduled" television between 1:30 and 2:00 PM every Tuesday and Thursday. These regular programs would not yet sell many sets. They consisted simply of the faces of men talking, laughing, and smoking.

As primitive as this was, it was way ahead of New York City's WRNY, which tried TV on its radio channel. It couldn't provide audio and video simultaneously so performers' images were telecast just before they sang or spoke.

Over in Passaic, New Jersey, W2XCD broadcast for sixty minutes a night, with forty-eight lines, scanning fifteen frames a second. One of its premiere programs was "Happy Irvine's Dramatic Recital with Music," and every night it somehow serialized Jack London's *Call of the Wild*. Surveying all this TV activity, a Schenectady newspaper reporter asked Ernst Alexanderson when he thought TV might be ready for the home. Alexanderson shrugged, "Sorry, I don't know. What I wonder is if the public really wants television."

In May 1931, American television scored an international "first"—the first marriage on television—live, of course. Grayce Jones and Frank DuVall had fallen in love in a television laboratory and decided to tie the knot in a ceremony broadcast all over the eastern seaboard. With a record of a wedding march in the background, the bride, dressed in white satin with a tulle veil held by a circlet of orange blossoms, stepped in front of a minister, the groom, a microphone, and an announcer, who began the ceremony: "Ladies and Gentlemen of the television audience, we have here a novel item and yet one with a serious aspect. It is a marriage."[7]

The Jenkins mechanical TV technique was promising enough that in 1931, William Paley's Columbia Broadcasting System (CBS) filed with the Federal Communications Commission (FCC) to do experimental broadcasts. At 485 Madison Avenue, they set up W2XAB, and on June 21 the tests began. First there were call letters, then some silhouettes, a still photograph, and a clock. After a month of this they were ready for a fifty-minute evening program, which featured Edwin K. Cohan, the technical director of the Columbia network, as well as the station's director William A. Schudt, Jr., who promised, "boxing bouts, wrestling, football games, art exhibitions, classic dancing, palmistry and news."*[8]

Announcer Ted Husing made the then-improbable suggestion that someday TV would be "two-way," with viewers able to "talk back." Mayor Jimmy Walker was there from his unofficial nighttime headquarters, the Central Park Casino restaurant, to formally open the station.

Starlet Natalie Towers won a non-election to become "Miss Television." Comedian Harry Burbig did a turn on "Little Red Riding Hood." None other than composer George Gershwin was there to play "Liza," and Kate Smith, the "Songbird of the South," sang "When the Moon Comes over the Mountain."

All this activity made the leaders of CBS look like broadcast pioneers; it was good for a press release. Behind the scenes, however, Paley expressed great pessimism about television, "It is hard to tell just how television will be handled, probably in movie theatres, because of the size of the theatre screen which would make television more enjoyable. Man is a social creature; he likes to rub shoulders with his fellows."[9]

In England, this mechanical television had been "broadcasting" for some time under patents held by the Baird Company. John Logie Baird was a Scotsman who, like Farnsworth, was something of a boy genius. At the age of twelve he had rigged up a homemade telephone. He never claimed to have invented television, but he was the first to take it out of the lab and get publicity for it. In the early 1920s, Baird experimented unsuccessfully in both the soap and the jelly business. Prior to that, he

*Keep in mind that this was the same year that W2XCD in Passaic, New Jersey, televised a fifteen-minute program called *The History of Television*.

had pursued ideas in artificial diamonds, undersocks, and something called "Baird's Speedy Cleaner." He had always been fascinated by radio and understood that technology well enough to realize there must be a way to send pictures by or with the radio. Working out of an attic, he borrowed $250 and made a very crude TV system using the Nipkow disc. In 1923 he placed an advertisement in *The London Times*: "Seeing by wireless. Inventor of apparatus wishes to hear from someone who will assist (not financially) in making a working model."[10]

Baird's contraption was bizarre by any normal scientific standards. Most of the parts came from his attic. The motor was held in an old tea chest, and an empty biscuit box housed the lamp. There was an old bicycle-light lens, some hat boxes, and a scanning disc cut out of cardboard. The whole thing was held together with sealing wax, glue, and string. It looked completely hopeless, but early in 1924, Baird got his first genuine TV picture: a flickering image of a Maltese cross.

A few days after his historic first broadcast of that Maltese cross, his landlord evicted him for failing to pay the rent. Years later, erasing any mention of the ignoble eviction, his town council voted to erect a placard: "Television: first demonstrated by John Logie Baird from experiments started here in 1924." Baird quickly found a cheap attic in Soho's Frith Street where he furiously worked on his makeshift invention.

On January 27, 1926, he called a press conference of sorts. He invited the science editor of the *Times*, as well as forty distinguished members of the Royal Institution. The scientists for some reason arrived in full evening dress, only to find they had to climb three flights of stone stairs and then stand in a drafty corridor while six at a time were allowed into the tiny attic that was Baird's laboratory. After the *Times* raved about television, dozens of newspapermen began arriving on the inventor's doorstep.

The first English TV star was a ventriloquist dummy named Bill. Within a year, Baird put a human face on TV, his office boy, William Taynton. The boy was reluctant and had to be bribed. Once the experiment worked, Baird changed places with young Taynton so that he could be the *second* human face on TV. After a successful public demonstration in Selfridge's department store, for which the inventor was paid twenty pounds a week, the press lauded Baird, and he began to receive financial backing. By 1929 the British Broadcasting System was sufficiently impressed to begin experimental broadcasts using the Baird scanning-disc system.

At the end of TV's first decade, Baird also successfully demonstrated the first video disc, using a standard wax phonograph record, as well as the first projection television system.

Baird was a success, but his ideas didn't come easily. When he needed to think out a problem, he would often go to bed for a week. It was in this hibernating mode that he had invented the "Baird Undersock," worn by soldiers in trenches during the First World War to prevent "trench foot." It was also in this mode that he conceived the adaptation of Nipkow's disc for his television apparatus. Sometimes when he emerged from his bed he had a great idea—such as the first transatlantic TV transmission—and other times he had a stinker. On February 10, 1928, he persuaded a London surgeon who had just removed a young man's eyeball to lend him the extracted organ to put into his television machine in an effort to rival nature. It was the weirdest experiment in the history of television. Wrote Baird:

> As soon as I was given the eye, I hurried in a taxicab to the laboratory. Within a few minutes I had the eye in the machine. Then I turned on the current and the waves carrying television were broadcast from the aerial. The essential image for television passed through the eye within half an hour after the operation. On the following day the sensitiveness of the eye's visual nerve was gone. The optic was dead.
>
> I had been dissatisfied with the old-fashioned selenium cell and lens. I felt that television demanded something more refined. The most sensitive optical substance known is the nerve of the human eye. . . . I had to wait a long time to get the eye because unimpaired ones are not often removed by surgeons. . . .
>
> Nothing was gained from the experiment. It was gruesome and a waste of time.[11]

On September 30, 1927, the first public broadcast was made from Baird's studio. The president of the Board of Trade, Sir William Graham, M.P., agreed to read a letter welcoming television to Britain. Unfortunately, the transmission momentarily broke down right in the middle of Sir William's reading. This was no great tragedy since the sound and picture were being transmitted separately. In March of the following year, Baird broadcast sight and sound simultaneously as music hall star Gracie Fields made her television debut.

The *second* play in the world to be televised was Luigi Pirandello's *The Man with a Flower in His Mouth*. Even though WGY's *The Queen's Messenger* in 1928 was clearly first, the BBC still calls their 1930 drama the "first." In any case, it was the first time that British TV audiences got to see more than the head and shoulders of a single performer. Now they got to see the heads and shoulders of *several* performers, and as with Alexanderson's *Queen's Messenger*, there was a special camera for hands and inserts. Blue, green, and yellow makeup were again used, and everything was ready until star Val Gielgud called in sick. Somehow the production went on as scheduled to an audience of fifty sets in the shops of local radio dealers.

The press reception to the Pirandello play was mixed, largely because Baird's associates bungled the press invitations. The influential *Manchester Guardian* was instructed to view the play on a television at a local radio shop. To hype the event, there was a lot of local publicity, and the shop was jammed with spectators giving no room to the newspaper critics. This is the *Guardian's* review in its entirety:

> My experience with the play was unfortunate, for not having a televisor of my own, I had to rely on the apparatus at a multiple store. This could only be seen by one person at a time; as there were over 100 waiting, and as the play lasted thirty minutes, our time before the machine was limited, and I, who was there professionally, as it were, arrived at the screen at the instant of a fade out![12]

In November 1932, Baird appeared on television for the second time. This time his co-star was not an office boy but a Danish film star,

Carl Brisson, and the broadcast was clearly seen in Copenhagen, six hundred miles away.

In September 1933, the BBC decided to take stock of their whole enterprise with Baird. They published the following announcement:

> The BBC is most anxious to know the number of people who are actually seeing this television programme. Will those who are looking in send a post-card marked "Z" to Broadcasting House immediately. This information is of considerable importance.[13]

The postcard census was a disaster. The BBC steadfastly refused to release a report on the number of postcards received, but a year later, the *Daily Express* followed up on it:

> No detailed information about the result is obtainable, but it is known that the figures painfully surprised even the most pessimistically minded at Broadcasting House.[14]

The Baird system was given a lot of tests by the BBC. There were many drawbacks, but experiments continued. In 1933 the BBC broadcast an infrared-ray technique that "stripped" cotton dresses off a line of dancing girls. The press teased the broadcasters about this unintended nudity. "Scientific progress took an unforeseen turn today," wrote the *London New Chronicle.*

Baird was always busy varying transmission techniques with the Nipkow disc. In his "intermediate film process," he photographed a BBC studio orchestra on film, which was immediately passed through a developing tank and scanned while still wet. The sound was recorded directly on the film and the broadcast of that film took place exactly sixty-four seconds after the event. On that particular orchestra broadcast, the musicians rushed from their brief opening performance into the viewing area to see themselves during the interval. The cello player, still holding his instrument, was wedged into the doorway with some of his fellow players, and the director had to stall in darkness to give the musicians enough time to untangle themselves and get back in place.

Baird's gift for publicity was shown at its best in 1936 when he put a Baird television on a Royal Dutch Airlines passenger plane and broadcast shots of passengers Paul Robeson and Charles Laughton from 4,000 feet altitude to London below. The BBC thought it was the "first" broadcast from an airplane. In 1939 RCA thought it did the "first" airplane remote, but the "first" had already taken place in Los Angeles in 1933.

The British public had actually purchased quite a few TV receivers, reasonably priced at forty pounds each. They turned out to be no bargain when Baird's mechanical scanning-disc method was doomed to extinction by the electronic systems. Anticipating this obsolescence, a Baird representative in 1934 invited Farnsworth to come to London and make a demonstration before a committee of Parliament. If Philo's system proved superior, Baird's representatives hoped to negotiate a license. The American inventor was all of twenty-eight years old, while most members of the committee were more than twice his age, and most were emotionally committed to Baird's mechanized broadcasting system. Emma Farnsworth remembered the dramatic scene.

Mr. Baird was extolling his mechanical method of television, when beyond the entrance door he saw the side of Philo's electronic TV screen. Mr. Baird became very still. He slowly advanced like one mesmerized, until he stood right in front of Philo's television set. He was staring silently for quite some minutes and then, he just turned and left without a word.

The next day, Baird paid Farnsworth $50,000 for a license, and the committee voted an appropriation to the BBC to establish television service for the full London area. Programs from Baird's studio in the Crystal Palace were quickly thrown together to capitalize on the favorable publicity. The Palace, a giant glass exhibition hall, was a popular English landmark. Baird's first telecast was a fashion show featuring the Duchess of Kent purchasing a hat from a London store.

Then, just as the Baird company was ready to hook up its newest transmitting equipment, a disastrous fire swept the entire Crystal

Palace. Everything was destroyed. This was a mortal blow to Baird. The BBC shut down, and when it finally reopened, it was firmly committed to a newer electronic technology that had been developed by EMI.

Joseph Dwyer McGee, the British scientist who developed a version of the cathode-ray tube for Electrical and Musical Industries (EMI), as well as the emitron camera, which became the BBC's workhorse for the 1930s, was a graduate student in nuclear physics during the 1931 depression. Jobs were scarce and the only one he could find was with EMI working in early television. His supervisor at Cavendish Laboratories, Dr. James Chadwick, told him, "Oh well, McGee you had better take it. I doubt if this television will ever amount to much, but at any rate it will keep you going until we can get you a proper job."[15]

A postscript for these pioneering BBC television efforts, was the remarkable admission, many years later by Lord Swinton, Britain's Air Minister during World War II, that public service television was promoted mainly because the government could see that war was on the horizon. Perfecting TV was a "peaceful" way to develop radar and have the technicians ready to operate it in case of war. In other words, TV in Britain in the 1930s was part of a secret government military plot to circumvent isolationist politicians by developing radar scientists and their technology.

Back in America in the early thirties, the brief boom in mechanical television continued with stations broadcasting all over the country. In New York, RCA was committed to electronic technology, but CBS had gone mechanical. In August 1930, Jenkins installed receivers for CBS in outdoor locations all over Manhattan for a special program featuring Ethel Barrymore, popular vaudevillian Benny Rubin, a chorus line, and New York Commissioner Heath. The first sports celebrity on TV was the giant Italian heavyweight, Primo Carnera. From that day—for almost two years—Paley's new network telecast at least three nights a week.

CBS was on the air every month from July 1931 to February 1933. Their regular stars were two actors billed simply as "Sally and Gene," who did musical plays, short sketches, and dramatic pantomimes.

Nowhere are their last names recorded. For three years, W2XAB of New York City presented just "Sally and Gene."

The first critical review of a CBS program came from *Billboard's* Benn Hall who reviewed a show called *Dramatic Moments* with Bert Hilliard. The verdict was rough: "Only when television performers realize television differs from radio should they attempt material of this sort." Hall saved his strongest vitriol for a CBS repertory dramatic group called the John O. Hewitt players: "Mr. Hewitt is undoubtedly sincere, either stupidly sincere or sincerely stupid. . . . His epics will, I suppose or hope, be buried."[16]

Of course there was nothing to bury. There were no tapes, no kinescopes, no surviving scripts. So rather than "bury" them and other early TV epics, William Paley, president of CBS, did the next best thing. He cancelled CBS television. The official announcement read:

> Further operation . . . offers little possibility of contribution to the art of television. It is our intention to resume our experimental transmission as soon as we are sufficiently satisfied that advanced equipment of a broader scope can be installed.[17]

Paley was mainly motivated by the fact that, in 1933, radio was making big money, and TV wasn't making any. Mechanical TV was a technical failure as well. Large capital was available only at RCA, where research pointed exclusively to the electronic methods of TV.

Earlier, Jenkins had moved his only remaining mechanical TV station, WZXAP, to Washington, where it could be better affiliated with his laboratories. This coincided with a deterioration in Jenkins's health. The Washington station faltered, losing its key alliance with radio station WMAL in 1932. After a long illness, Charles Francis Jenkins died and with him died mechanical television in America. His TV system would have died anyway, but without its inventor to promote it, the death was quick and relatively painless except for the financial impact on the consortium of Lee De Forest and several New York bankers who had invested $10 million in 1928. Their money was gone, and the research deemed worthless.

Mechanical television died simply because it wasn't good enough. There was no conspiracy of big corporate monopolies; no Lone Ranger inventor stymied by short-sighted moguls. It just stank. The receivers sold for an affordable price, but people eventually were willing to pay a lot more for a cathode-ray tube receiver because it was real television and not some flickering fad in a hundred-dollar box. It would be nice to conclude that electronic-television pioneers learned something from their mechanical TV predecessors. They didn't. Electronic TV evolved separately.

There was one last curiosity as the BBC brought down the curtain on mechanical television in 1935. The Postmaster-General, Sir Kingsley-Wood, made a personal on-camera appeal to the public to allay the widely expressed fear that TV was a Peeping Tom. Sir Kingsley-Wood assured viewers that there was no possibility that the BBC was looking into people's houses. Decent, honorable citizens could rest easy and so could the indecent, dishonorable ones.

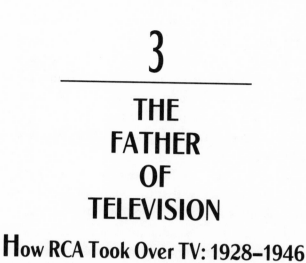

3

THE
FATHER
OF
TELEVISION

How RCA Took Over TV: 1928–1946

One of the first "performers" on electronic television was Tom Sarnoff, son of General David Sarnoff, the guiding force behind the Radio Corporation of America (RCA) and its broadcasting subsidiary, the National Broadcasting Company (NBC). In 1926, as a birthday party surprise for the boss, Sarnoff's employees rigged a TV camera in his dining room and put a receiver in another. Four-year-old Tommy Sarnoff, dressed in a sailor suit, stepped in front of the camera and sang "Happy Birthday" to his father.[1]

Four biographies have described General Sarnoff as the "Father of Television." This is a flattering overstatement, but understandable since many of these books were written by his old friends and colleagues. What can be said for sure is that Sarnoff always planned on becoming the dominant power in TV, much as he had become the dominant power in early radio. Although he wanted credit for being the "Father of Television," he wanted his baby to grow at a rate of speed that he could control. He wanted as close to a monopoly as he could get, but at the right price.

One of Sarnoff's principal inventions was his own legend. He long claimed that at the age of twenty-one he picked up the first distress signals from the ship that was trying to rescue the *Titanic* and its passengers. According to Sarnoff, he'd had a lonely vigil for seventy-two hours at the Marconi station on the top of the Wanamaker Building in New York City.

In 1977 Carl Dreher, an RCA engineer, revealed in his book, *Sarnoff: An American Success*, that the Marconi wireless station in the Wanamaker Building was closed the night of the first *Titanic* message. In fact, the Marconi company had closed down the entire Wanamaker operation to prevent interference with its coastal receivers. Sarnoff's "first big break" was later exposed as his first big whopper.

To properly separate Sarnoff's public persona from the inner workings of RCA, it is helpful to look at several of his friends and enemies. First, a friend in radio, then, a rival in broadcasting, and finally, an enemy at the FCC.

Sarnoff met Edwin Armstrong in 1913 when they were students together, and decades later the general would list Armstrong as one of his few close friends. Edwin even married Sarnoff's secretary. A tall, imposing young man with a drawling voice, he was a master of argument and liked to demolish his opponents. Sarnoff enjoyed that quality in Armstrong, so it was ironic that Sarnoff would eventually demolish his close friend.

Armstrong was a scientific genius. His experiments in shortwave transmission produced the superheterodyne, which Armstrong personally patented. It was a regeneration circuit that finally made precise tuning possible by the mixing of radio waves. He then introduced an improved vacuum radio tube that produced much better radio reception. When Armstrong demonstrated his invention to Sarnoff in 1922, Sarnoff bought the patents, giving his friend $200,000 and sixty thousand RCA shares. Armstrong instantly became the largest noncorporate stockholder in the company.

With a secure monopoly on radio receivers for RCA, Sarnoff put his friend to work developing a better broadcast technology than the AM band of radio. Armstrong took a dozen years to complete his assignment, developing the technology we now call FM. With Sarnoff's support, Armstrong went so far as to build an operational FM transmitter in RCA's space at the Empire State Building.

Sarnoff had grown to love AM, not because it was technically satisfactory but because the National Broadcasting Company (NBC), the broadcast division of RCA, had two of the three AM networks (NBC's "Red" and NBC's "Blue"), and was selling or licensing most of the radios in the marketplace. It was a sweet deal and getting sweeter. Why should FM, which would throw open hundreds of new broadcast frequencies, be rushed into the marketplace?

At the 1935 stockholders' convention, Armstrong was baffled that Sarnoff spoke glowingly of the future of AM radio and television, but never mentioned FM. Armstrong was even more surprised a few days later when Sarnoff instructed RCA to stop producing FM sets. Armstrong was then evicted from his own studio and notified that the space he had occupied would be used to develop television technologies.

Sarnoff had failed to consider that he did not own Armstrong's FM patents, having only made a deal for the vacuum tubes. When, on his own, Armstrong began building a fifty-thousand-watt FM station in New Jersey, Sarnoff decided to offer his former partner a million dollars for his patents. It was a very large sum to pay for a technology for which Sarnoff had no immediate plans. To justify his huge offer, Sarnoff said that he needed FM frequencies for TV sound. By this clever move, he made himself appear to be a TV pioneer rather than a radio monopolist.

Armstrong smelled a rat, spurned the offer, and sued RCA. The lawsuit lasted fifteen years and left Armstrong broken and penniless. Ironically, he sold all of his RCA stock to pay the lawyers that were suing RCA.

On a winter evening in Manhattan, in 1954, Edwin Armstrong wrote a note to his wife, opened a window in his apartment, put on his overcoat, hat, and gloves, and jumped fifteen stories to his death. No one heard him, and his body wasn't found until three hours later. The suicide note ended, "God keep you and may the Lord have mercy on my soul."[2]

Carl Dreher visited Sarnoff after he received the news. He wrote, "When I saw Sarnoff he was his usual direct self. Looking into my eyes, he put his hands on his chest and said, 'I did not kill Armstrong.' " Another associate, Kenneth Bilby, later shrugged off the suicide with this explanation: "Unfortunately, he [Armstrong] lacked the Sarnoff stomach for prolonged battle."

Sarnoff was first and foremost an astute businessman. Just as he squelched FM to preserve his radio empire, so also did he take cautious, even foot-dragging steps in the development of television to preserve his first-place position.

Sarnoff's only rival, William S. Paley, did not start the Columbia Broadcasting System. It was an offshoot of the old Columbia Phonograph Company. But in 1928 when that company was going broke, Paley bought it with $145,000 of his family money. At the age of twenty-eight, William Paley owned a network of fifty radio stations. CBS experimented with television in 1931, using the Baird mechanical process, but terminated the experiment by 1933, awaiting better technology. Sarnoff was using better technology and to herald RCA's technical progress, Sarnoff built an exclusive transmitter on top of the Empire State Building, the tallest in New York. Even though he had no immediate broadcasting plans for CBS, Paley ordered a taller transmitter built on top of the Chrysler Building. When Sarnoff raised his, Paley, in some kind of phallic frenzy, also raised his.* Throughout this jungle war of transmitters, the federal government did nothing to regulate the television pioneers.

In 1944, RCA's total revenues—radio, TV, and the war effort included—amounted to $325 million. By 1946, having terminated their profitable production for the war department, revenues were down to $236 million, almost all of it from radio. Radio sets were cheap to produce and so were the programs. Radio was a license to

---

*Sarnoff's hold on the Empire State Building lasted until 1949. Other transmitters were spotted all over the city. ABC's first one was atop the Hotel Pierre.

mint money. Television, on the other hand, was a drain. Two hundred million dollars had been spent just for research and development. And while RCA sold more TV sets than its rivals, by the end of 1946, the total cumulative retail sales were less than $5 million. Sarnoff felt that TV would only be worth his investment if his payoff was secure. Security rested with the FCC. None of his monopolistic development of radio during the 1930s could have taken place without a docile FCC (originally called the FRC—Federal Radio Commission).

The framers of the Sherman Antitrust Act fifty years earlier could not have imagined radio, or the easy avenue to monopoly inherent in the concept *network* radio. Furthermore, network radio was something that politicians were just beginning to see as an avenue for personal political power. Because politicians needed the airways, they treated Sarnoff and Paley with kid gloves. By 1940 Sarnoff's power and his monopolistic practices began to make President Franklin D. Roosevelt very nervous. Roosevelt decided to appoint an "activist" FCC chair, James Fly.

Fly, a solid New Dealer, was feared by Sarnoff, who described him as "irresponsible, dangerous and socialistic." Fly believed the chief duty of the FCC was to take its licensing functions seriously, fostering competition and restraining any tendency toward monopoly. He felt that information media like radio or television should, at all costs, resist concentrations of ownership. Fly's first priority was to break up NBC's Red and Blue radio networks. In 1941 Congress passed a law outlawing any network organization that "maintains more than one network." Since this applied only to NBC, and since the Constitution and legal tradition opposes any law that applies only to a single entity, Sarnoff hoped the rule might be declared unconstitutional. But the Supreme Court upheld the FCC, and NBC was forced to sell its Blue network to the new American Broadcasting Company (ABC).

Troublesome as the radio breakup was, Sarnoff feared a stronger FCC under Fly would obstruct his dream for an NBC television empire. Could a newly activist FCC undo Sarnoff's radio empire and nip his TV ambitions in the bud? The answer was certainly "yes" because Fly backed his regulatory ideas with incredible energy. He was persuasive, resourceful, even Machiavellian, when he had to be. All this was concealed behind a plain, simple quizzical expression that went perfectly with his Texas drawl.

When Sarnoff ordered his RCA factories to start building TV receivers, it was an aggressive move against the FCC, which had yet to approve uniform standards for TV receivers. Sarnoff's plan was to sell enough sets to the public to make the FCC's opinion moot. If RCA could get all these new sets into American homes, and if NBC had the majority of America's broadcasting stations, Sarnoff would have repeated exactly what he had done in radio a decade or so earlier. He was the first man in the entertainment industry to understand the importance of controlling what today is called "hardware" and "software." Sarnoff threw up a smokescreen, calling the FCC accusation of monopoly building a "mildewed red herring." Sarnoff had underestimated the conviction and the tenacity of Fly, who was not buying this. Given a free hour on the new rival, Mutual radio network, he laid out his complaint against RCA's monopolistic tactics. "Big business," meaning RCA, was "bullying the little fellows." He ordered RCA to recall all TV sets already sold. Sarnoff must have held a bundle of political IOUs, because within two months Fly rescinded his order under pressure from Congress. Shortly thereafter, NBC's experimental W2XBS was renamed WNBT, becoming the first commercial television station in the country—just what Sarnoff wanted, and the last thing Fly could have wanted.

After the war, Sarnoff's monopolistic hopes rested more in broadcasting than in set sales. Though UHF technology existed, with its eighty or more possible channels, RCA fought hard for VHF with its limit of a dozen channels. Final approval rested with the FCC. Could Sarnoff succeed in taking UHF off the market, just as he had tried to block the spread of FM radio?

Without warning, the troublesome James Fly quit the government. He accepted a generous offer to head the Muzak corporation, which made bland music for elevators and department stores. People at RCA openly acknowledged that Sarnoff had influence over the board of Muzak and had used this influence to get Fly off the FCC.

Later there were other instances of Sarnoff's influence over the FCC. Fly's successor, Charles Denny, after making a series of decisions favorable to Sarnoff, resigned as FCC chair to become an RCA vice-president and general counsel. He was followed in his FCC post by David Lillienthal, a close friend of the general. A few years later, Lillienthal graduated from the FCC to serve as a consultant to RCA.

Since the most important television pioneering work was done by Philo Farnsworth, Sarnoff was poorly described as the "father of television." With all his power however, he was able to personally postpone the development of UHF, FM, and quality color television. When CBS tried to block Sarnoff with accusations that the RCA color system was not compatible with existing black and white sets, Sarnoff promised the FCC that within six months his engineers would be able to demonstrate a compatible system. Later asked how he knew they would have it ready, Sarnoff answered, "Because I told them to."

4

SPREADING
THE NEWS
NBC Programming: 1933–1936

I n 1933 RCA chair David Sarnoff took a grand tour of his five major radio stations. He took with him a prototype of a projection television. It was eighteen feet long and eighteen feet high, a veritable King Kong standing on the stage. After St. Louis and Cincinnati, he went to Nashville, inviting the entire staff of WSM radio to his public TV demonstration.

WSM had a daily program with a high school senior named Frannie Rose Shore. She was fifteen, and her show was called "Our Little Cheerleader of Song." Everyday after school she would head over to WSM for another live broadcast.

Frannie had been singing at home for years. Her mother, Anna, possessed a fine contralto voice, and Frannie used to imitate her, even when people wanted her to keep quiet. She'd practice a lot with her ukulele, and in eighth grade assembly she made her debut, singing

"My Canary Has Circles under His Eyes." Soon she sang for the Ladies Aid Society and the First Presbyterian Church choir. At Hume-Fogg High School, she was throwing herself into student productions and cheerleading. Then she was given a chance to sing for a salary at a small Nashville nightclub. After that came radio station WSM.

Frannie's father, Solomon Shore, had a successful department store. The Shores were one of the few Jewish families in the neighborhood that had assimilated to the extent that Solomon was active in the Masons. Frannie had a comfortable life even though she hated her name Frances. "Franny" often became "Fanny" and that led to endless teasing. Like most adolescents she longed for a new name.

The day that Sarnoff came to town, Frannie was greeted after her radio program by her boss, Ed Kirby, who asked her to join the staff of WSM for a press conference on the stage of Nashville's biggest movie palace. Kirby assured young Frannie that a photographer from the Nashville *Banner* would be there, and with Sarnoff coming, Frannie's picture would be sure to make the front page. Frannie recalled the event:

> Sarnoff told us that this was not a working TV, but that someday TV would be like what we saw. The general explained that instead of first hearing the story you were going to see the story. Instead of just hearing the music, we were going to see the musicians playing it. Everyone thought it was absolutely the most revolutionary idea. I never dreamed I'd be part of television myself.[1]

Sarnoff didn't meet Frannie that day, and it would be more than a decade before they would meet. By then Frannie had become one of NBC's biggest stars: Dinah Shore.

Several summers later, after her mother died from a heart attack, Frannie went to camp in New Hampshire. She scrupulously saved the candy money her father sent her and sold her Brownie camera to a fellow camper. The $253.73 she netted was enough to finance a stopover in New York on the way back to Nashville. In her camp duffel she had squirreled away a letter of introduction from the WSM program manager, Harry Stone.

That letter got Frannie a big tour through the Radio City Music Hall and a VIP pass to an NBC radio program. "The letter said 'This will serve to introduce Miss Frannie Rose Shore. Anything you do for her will be greatly appreciated,' " recalled Shore.* The letter worked wonders. It even got her a singing audition.

> I didn't do well. I was too scared, but they were nice enough to send me across the street to CBS. No luck there, but I did get directions to independent radio station WNEW. That station was always looking for new talent.[2]

Across the street at WNEW, Frannie Rose auditioned along with fourteen young ladies in front of a producer, Martin Block. Frannie Rose sang *Dinah*.

"Dinah?" said Block after all had finished. "You!" he said, pointing to Frannie Rose. "Dinah, come here."

The high school girl from Nashville took a deep breath. She would never sing with the name "Frannie Rose" again. "You'll start tomorrow morning at nine, Dinah. Your second program is at noon. You'll get the same pay as our other singer: Seventy cents a week."

At home Dinah had never had to ask her father for money. "There had always been dollars in my pocketbook because Daddy put them there." This time would be different. Daddy didn't know that his girl was in New York, much less that she had gotten a job. Before calling home, Dinah checked into the Barbizon Hotel on Lexington Avenue, a nice hotel catering to unmarried women. This hotel provided a safe location that her father reluctantly approved of. Dinah told him her singing job would pay for her room (a lie).

The next day, Dinah was introduced before air to bandleader Jimmy Rich and a skinny twenty-year-old who would be singing with Dinah on the radio show. His name was Frank Sinatra. According to Dinah,

---

*As Dinah noted in her recollection: "This spoke highly of my talent, right?"

There was this aura about him despite his skinny frame and square shoulders. He was very sweet and gallant but that first morning Frank could never remember my name. He'd call me 'Honeybell' or 'Dixie,' never 'Dinah.'[3]

The work was exciting, but Dinah couldn't afford the Barbizon and moved to cheaper quarters, sharing a one-bedroom apartment with three other girls.

Two of them were pretty models. They didn't have to save money for food because they always had dinner dates. I was awfully jealous. One day a fellow who remembered my audition at Radio City came by and asked me and Frank if we wanted to be on television. I said 'sure' but Frank just laughed.[4]

It's surprising that Sinatra had no interest in TV exposure, because at that point in his career he was doing *anything* for exposure. On radio in hometown Hoboken, New Jersey, he sang for free. In New York City, he used to follow musicians into performing halls and beg to carry their instruments so he could sneak inside and audition with their orchestras.

Dinah's enthusiasm for television was dampened when she learned that her "debut" was just a demonstration to be broadcast internally within NBC. The next day after her noon radio show, Dinah went to NBC where she was escorted into a very small studio on the seventh floor. Martin Freeman came along to provide piano accompaniment.

It took a long time to set up the lights. Dinah could see them adding more and more. It seemed enough to light Yankee Stadium. Then the makeup man put her in the chair.

I was horrified. The man was covering me with green makeup and then adding black lipstick and black eye makeup. I was ready to cry. All my life I'd had a tan. I'd been a swimmer, a tennis player, and here I was made up like some kind of clown.*[5]

---

*Early television was not successful with the color white. In the 1930s everything that was supposed to be white had to be painted green.

Dinah never liked her looks from earliest childhood. She was born with very black hair, a dark complexion, and she always thought herself too skinny. "When I was a teenager, all I had to do to realize that I was no beauty was to look in the mirror." Radio had been a comfort to her because she could sing her heart out without concern for what the listener might think of her looks. Now she was being seen, she had no idea by whom, and she looked worse than she could ever have imagined.

The studio was so cramped that the technical crew was embarrassingly close to Dinah when her performance went on the air. Arthur Hungerford, a technical assistant in the studio, sat at the base of the camera and watched as Dinah sang her three songs. It was hot and getting hotter. He began to worry that young Dinah was scared out of her wits. He wondered if she would collapse on them. From Dinah's viewpoint, it wasn't fear; it was the heat:

> The mascara came off. The lashes came loose—they were falling down. My eyes were burning. No wonder I was in tears. It was almost impossible but somehow I went on. I thought that TV would never work if performers had to look as ugly as I did.[6]

But she kept singing. Hume-Fogg High School's "best all-around girl" kept singing in that dreamy, rich, slow, thoughtful style. It wasn't loud or powerful. It didn't need to be. Art Hungerford knew his microphone would take care of that. What impressed him and the other technicians that day in NBC was how "truthful" her singing was.[7] The voice that a nineteen-year-old girl described as "just ordinary" would later charm millions for NBC television the way it had charmed the handful of NBC technicians at W2XBS in 1936.

During the next year, W2XBS needed to find more unknown performers who would be willing to subject themselves to the heat and the potential embarrassment. One eager unknown was Eddie Albert, who in the 1960s would gain permanent TV fame in *Green Acres*.

In college in Minnesota in the early 1930s, Albert got a job as an assistant manager of the local movie theater. Between shows he used to sing and do magic acts. "I wasn't learning anything practical in college so I dropped out and ran the movie theater full time." The highpoints in his early performance career were movie promotions. Whenever the theater played a *Rin Tin Tin* picture Eddie would go on stage and raffle off a dog. From this modest debut, Eddie had his heart set on being a performer.

Eddie Albert arrived in New York with $4.00 in his pocket, and on warm nights he slept in Central Park. With Grace Bradt he quickly developed a modest nightclub act called *The Honeymooners*. The material he and Grace performed seemed perfect to talent scouts from NBC and General Foods.

Eddie and Grace had high hopes at the beginning of their interview for NBC. They were looking for a break in radio—and no wonder. Fame and fortune came quickly with an NBC radio program, even if it had to begin as a local one. But in their meeting with the studio and agency executives, the talk was all about television. Grace and Eddie had read about experiments in the new medium—but they had never seen a TV set, and they didn't know anybody who had. Quietly and patiently the executives outlined what they had in mind.

Eddie would write a small series of half-hour domestic sketches for the two to "star" in. "Stardom" was a loose concept here since the broadcast would never leave the RCA building. They would broadcast to half a dozen sets at most and would be seen by no more than fifty people. This was a smaller audience than the two had for their little cabaret act downtown. The "fifty people," it was explained to Grace and Eddie, were VIPs, advertisers, and broadcasters who would be making the decisions that could someday make them *real* stars. The fact that the couple would be appearing in a sketch tailor-made around General Foods products was a sure way to appeal to those VIPs. Finally, they were promised a fee for jointly appearing and writing their own material. They would share ten dollars.

To Eddie it was a king's ransom, and he plunged into script writing, unaware that his first effort, *The Love Nest* (1936) was to be a milestone in TV history. It was the first original "drama" written for the new medium. While Eddie was writing his script, RCA asked him to come

come up to the studio for some camera tests. He remembers being paid
five dollars to do these tests:

> It was hot as hell, and they were putting strange colors on my
> face. The basic makeup was greenish and they also put purple lip-
> stick on me. They told me that they'd done the same for Betty
> Grable, so who was I to complain? They'd go into another room
> to look at me on the tube and then come back shaking their
> heads. There was no tape at that time, of course, so I never got to
> see what they were doing. In fact, they never invited me to see
> any of the other shows they were producing. I was flying blind.
>   Then on the scheduled day, Grace and I set up in the studio.
> We wouldn't memorize our lines until after the agency approved
> the script. I asked who was going to direct us, and we were intro-
> duced to a guy in a suit who emerged from a back room.
> Everybody was coming out of back rooms in early TV. This fel-
> low asked us what we were going to do. We showed him the
> script, but he didn't seem much interested. It was becoming clear
> that Grace and I were expected to direct ourselves. This guy
> would at least know what to do with his cameras.[8]

For most of the people in NBC Studio 3H on September 21, 1936,
The Love Nest was just another job. For many of the technicians, it
didn't matter what happened in front of the cameras, they just needed a
warm body or two. Most of the work was designed to test new
iconoscope tubes, sometimes ten at a time. For the General Foods
agency people, it was a chance to test video commercials without
embarrassment. *The Love Nest* showed Grace serving her husband
Eddie a vitamin rich dinner consisting of vegetable soup, nuts, and
carrot fluff for dessert. When Eddie wouldn't touch this overly healthy
dinner, the two left to eat in a restaurant.

There was one person in the studio the day of *The Love Nest* who
took television seriously. He was the man who had squatted beside the
camera while Dinah Shore cried her eyes out. A twenty-nine-year-old
whiz kid in sound, he was very excited to be on "the end of the fish

pole" at NBC. He thought he was making history, so every night he added to a diary of the day's events. Sometimes when a director chucked his notes into a waste basket, Arthur Hungerford would retrieve them. This is valuable stuff, he thought. Someday people might want to know how it all began.

NBC's Studio 3H was a two-story room measuring about 20-by-40 feet, with a control booth elevated on the second-story level, and featuring a glass window. It had been built in 1933 as a radio studio in Rockefeller Center's Radio City, but two years after it was completed, Chairman Sarnoff had it remodeled for television.

Inside the control room sat the director, who would give instructions to the technical director, who would relay them by headset to the cameraman. There was also a sound engineer and usually a script girl. On the floor was a stage manager with his own headset. The studio had primitive air conditioning, but the ducts were in the roof, and even when the system was turned up double, not much cool air came onto the stage floor.

There was a lot of secrecy about TV in 1936. Only RCA technicians had keys to Studio 3H. They were sworn not to lend their keys to anyone for fear that they might be duplicated. Even though TV experiments from this studio were still very primitive, NBC firmly promised an elaborate show to be broadcast closed circuit to high officials of the radio industry. With no script at hand, no cast, and only a few experienced technicians, Chairman Sarnoff scheduled a broadcast time of 3:00 P.M., July 7, 1936.

In June, RCA inaugurated a series of field tests utilizing studios in Radio City and a transmitter atop the Empire State Building. Simple test programs were broadcast to "audiences" of RCA engineers and executives. Sarnoff knew he could deliver the goods, but he was not so sure he could do it with quality. Only twelve engineers were assigned to the television project, and four of these had to be at the Empire State Building. That left eight in Radio City—where nobody had any TV production experience.

Picked to be the sole cameraman was A. W. Protzman, a radio sound technician. His assistant was Nick Kersta, recruited from the

Sales Promotion Department. These appointments were made by Bob Shelby, a veteran engineer. Protzman looked around the building to find someone to operate the boom microphone. In the accounting department he found that eager young man who was engrossed in writing an unsolicited history of television, Arthur Hungerford. Every night Hungerford went home and added to his diary every detail he could remember about early television productions:

> Shelby had no problem putting together the production staff. He knew what he was dealing with. But programming was a mystery to all of us, so he brought over Bill Rainey who worked in radio production. His secretary, Mary Kennedy, doubled in props and casting. She'd had no experience in either.[9]

The format of the July 7 show was designed by Rainey. Fortunately for everybody concerned, it needed little original material. It seemed easy to put together and hard to screw up. Eliminating the possibility of mistakes was a priority since this show had to begin with the Big Boss himself, David Sarnoff.

A technical run-through was scheduled Sunday, July 5, two days before airing. No one dared to ask Sarnoff to stand around for camera blocking, so three men and three women were stand-ins for the technical rehearsal. Marks on the floor were made for close-up photography, and Mary the prop mistress dressed the simple office set. The next day, Monday, saw a real rehearsal. Radio's celebrated Pickens Sisters sang "Carry Me Back to Old Virginee" followed by a spoof on grand opera. Rainey pulled Sarnoff aside to whisper to him that the sisters were donating their time, and Sarnoff beamed approval. Sarnoff then rehearsed his spot with Major Lenox Lohr, president of NBC. Offering advice was General James G. Harbord, RCA's chairman. According to Hungerford: "All these guys wanted to be in on the action."[10]

Henry Hull, appearing in the Broadway production of *Tobacco Road*, did a monologue from the show in his character as Jeeter. He used no scenery, just a stool and a plain background. The only filmed record of this landmark telecast is a remarkable and brief 16-mm newsreel clip from behind a camera as Hull gets in place for a rehearsal and the cameraman waves him into position.

During the long rehearsal, everyone kept stopping and starting because of technical adjustments. The entire Radio City Rockette chorus line had been advertised as "120 dancers long." Unfortunately, there was only room in the studio for three of them. They waited patiently at the side of the studio, under the watchful eye of their mentor Russell Markell. The rehearsal crew was finally ready for the dancers shortly after midnight, after blocking "Betty Goodwin's Fashion Parade."

By 1:00 A.M. Sarnoff was sure this debut show would be a disaster. There was no time for a nonstop run-through. There was no official timing for a show like this. Mary Kennedy had timed *radio* shows, and they were easy. What kind of rehearsal was this?

At 9:00 A.M. the next morning, everybody dragged into 3H to block the two remaining acts: Green and Wiltshire, followed by Graham McNamee and Ed Wynn. The veteran stage performer Wynn was the only performer who was nervous—and he was *very* nervous.

Visitors began arriving by noon to the twentieth floor of the RCA Building. First were 250 members of the press, who were seated in the main hall with dozens of TV sets. The front row had new 12-inch sets, enclosed in mahogany cabinets three-and-a-half feet tall with several white knobs below. The remaining rows had smaller sets with mirrors attached to make the pictures larger. The next group to arrive was the RCA licensees, followed by a group of advertising agency executives.

At 2:00 P.M. the room suddenly darkened and the TV screens came to life. Viewers could see a sharp picture in black and white of two small children, representing NBC and RCA, drawing aside a curtain to reveal Betty Goodwin making preliminary introductions. Lenox Lohr then spoke: "What you will see today is the result of tireless effort on the part of every man and woman and the expenditure of huge sums over a period of many years. At last television is out of the laboratory and into the field."[11] Sarnoff quickly summarized

NBC's progress and leadership over ten short years. He said that sets were not available yet—and would not be made available until the cost could be brought down. He then introduced a newsreel to show how the system would handle movies. Film clips were essential to early television, since they allowed time for one show to set up while another show left the stage. On July 7, the film clips began with "Mercury," a streamlined train, and ended with a montage of army maneuvers.

There were many limiting factors to Sarnoff's debut program. With only one camera, each performer had to stand in the same spot to do his or her number. The dark drapes in the background looked fearfully somber, and of course the green makeup and black lips demanded by the iconoscope camera tended to give a weird pall to the proceedings. On the bright side, each segment finished on time, and there was no major disaster.

Sarnoff sat quietly in the studio, not sure what he had done. The studio lights had been so hot he was soaking wet, even in his third shirt. Many performers had removed their jackets, but the NBC executives kept theirs on as long as Sarnoff kept his vest buttoned and his jacket on. A watch and chain extended across his forty-seven-inch chest. For his entire career, he would never be seen any other way as long as there was a photographer present.

Finally as the studio emptied out, Sarnoff made his way to the packed control room. The technicians had been happily celebrating the snag-free show. When he entered the booth, there was an abrupt silence.

The phone rang.

It was the president of Standard Brands, a potential sponsor. He loved the demonstration. All praised the "casual, informal, and intimate" nature of this show. Hungerford summarized the triumph in his diary:

> There was undoubtedly a feeling of informality in the proceedings. Perhaps unknowingly this very informality contributed to the success. Each member of the audience gained a feeling that

this performance was for himself alone. Television had become a friendly medium.[12]

The reaction of the press was mixed. Most of the criticism mercifully bypassed the program itself and concentrated on the technical state of TV. The *Herald Tribune* said it was like watching a "radio shadow show." It sarcastically quoted Sarnoff saying, "Television is today an unfinished product." The picture had a "greenish-hue." Those scenes that didn't "flicker" were "blurred and foggy."

The *New York Times* was more enthusiastic. Headlining "Television Stages First Real 'Show,' " it emphasized the fact that the "private" demonstration was "eavesdropped" on by dozens of set owners in the metropolitan area. The *Times* quoted a prominent radio industrialist: "It was an extremely interesting demonstration but it is a long way off before it reaches the house."

By the middle of 1937, Sarnoff's experiments were gaining better publicity. NBC introduced a Milwaukee girl who went to Paris and became famous as a *chanteuse* with "Je vous aime beaucoup." Her professional name was "Hildegarde," and she enjoyed her TV exposure so much that she volunteered for everything including the test pattern. John Royal was the NBC program vice-president who had discovered Hildegarde, and with his poorhouse budget he thought he was onto something—TV could create its own stars.

Nevertheless Sarnoff demanded the publicity value of big names, so Royal went after several Broadway plays and landed *Susan and God* with British star Gertrude Lawrence, who had gained fame in many plays on London's West End, as well as on Broadway.* Royal found John Golden, the eminent Broadway producer of *Susan and God* in his office in the Forty-third Street theater that today bears his name. Golden was a portly gentleman. All the features of his face were oversized, his lips, his nose, even his eyebrows. He sat quietly at his desk as the NBC executive spun his web.

*Lawrence was actually making her second TV appearance. The first was on Baird's mechanical system in England. Her famous life in the theatre was portrayed in Robert Wise's TV film *Star*, with Julie Andrews.

"Imagine this. The opening card: John Golden Presents Gertrude Lawrence."

The implication of equal billing with the great stage star caused Golden to blink. On the theater playbill his name was a third the size of his star's name. "What about NBC?"

Royal continued, "Just a modest 'through the facilities of' card. This is your show, Mr. Golden. In fact, Sarnoff wants you to appear on camera to introduce your show."

That did it. All that remained was to set the date.

As usual the production budget was laughable. Art Hungerford and the designer painted the scenery themselves in a rush job, using templates to get the effect of wallpaper patterns. There wasn't enough time for the paint to dry and when Royal made his last minute inspection he was horrified.

" 'This place stinks' " he announced, according to Hungerford's account, and handed Art fifty dollars. "Royal told me to get a bottle of the star's favorite perfume, and we sprayed the studio. We probably spent more on the perfume than we had on the damn set."

It was blistering hot June 7, 1938, in the Radio City studio. Hungerford had been keeping an eye on the weather outside. Static-infested clouds were rolling in from the west, taking dark shapes by the Palisades across the Hudson. He and the other novice TV technicians had enough radio experience to know what static could do to radio soundwaves, but they were comforted by the fact that the ultra-shortwaves that carry TV pictures were oblivious to atmosphere static.

Inside 3H's hotter-than-hot studio, the clock was 3:00 straight up, and the red light came on over the title-card camera.

"John Golden presents Gertrude Lawrence." The credits were, as promised, of equal size and a smiling Golden was revealed in front of a desk backed by a dark, velvet drape.

"My name is John Golden and I wish to welcome you all to a new and glorious era in the world of theater."

Golden never asked how many people would be watching the outsized letters of his name and listening to his inflated delivery. Royal knew that the truth was undramatic to say the least. An audience of forty-three sat in front of telereceivers in Radio City and a few dozen more had the program available to their home sets, scattered through the metropolitan area. Maybe sixty people in all.

"I welcome the new science of electronic photography," the Broadway producer said, without evidence of any fear in his voice. "A new medium of many sizes and many values. Wasn't it Shakespeare who said, 'All the world's a stage'? And *now*," Golden gave a hammy wave of his hand, ". . . and now, *on with the play!*"[13]

Anticlimactically the show switched back to the title-card camera on which a seemingly endless printed synopsis of the Act One plot of *Susan and God* slowly crawled along to bring the television audience up to the point of the extracted scenes.

Finally the director switched to a bedroom set, the one Art Hungerford had so recently painted and perfumed. As pathetic as it looked to the naked eye, over the 365 scanned broadcast lines, it looked like a reasonable facsimile of the Broadway stage set. There in clear detail were Gertrude Lawrence, Paul McGrath, and Nancy Coleman. The decision of the stars to wear their regular Broadway makeup was also a revelation. It worked. Goodbye forever to green cheeks and black lips.

Royal chose to watch the production with the forty-three people in the room of telereceivers—and not in the control room.

It was playing well. Spectators were actually applauding the end of every scene. The principals had not altered their Broadway techniques, except in volume. Everything looked reasonably realistic.

But, Royal was bothered by the absence of laughter for what was normally received as a comedy. The humor of the play was not "catching" the forty-three spectators. Was the synopsis too brief, or did the wave of words move too fast? Perhaps it was these technical marvels that just put the audience into a "spell." Well, applause was applause. The performers were surviving the intense heat of the studio lights (though near the end, Miss Lawrence looked tired), and in twenty-two minutes it was all over, to another great round of applause.[14]

The next day critics called it, "A rainbow across the sky." The *New York Times*, which had harshly reviewed NBC's earlier television attempts, gave considerable praise. Art Hungerford had two great rewards, a cover spread on the whole show from *Electronics* magazine, which just happened to be edited by an old fraternity brother, and a personal thank you from Gertrude Lawrence herself.[15]

For the next two years, Art Hungerford was usually on the floor as boom man or stage manager. He has often remembered the tension in the booth.

> Once Warren Wade got a phone call from his wife while we were on the air. It was right after we started using two cameras. Warren was getting very creative and working on lap dissolves. The call from his wife was to complain about a shocking thing that had happened on the TV set in her own living room. 'Somebody's jamming your signal, Warren,' she screamed. 'I'm getting two pictures at once!'[16]

In the same studio, Hungerford remembered Louis Hector as Sherlock Holmes in *The Three Garridebs*.

> He was going great guns until the second act when he went up on his lines. Totally blank. He looked to Watson for help, then to me. The 'dead air' seemed like an eternity. The one man who should never be at a loss for words was the Great Sherlock. I used my headset to signal our director Tom Hutchinson to kill the sound. Then I read Louis the line, Louis repeated it, but only half of the line made it 'on the air.' The result was so confusing that the home audience thought whatever had gone wrong was NBC's fault and not the actor's.[17]

This popular perception—that early television was constantly falling apart—saved the reputations of many performers and technicians who were themselves falling apart.

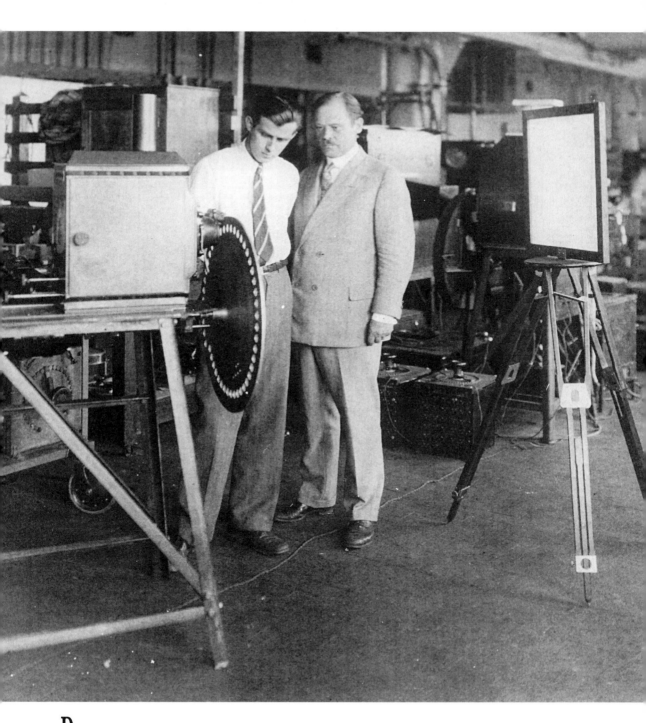

Dr. E.F.W. Alexanderson (right) and Ray D. Kell pose here with a General Electric mechanical scanner in 1927. Almost immediately, the work of Philo T. Farnsworth and Vladimir Zworykin made such devices obsolete. (COURTESY HALL OF HISTORY)

ABOVE: *The Queen's Messenger* was the first television drama shown on WGY in Schenectady, New York, September 11, 1928. The cameras couldn't move and neither could the actors, so a third camera conveyed the hand actions of a double. On broadcast night the picture traveled only a few miles but the sound could be heard on short wave radios in California. (COURTESY HALL OF HISTORY)

LEFT: Most histories of television list Franklin Roosevelt as the first president to go on TV, but Secretary of Commerce (and future president) Herbert Hoover appeared on TV in 1927 in a two-city hookup. He was followed by an Irish comedian in black face.

(COURTESY BETTMANN ARCHIVE)

P hilo T. Farnsworth invented electronic television when he was a high school student in rural Utah. He is shown here with his dissector tube and a 1929 receiver. NBC reluctantly licensed his patents and at age twenty-three Farnsworth was a prototype of the American Dream.

(COURTESY BETTMANN ARCHIVE)

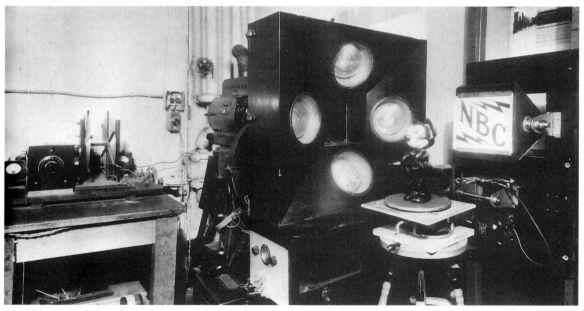

I n 1930, using primitive electronic technology, RCA's New York transmitter (W2XBS) could actually broadcast *Felix the Cat* (on the turn table). (COURTESY GLOBE PHOTOS)

T he earliest television sets had gigantic cabinets and tiny five-inch circular screens. They could be viewed from a standing position or a tall stool. The concept of "couch potato" was decades away.
(COURTESY DAVID SARNOFF RESEARCH CENTER)

ABOVE: NBC broadcast many hours from the 1939 New York World's Fair. RCA Chairman David Sarnoff called it "one of the most significant theatrical and social advances of modern times." Shortly after this, Burr Tillstrom's puppets performed *St. George and the Dragon.* (COURTESY DAVID SARNOFF RESEARCH CENTER)

RIGHT: David Sarnoff with Conductor Arturo Toscanini. Sarnoff tried to lure the maestro to conduct the NBC Symphony on television by giving him his own TV set. Toscanini preferred wrestling to cultural events. (COURTESY DAVID SARNOFF RESEARCH CENTER)

LEFT: Hugh Downs pioneered in Chicago television while holding down an NBC radio job. WKBK was unique with an air conditioning system that kept the temperature at 30° until the studio lights were turned on zooming it over 100°.

(COURTESY HUGH DOWNS)

BELOW: Hildegarde, or rather "The Incomparable Hildegarde" was a girl from Milwaukee who, as a "French chanteuse" became one of the first TV-created stars in 1938.

(COURTESY GLOBE PHOTO)

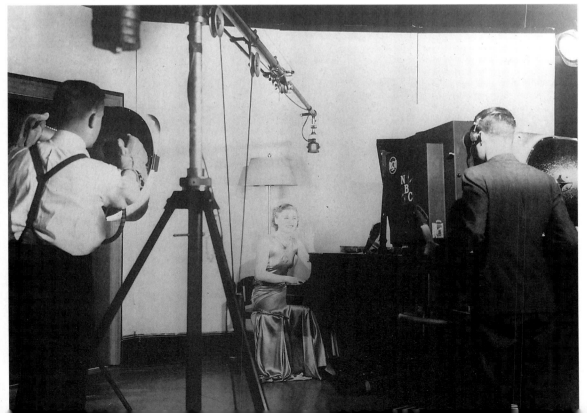

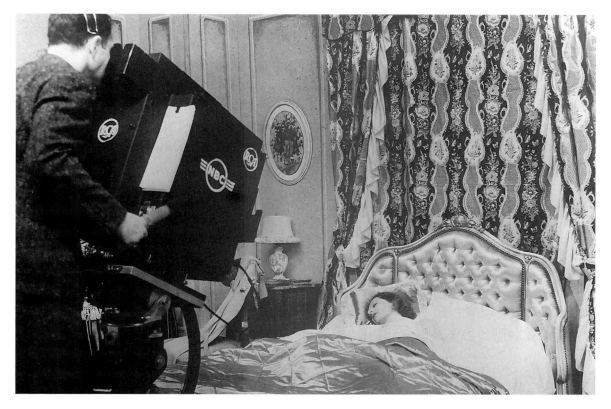

ABOVE: Gertrude Lawrence in NBC's 1938 broadcast of the Broadway play *Susan and God.* Wallpaper was too expensive so the walls were stencil painted. The smell of the paint was so bad that fifty dollars was spent on the star's favorite perfume to fumigate the set. (COURTESY GLOBE PHOTOS)

RIGHT: Broadway producer John Golden approved TV scenes from his hit play *Susan and God* after NBC promised to make his appearance as prominent as that of Gertrude Lawrence. Here he is on camera with David Sarnoff.

(COURTESY GLOBE PHOTOS)

Eddie Albert and Grace Bradt in 1936 performed Albert's *The Love Nest*, TV's first original drama. The boom man kept a diary of NBC's first experimental year.

(COURTESY ARTHUR HUNGERFORD)

On May 11, 1938 W2XBS in New York broadcast *The Mysterious Mummy Case.* Twenty-year-old Dorothy McGuire made her TV debut opposite Burgess Meredith in this melodramatic story of a cursed coffin. (COURTESY NEW YORK PUBLIC LIBRARY)

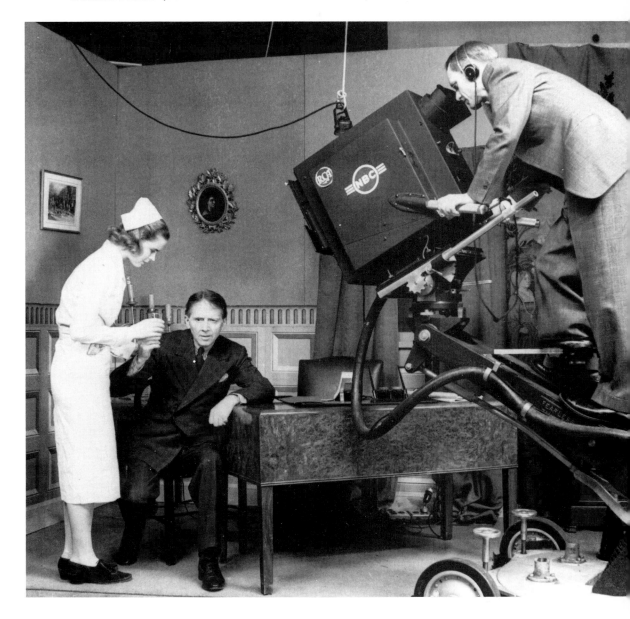

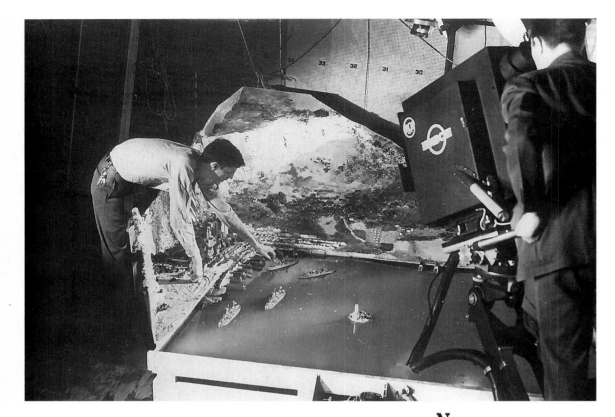

ABOVE: **N**BC special effects wizard, Capt. William Eddy, designed this elaborate diorama. The ships were actually less than five–inches long, and wires kept the ships anchored. To hide the wires, Capt. Eddy submerged small turtles to stir up the water. When the studio lights unintentionally heated the water, the "Giant Turtles" surfaced. (COURTESY GLOBE PHOTOS)

LEFT: **A** Sherlock Holmes story *The Three Garridebs* starred Louis Hector as Holmes. Hector, a popular radio actor, kept forgetting his lines so he worked out a system with the stage manager for prompting. A wild gesture from Hector and the director would cut off the broadcast sound long enough for the prompt. "Hector often looked as if he was saluting the Pope." (COURTESY NEW YORK PUBLIC LIBRARY)

John Logie Baird, who has a plaque in London commemorating his first TV experiments in 1924, makes an on-camera appearance in 1932 with Danish film star Carl Brisson. Baird had invented early mechanical television after two long years on other gadget creations, including special socks for trench warfare. BELOW: The BBC ran a contest in 1935 for TV hostesses. The search was for two single "super women" with charm, tact, and without red hair. From an avalanche of applicants, Elizabeth Cowell and Jasmine Bligh were chosen. (COURTESY BBC TELEVISION)

ABOVE: In 1932, using Baird's mechanical system, the BBC featured "The Paramount Astoria Girls." Cecil Madden, who later became program organizer for the BBC was known as "Legs" Madden, because of his strong belief in the success of "Leg" shows on television. To impishly prove his point, he engaged for an April Fool's Day every all-male act he could find. Not one woman appeared on the entire day's programming!

(COURTESY BBC TELEVISION)

LEFT: In July, 1930, the BBC produced its first drama, Pirandello's *The Man with a Flower in his Mouth.* One critic described the TV scanning lines as giving "the feeling of looking through a cabin keyhole on a rather rough day at sea."

(COURTESY BBC TELEVISION)

RIGHT: The BBC was far ahead of the United States when it began all-electronic programming in 1936. Here are *Eric Wild and His Tea Timers*. Note that the BBC iconoscope cameras were smaller than their American counterparts. The dolly is also state-of-the-art with pneumatic tires.

(COURTESY BBC TELEVISION)

BELOW: Compared to American TV in 1937, the BBC was big time show business. At its studio at Alexandra Palace, actor Tom Costello has an orchestra and a genuine studio audience. In the first half of the same year the BBC was doing five abridged Shakespeare dramas using the Baird mechanical system and by mid-year did their first all-electronic drama.

(COURTESY BBC TELEVISION)

Ballet was always a problem—even for the always ambitious BBC. Here in 1939, the cramped Covent Garden ballet finds eight of its dancers striking poses off camera. It was worse in the U.S. where only six of Radio City Music Hall Rockettes could fit into the NBC studio.

(COURTESY BBC TELEVISION)

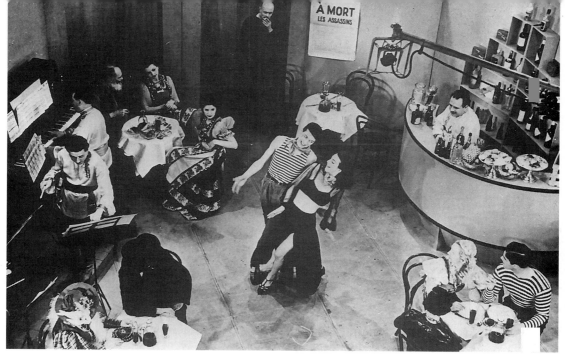

Television's first regular variety show was *Cafe Cosmopolitan* on the BBC in 1937 starring Ernest and Lotte Berk.   BELOW: BBC's *Will Shakespeare* with Nancy Price as Queen Elizabeth (1938). The quality of British TV drama had great impact on home viewers. People watching *Night Must Fall* found it so realistic and intense, that not many were obliged to switch off their sets.

(COURTESY BBC TELEVISION)

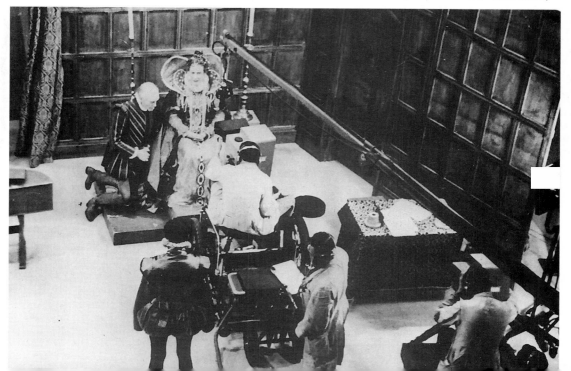

On August 29, 1939, the BBC had an artistically elaborate triumph with *Prison Without Bars*. Three days later, with the outbreak of war, they abruptly stopped transmission in the middle of a Mickey Mouse cartoon. (COURTESY BBC TELEVISION)

5

CURTAIN UP
AT THE
WORLD'S FAIR

Early television at the crossroads: 1939

I t was half past noon on Sunday, April 30, 1939. The Nazis were spreading into eastern Europe, and Japanese soldiers were all over China. America was still at peace, and on this sunny spring day, the feeling was not the dread of war but a patriotic pride in American know-how. America had pulled itself out of a depression. One in three families had a telephone, one in two had a radio. A man's Palm Beach suit at Weber and Heilbroner cost $15.50. The big summer attraction announced for the Paramount Theatre in Times Square was Phil Spitalny and his World Famous All Girl Orchestra. And the biggest deal in New York City that summer was the 1939 World's Fair, built on a reconditioned Long Island swamp to proclaim a vision of peace and progress.

This World's Fair was a true crossroads. Everybody was there. The famous and the soon-to-be famous. The highest was the president of the United States; the lowest was Gregory Peck, a twenty-five-cents-an-hour gate guard. A day at the fair cost around $8.00, or it required a lot of ingenuity. An eighteen-year-old Hugh Downs from Chicago pretended to have a press pass. He passed by the family of an eight-year-old boy from Long Island named Roone Pinckney Arledge, Jr. He would grow up to be the head of ABC television.

There was, of course, a time capsule at the fair. It was twice as tall as a man and pointed at both ends. It was carefully lowered into a hole officially called the "Immortal Well." When opened five thousand years later (6939), it would show future peoples what was meaningful to Americans as they approached midcentury. There were, among other things, a Mickey Mouse cup, a wind-up alarm clock, a copy of *Gone With the Wind*, and a film newsreel. There was no radio and positively no television.

From the far end of the reflecting pool, the thematic Perisphere looked as if it were held up by the jets of water from the pool. The Trylon, alongside it, looked like a rocket ship poised for take-off.

At Democracity, an enormous white building, a thousand-voice chorus was piped in with the fair's theme song, extolling "a brave new world, tomorrow's world, that we shall build today." Tomorrow's world consisted of a core city, Centertron, encircled by satellite cities known as "Pleasantvilles." More industrial areas were known as "Millvilles." An assortment of greenbelts added to a sum total of a future industrial wonderland free of congestion and pollution.

Nearby in the General Motors exhibit, the popular Futurama showed more such utopian city planning. It was of, by, and for the automobile. Visitors waited in line two hours for the tour and on exiting received a button saying "I have seen the future."

The most popular exhibit was *Amazon Warrior Women*. Outside a barker hustled the crowd: "Nudity, yes, ladies and gentlemen; obscenity, no." The bare-breasted warriors were considered an "educational exhibit," alongside the Ice Act where two beautiful girls were "frozen alive."

In what today would surely win the bad taste trophy, black dancer Bill "Bojangles" Robinson, Shirley Temple's famous co-star, challenged

Chinese rickshaw runners to a 75-yard foot race. The rickshaw runners were in track suits, Bill was in a business suit. Bill ran the race *backwards* and celebrated each night's victory with a tap dance.

Broadway's most famous showman since Ziegfeld, Billy Rose, staged a stupendous aquacade, and between performances a large bandstand featured Les Brown and his "Band of Renown," with Jack Haskill and a very young Doris Day. Beyond that was a show of Antarctic penguins and "infant incubators" where for 25 cents one could see an exhibit of premature babies in shiny oxygen tanks. Outside the building was a giant thousand-pound baby made of stone, depicted lying on its back waving legs and arms. Inside nurses dressed in white were peacefully guarding tiny babies bathed in soft warm light. Had it not been for the recent invention of this infant incubator, many of these premature babies would have died. It had been invented by Philo Farnsworth, whose other greater invention—television—was on display a few blocks away with no credit to the inventor.

Around the fair you could try the first electric razor (it needed lots of talcum powder to work), see the first florescent light bulb, see the "real" Elsie the Borden cow, and taste the first aerated Wonder Bread. Kodak was demonstrating the first Kodachrome transparencies, Du-Pont was demonstrating the first uses of Nylon, Lucite Paint, and Plexiglas. At the Public Health Building there was a huge plastic man with all his giant organs visible except his genitalia. Nearby you could see cows being milked and Cokes being bottled. On opening night at the fair, Albert Einstein threw the switch to illuminate the entire twelve-square miles.[1]

The highlight of the fair was the RCA pavilion just to the west of the "Court of Peace," located on the "Avenue of Progress." It was shaped like a giant vacuum tube. Within the pavilion, thousands gathered at twelve special receivers, with picture tubes of five and nine inches and prices ranging from $200 to $600. In addition to the twelve TV sets at the fair, there were two hundred television sets in use in the New York metropolitan area. On this Sunday afternoon, no doubt all two hundred and twelve sets were operating as President Franklin Roosevelt delivered the opening address.

Roosevelt was not the first president on TV. As we already know, in 1927, Hoover, who would be elected president in 1928, had appeared on an experimental hookup between New York, New Jersey, and Washington. In keeping with the unpretentiousness of TV in those early days, he had been followed by an Irish vaudevillian who told jokes in black face.

In anticipation of the hugh promotional value of the World's Fair, NBC announced "regular television broadcasts" from the day the fair opened. Most of the programs originated at Studio 4H in Radio City. They were then sent down Fifth Avenue by underground cables to transmitters in the Empire State Building. In charge of the transmission operation was a tall young man named T. J. "Buzz" Buzalski. His domain was the mostly vacant eighty-fifth floor. The RCA labs were a mass of panels with disks, radio tubes, and coils of wire. Part of Buzz's job was to keep an eye on the aerial atop the Empire State Building. He liked this part. In those days you could walk outside at the highest level, and there was the NBC aerial, 260 feet above the souvenir counter, with its four stubby, torpedo-shaped arms of stainless steel.

Buzz had been on the job February 26, for the first test pick-up from the fairground. Carpenters and painters were still painting the finishing touches on the RCA pavilion, while Charles Correll and Freeman Gosden were trading one-liners, in black face, for an experimental TV broadcast of *Amos n' Andy*.

On opening day, President Roosevelt was followed on the podium by David Sarnoff, chairman of the board of RCA, who was introduced as the "father of American radio" along with the spurious story of how he "relayed wireless messages from the sinking Titanic." Broadcasting to two hundred and twelve sets but playing for the much larger audience at the fair, Sarnoff spoke directly to the live camera:

"Good morning, ladies and gentlemen. It is fitting that the greatest World's Fair in history should be the scene for the first public showing of one of the most significant theatrical and social advances of modern times. On April 30, the National Broadcasting Company will begin the first regular public television program service in the history of our country, and television viewing sets will be in the hands of merchants of the New York City area for purchase. It is with a feeling of humbleness that I come to this moment of announcing the birth, in this country, of a new art so important in its implications that it is bound to affect all society."[2]

The press did not respond with the reverence that Sarnoff hoped for. The *New Yorker* sneered: "Doubtless it will throw you into gales of indifference to learn that NBC plans to begin regular television broadcasts on the day the World's Fair opens."[3]

Three young men—all from Chicago—stood in the back of the audience, and a decade later all would be in the thick of TV. Hugh Downs had a cousin working on *The World Telegram* who had wrangled a press pass for him. Downs stuck it in his hat and moved freely through the RCA exhibit. He passed by a thirty-four-year-old man named Leonard Goldenson, who was a vice-president of Paramount Pictures theater division. Four decades later, Goldenson would be Downs's boss as chairman of the American Broadcasting System. At that moment, however, Goldenson didn't have much of a clue about television. He thought the live broadcast of FDR was coming from the White House when in fact it was a direct feed from another section of the fair. Goldenson, whose company owned a TV station in Chicago, was not aware of another young Chicago performer who waited in the RCA pavillion to make a brief TV appearance. Burr Tillstrom operated "Kukla and Ollie" in a puppet show of "St. George and the Dragon," presented by "The Kuklapolitan Players."

For a long time Hugh Downs stared at an RCA receiver, the TRK660. He was a radio buff and had a thousand questions. He was about to ask them when he realized the press pass in his hat might lead to an "interview" he didn't want to have. He gazed at himself on the TRK660's screen and thought, "My God, TV is a reality." Up to that point he had only known TV as a futuristic prop in Hollywood movies.

Hugh then tried the Parachute Drop, the longest and highest free-fall thrill ride ever. Unfortunately for this eager young man, the parachute failed to open completely and he dropped three times the intended speed, nearly breaking his back. Later he stumbled on and joined the eight thousand spectators who, each hour, went up the world's two largest escalators to the Helicline, a curving ramp down the Trylon to an overview of the fairgrounds.[4]

Downs was fascinated by something in the amusement area called an "all-electric band," which was performing at the other end of the amusement area. Tom Adrian Crocraft's All Electric Orchestra was indeed the orchestra of tomorrow. It was an "amplified" band. A news report described "the original vibrations picked up electrostatically, translated into electrical voltages, and then into sound by amplifier, controls, and reproducer." By September the All Electric Orchestra needed a vocalist, and signed on twenty-year-old Dinah Shore. Of all the performers and guests at the fair, Dinah had the least interest in the RCA television exhibit. Two years earlier she had "appeared" on television and hated the experience.[5]

A fourth young man—not from Chicago—was an inventor who had not been officially invited to this World's Fair spectacle, even though some of his inventive magic was on display. He was a tall family man from Passaic, New Jersey, and his name was Allen B. DuMont. As early as 1930, while working for the De Forest Radio Company, he had conducted experiments related to the development of television technology. Philo Farnsworth, the inventor of the incubator, had invented the image dissector tube, the basis of modern TV, but it burned out too quickly. In 1931, in his own basement, DuMont perfected the cathode-ray tube, a relatively inexpensive tube that lasted for more than a thousand hours. Not much by today's standards, but back then it was a big breakthrough. By 1939, DuMont had an experimental station going in Passaic, W2XWV, and was distributing a DuMont receiver to stores that was of higher quality than the RCA sets on display at the fair. Press releases from DuMont that preceded the opening of the fair attempted to steal attention from the RCA pavilion. They pointed out that DuMont sets, with an 8-by-11-inch screen, were bigger than RCA's and had a better picture. DuMont started experimental broadcasting in June, as did CBS, in an attempt to curtail Sarnoff's dream of a monopoly for NBC.

At the first night for the RCA building, Mayor Fiorello LaGuardia was saluted by a San Antonio, Texas, girls pep and marching squad—two hundred strong—who shouted "Hip, hip, LaGuardia!" at the top of their lungs. Then RCA conveniently voted the mayor the "most tele-genic" man at the fair. Twenty-three-year-old Betty Furness, who was hoping for a solid career as a screen actress, skipped the RCA exhibit, because she thought "television" was simply a device for people using telephones to see who they were talking to.[6]

The Trylon monument was on the "Avenue of the Patriots," and cameras from the RCA pavilion could aim up the avenue and keep it in the background of their popular radio show "Vox Pop," which was debuting on television. This was TV's first "man on the street" show. Parks Johnson and Wally Butterworth broadcast all through the summer. But for these performers, keeping the World's Fair background on camera was less important than keeping their pipes filled with their sponsor's Kentucky Club Tobacco. Even though the FCC said television had still to be "non-commercial," Kentucky Pipe Tobacco was plugged throughout this fifteen-minute show.

Visitors to the RCA pavilion saw a lot of remote broadcasts beamed to the fair from RCA's Manhattan transmitters. On June 1, NBC broadcast a boxing bout between Max Baer and Lou Nova. Nova squarely knocked out Baer in the eleventh round, but announcer Ed Herlihy spent most of his time raving about the RCA technology that made the broadcast possible. Herlihy's silvery voice was already familiar to newsreel audiences. When the first experimental *Kraft Television Theatre* tested on June 6, 1940, it became the first of the 1,423 times Herlihy would wrap his tongue around the word "Velveeta."

Burke Crotty, a producer for NBC at the fair, was dubious about how much the RCA exhibit would help the sale of receivers. "They may have been for sale, but not very many of them were bought," he recalled. The only set worth buying, according to Crotty, was the TRK660, a huge thing, four-and-a-half-feet high. The top was a hinged lid with a mirror reflecting the image on the tube below. It wasn't that the mirror enlarged the picture. It didn't. It was that the tube was so long, the only way to put it in the box was upright. Crotty scoffed, "I'd just bought a new car for $1,000, and they expected me to pay $660 for this elephantine TV!" Crotty, working for RCA, had never seen DuMont's fourteen-inch sharper image in a smaller cabinet, a unit he called the "Clifton."[7] It was great TV for its time, doomed to failure simply because DuMont didn't have the money to advertise it.

By October the leaves were falling off the trees, and NBC wrapped up their World's Fair programming with a self-congratulatory brochure listing their proudest achievements:

> The King and Queen of England.
> Grandmother's Night-off Club.
> Secretary Cordell Hull.
> Dairymaid's Beauty Contest.
> Parade of the U.S. Mechanized Cavalry.
> Musical Ride of the Canadian Northwest Mounted.

The fair was indeed a crossroads. Sarnoff pretended that it was television's debut. But hundreds of visitors to the fair, from Sarnoff himself to Dinah Shore, from Allen DuMont to Philo Farnsworth and Kate Smith, had all seen the future many years before. The electronic camera and reliable cathode-ray tubes were perfected by the end of this decade. Blistering hot lights were still a problem, and engineers from every company were hard at work to solve it. Television was being integrated with interlocking areas of ownership, programming, and sales. The "chicken" was ready, and the "egg" could take a bow.

All the forms of TV programming that we might list today were introduced before 1941: news and sports remotes, dramas and comedies, musicals, variety shows, and quiz shows. Even two-way home-shopping television had been introduced. But early TV programming was a series of flawed one-shots. Television was not going to be a mass medium until certain economic and policy problems could be solved. Economic troubles could be solved by more and better advertisers, as well as by the production of more receivers. Public relation problems could be solved by a green light from the FCC and a little less competition among Sarnoff, Paley, and DuMont. But through all this, day after day, the ever-hungry jaws of the one-eyed monster would have to be fed.

6

THE GAME'S AFOOT

1939–1947

The concept of broadcasting "real people" goes back to that radio program *Vox Pop*. It began in Houston, Texas, where Parks Johnson and Jerry Belcher dropped a microphone out the window of KTRH's studio in the Rice Hotel. Initial interview subjects were very skeptical that they were actually on radio; a decade later people were just as skeptical that they were on TV. At first *Vox Pop* paid their guests in dollar bills, then but Johnson's wife, Louise, hit on the novel idea of prizes. There was no prize too unusual. Her prizes ranged from puppies and silverware to lawnmowers and rugs. The audience-participation show, as we know it today, was born. *Vox Pop* made the transition to television at the RCA pavilion at the 1939 World's Fair, and by 1947, the show had been exported to Europe and Central America. In 1939, when *Vox Pop* debuted on television at the fair, it was already less of a "reality" show than when it began. The interviews were all scripted, and the guests were scouted and screened in advance. *Vox Pop* was widely and easily imitated.

At DuMont in New York in 1941, announcer Dennis James did his first "man on the street" by simply pointing the camera out of the window onto Madison Avenue. He claimed he was TV's first "man on the street."[1] On radio this kind of reality programming had sprung up everywhere. In Cincinnati, a young sportscaster named Red Barber working for WSAL traveled neighborhoods with a hand mike attached to a large white mobile trunk. In Pittsburgh, another sports announcer, Bill Cullen, Jr., (later a panelist on *I've Got a Secret* and a host of countless TV quiz shows including *Name That Tune*), brashly promoted himself into a sidewalk interview show called *Have You Got It?* And in New York in 1937, the man-on-the-street format was combined with quiz questions on *Professor Quiz*. It provided a network break for a young announcer from Washington named Arthur Godfrey.

Another voice all over New York radio was the twenty-six-year-old Ralph Edwards. In the 1950s and 1960s, he would star in *This is Your Life* and produce popular game shows, but in radio in 1939, he was a "voice for hire" working over forty shows a week, including *Life Can Be Beautiful* and *Against the Storm*. Ralph was not content with this radio-acting success. He wanted to be the boss, not just another well-paid voice. Coming into contact with agency people every day, he knew he could draw up a fresh program idea and sell it as daytime programming. He knew it had to be some kind of game show—something like a quiz but more like contest. The idea Ralph Edwards came up with became such a radio success that a New Mexico city was named after it. On July 1, 1941, at 9:30 P.M. Ralph Edwards presented the *first* television game show, *Truth or Consequences*.

The idea came to Ralph one evening at home with his wife, Barbara, and her parents, who were in town for a visit. During all the family small talk, Ralph sat in his chair staring straight ahead thinking a single phrase over and over: "Heavy, heavy hangs over thy head." It was a song he remembered as part of a game he played as a boy in Colorado. The game was called "Forfeits" and to play you had to get five or six friends of both sexes each of whom contributed a secret object to the questioner. He would then hold the object over someone's head and sing a song:

> "Heavy, heavy hangs over the head.
> Is it fine or super fine?
> Tell the truth or pay the consequences."[2]

"Fine" identified a boy's article, "superfine" was for a girl's, and if you guessed wrong, you had to "pay the consequences," which might be to run around the barn or sit on a girl's lap.

A friend at the Compton Agency liked his idea, and in less than two months the show went on the air with Edwards and staff announcer, Mel Allen. The show was a huge success and ran for years on radio and TV, and the outrageous stunts frequently made newspaper headlines. The irony of Edwards's creation was that he intended *Truth or Consequences* to be a send-up of the big-money radio quiz shows that were popping up everywhere. *Truth or Consequences* ultimately became the thing it satirized, spawning dozens of imitations.

When ABC entered television after the war ended in Europe, it didn't have its own stations, and it didn't have much money, so it resorted to low-budget game shows broadcast on the facilities of DuMont and General Electric.

On February 25, 1945, while ABC was still the "Blue Network," it promoted a video version of a popular radio quiz show, *Ladies Be Seated*, with Johnny Olsen. Johnny is known today as the offstage announcer on *The Price is Right*, but in 1945 he was also an unknown radio voice. *Ladies Be Seated*, like Ralph Edwards's pioneer effort, was a stunt show. Blindfolded housewives raced through messy bowls of spaghetti while their husbands tried to fill in the missing words to songs.

In this book's introduction, it was pointed out that there are no filmed records of pre-1948 television, and that nearly all of the scripts were destroyed long ago. One of the few scripts that remains is the very first episode of *Ladies Be Seated*, starring Johnny Olsen, which was broadcast over WRGB in Schenectady, New York, on February 25, 1945.* The script is interesting for its technical detail, and also because it reveals that there was carefully *scripted dialogue* in what appeared to be an all ad-lib show. After reading this rare script, it is apparent that everyone involved with *Ladies Be Seated* took the show seriously, even if the home audience only remembered contestants in red flannel pajamas dancing with inflatable partners.

Quiz Kids was another radio show that easily transferred to television. The panelists ranged in age from six to sixteen. The biggest kid star in both radio and TV was Joel Kupperman, who was ten and had an IQ over 200. He answered algebra problems almost instantly with no pencil or paper. His amazing math skills had radio listeners worried that *Quiz Kids* might be fixed. It wasn't until they saw Kupperman on the TV version that viewers were convinced of his honesty. Seeing was believing. Or, at least that would be true for the next ten years.

By the 1945–46 season, there were three new game shows on television: *Cash and Carry*, *Play the Game*, and *See What You Know*. None lasted more than a few weeks. The weirdest was a patriotic variety game show *Letter to Your Serviceman*, with the most unusual slate of hosts in television: burlesque comic Joey Faye, composer Burt Bacharach, and actress Helen Twelvetrees. They lasted ten weeks.

The following year, DuMont tried an "amateur hour" contest called *Doorway to Fame*, but the real *Amateur Hour* was a year away. WNBT was still trying for a cultural quiz show borrowing from *Author Meets the Critics*, the recently revived radio quiz show of the same name. This unique show brought book reviewers face to face with an author, who was given a bell to ring whenever he was in disagreement with a critic.

By 1947 charades came to television in the form of a telephone quiz show called *Telequizzicals* at WBKB in Chicago. There is no record of how this show actually worked, but there is lots of documentation that Commonwealth Edison, the sponsor, tied in endorsements for electrical appliances with almost every question. When Mike Stokey's *Pantomime*

*See Appendix C.

Quiz became successful in Los Angeles in 1947, it was immediately copied by DuMont in New York. Bill Slater, a popular sportscaster, headed the company of actors on *Charade Quiz*, which had a maximum prize of $150, making it the biggest prize in television to date.[3]

Over at NBC, producer-director Fred Coe took a break from dramas to create *Seven Arts Quiz*, a high-brow panel show that was led by Bill Slater. Slater, a cool sports announcer, was an odd choice for a high-brow show. His attitude can best be described by an incident during a pharmaceutical commercial. A girl dressed as a nurse fainted in the middle of this live advertisement. The director "went to black" and the stage manager frantically signaled for Bill to "cover." "What's the big deal?" shrugged Slater, coming on camera. "She just fainted."

"What's the big deal?" was not only the watchword for studio accidents, it became the ongoing answer to any questions about "staging" audience-participation shows. If *Ladies Be Seated* wasn't as spontaneous as it looked (see Appendix C), then "what's the big deal?" A decade later, this flippant defense would get many game-show producers in big, big trouble as their world faced collapse amidst revelations of rigged quiz shows.

7

THE BIRTH
OF
THE BBC

1929–1946

Regular BBC programming began in 1929 when the British Broadcasting System joined Baird Television for broadcasts with mechanical TV—using a 30-line screen and twelve-and-a-half pictures per second. Sound was added in 1930. Since two widely separated wavelengths were needed for transmission—one for sound and one for picture—BBC television could only broadcast after 11:00 P.M. at night, when BBC radio went off the air.

Late in 1935 Baird was still working with the BBC, this time using several systems including a version of *electronic* television based on Philo Farnsworth's patents. Also working with the BBC was Marconi-EMI Ltd., recently formed in 1934 with a rebuilt research staff to tackle television. It was using electronic technology based on Vladimir Zworykin's RCA patents. The two systems, Baird's and EMI's, broadcast on alternating weeks. The BBC announced that one of these competitors would be picked as the sole BBC technology within twelve months.

In 1935 the *Daily Telegraph* reported that the BBC was casting for a female television announcer to be the "signature" for the new television system. The press called it the search for a "super woman." Specifically, the winner would have to have outstanding personality, charm, tact, and memory. She had to photograph well, have a mezzo voice, and be equally acceptable to women and men. The two unwavering demands of the contest were that the super women could not be married and must not have red hair. The hair restriction had to do with the difficulty in transmitting the color red, and the marriage restriction was the result of some malarkey about the demanding nature of the job. In any case, hundreds of thousands of women applied—from all over the world. In May 1936, the BBC settled on Jasmine Bligh and Elizabeth Cowell. Each was given a contract for six months. They were also given a yearly clothing allowance of thirteen pounds, but since they were only to be photographed from the waist up, they jointly agreed to buy only tops, wearing their own skirts.[1]

The BBC "preview" on August 26 at Alexandra Palace was a big hit with the press, which had heretofore been skeptical about all the corporation's efforts. Insiders always suspected that the press's hostility was partly because the in-town Broadcasting House was only for "the teetotalers"—no alcohol could be served. Alexandra Palace was sufficiently remote, and there was lots of liquor for the gentlemen of the press.

The pampered press proved to be very forgiving. The demonstration began with a blown fuse, and there was a delay of two hours. What's more, the widely publicized "super women" were no-shows. Jasmine Bligh had been rushed to the hospital for an appendectomy, and Elizabeth Cowell was home with a throat infection. Thank God for the booze!

While the super women were recovering, male announcer Leslie Mitchell filled in. He faced each breakdown with resource and courage. Once he was rushed back onto the studio floor with instructions that the picture had broken down but that the sound was still operating. As

Mitchell slowly walked through a string of jokes for all occasions, the director interrupted on the studio's intercom speaker: "What do you think you're doing? The picture's all right, it's the *sound* that's gone!"

Mitchell's most undignified moment occurred several days later while announcing a fire-fighting demonstration from atop the ladder of a hook and ladder truck. The extension ladder caught Leslie's pants and methodically tore them into strips. Mitchell became the first man in TV history to be photographed with his pants off.

Midway into a ten-day demonstration, which for mysterious reasons the BBC called *The Radio Show*, saboteurs struck. First, a wad of tinfoil was stuck into a vital plug point, then there was a dead mouse wedged into the equipment in a location which the rodent could never have reached on his own. BBC officials suspected the saboteurs were working for rival trade interests. Or could Baird's people have been wreaking havoc on EMI people—and vice versa?

On August 31, Elizabeth Cowell was fully recovered from her throat problem. The first BBC Superwoman was at last ready to go. Appropriately there was mass confusion and no rehearsal time. First Cowell announced singer Helen Mackay with a grand gesture to her right. Miss Mackay promptly entered on the *other* side. Then famous baritone Peter Dawson was introduced and began his act in a shot so wide that it still included Miss Cowell and the studio telephones. Unfortunately it didn't include Dawson's head, and the singer was so tall that a second fixed camera only had him covered from the neck down. The phone rang. It was an assistant director telling the hostess to get Dawson to sit down. Elizabeth, thinking she was off-camera, amateurishly pantomimed to the singer to consider a stool behind him. In mid-song Dawson shrugged off what he thought was simply a courteous invitation. The close-up camera never did get a shot of more than what newspaper critics referred to as "the Headless Baritone."

On October 8, just before the BBC began regular service, Cecil Madden introduced *Picture Page*, which became the BBC's most popular show in the prewar period, running over six hundred performances. The premiere show of this anthology series had a troubadour, a suffragette, and a prizewinning Siamese cat named Prestwick Pertana.

That night the BBC measured the broadcast range of its electronic TV at twenty-five miles.

The Alexandra Palace broadcasting station officially opened on November 2, 1936, with two hours of programs, everyday at 3:00 P.M. and 9:00 P.M. Within four months, a Television Advisory Committee gave Marconi-EMI the contract, and Baird was sent packing. With approved standards in place, a handful of Londoners were eager to buy TV receivers at a cost of from $500 to $1,000 each. Set ownership was limited to the very wealthy and the owners of pubs.

The BBC itself didn't have much interest in selling TV sets. Without regard for payback, it had spent four million dollars for two years of experimental production, and it was prepared to spend a lot more. For a variety of reasons—not all of them above board (such as the secret radar research)—the British government had a vital interest in the progress of early television.

As with American television, what the BBC home viewer saw on his screen gave no clue to the backstage hysteria that led up to the program. Rehearsals for dramas were limited to two hours each, and attention was focused exclusively on technical matters. During the three years that preceded World War II, the BBC set off fearlessly into the Great Unknown. Cecil Madden, the BBC's television program organizer summed that time up in an interview with American producer Richard Hubbell:

> In the early days, it was to some extent a matter of trial and error. With the tremendous variety of subjects open to us in 1936, it was almost impossible to lay down any rules about what was good and what was bad television. Right from the beginning our object was everything—real variety. In the very first television program we did, we had a complete variety show in which we showed everything, even the orchestra. I created a series called *Starlight* to exploit the biggest stars of variety, cabaret, or music world: Paul Robeson, Pyatigorsky, Alice Marble, Lou Holtz, Sophie Tucker, Bebe Daniels.[2]

Bebe Daniels, an American movie star from the great Warners-Busby Berkeley musicals, worked often for Cecil Madden, trying out songs, sketches—even special effects. Madden featured a series of "all-American programmes" called *100 Per Cent Broadway* with truncated chorus lines tapping out minimally rehearsed numbers.

His variety shows under control, Madden branched out into ballet, recruiting the world-famous Vic-Wells Ballet and its prima ballerina—Margot Fonteyn. His production of the *Sleeping Princess* was so big it needed two stages. Since there were no intermissions, Miss Fonteyn once had to dash down a fifty-yard corridor from one studio to the other while the studio orchestra held the longest chord in television history.

Cameraman Stanley Lake remembered one continuous "take" on his camera 2, in studio A,

> It lasted about one hour and twenty minutes—compared with a movie cameraman, whose average camera shot cannot be more than two minutes. There was the strain of continuous focusing, and there was also the psychological strain, because the camera viewfinder showed the scene upside down. Then there was the continuous panning of the camera from left to right. It was rather like waking up from a dream when the production was all over.[3]

The first BBC drama of the electronic era was a film clip of Laurence Olivier in *As You Like It*. The same broadcast had a live excerpt from a current West End play, *The Two Bouquets*. For the next three years the BBC experimented with four hundred different television dramas, many of outstanding length and quality. During the same period, America's NBC had only made sixty-three. RCA had not yet begun a push for the public to buy television sets, whereas in Britain, TV sets were already in demand. The BBC concentrated on fine programming, not set manufacture and sales, leaving these areas to independent entrepreneurs. Ownership of receivers in 1936 was an astounding twenty-three thousand.

The quality of the acting was so good that some productions produced unexpected results. *Night Must Fall*, a thriller about the menacing of an elderly lady, got several viewers "too excited." They wrote to the BBC to say they were "obliged to switch off" their sets.

Scenic values eventually came up to the level of fine acting. Set designer Peter Bax began with a budget only for curtains. This budget was expanded, and soon Bax could afford wallpaper. Then he convinced Cecil Madden that studio sets could be reused, and the BBC opened its purse. The elaborate forest in *Tristan* was featured a week later in *The Emperor Jones*. American reporter Edward R. Murrow, a TV skeptic himself in the early days, interviewed Bax about many special visual effects the BBC had achieved, including, what Bax described as:

> revolving stages and rolling ships and shaking railway carriages, smoking fires, real fires, and all the rest of it. And our visual effects, just as they do in the movies, came from a combination of mechanical design and optical illusion.[4]

Actors on the BBC, used to honing their craft in the theatrical West End, were frustrated by the lack of rehearsal time for television. Those few hours available were always taken up by technical matters, and on-the-air technical disasters frequently caused actors to dry up. In 1937's condensed *Othello*, for example, the actress playing Desdemona panicked because she had never seen a TV camera before. Frequently performers got stuck in the fog or traffic—or both—and would go on the air without rehearsal. Sympathetic cast members often tried to help. BBC makeup artist Christine Hillcoat remembers an elderly actor telling another elderly colleague, "If you dry up, old boy, just carry on mouthing words. The audience will think it's a technical fault, and they've lost sound." Sometimes actors hid little pieces of paper with their lines all over the set; in drawers, on lamps, wherever. This, of course, left them wide open to sabotage by their fellow actors. Wrong cues were often followed by dead silence.

When a BBC program didn't have room for live music, producers resorted to player pianos with their pianist-operators tucked away in an adjoining studio. Once in 1937, John Snagge, who worked for the BBC as early as 1924 and didn't retire until 1981, had just left his control room when one such piece of background music turned into a strangled discordant mess. He returned from the men's room toilet to the music studio to see one of his colleagues gasping for air because his tie was caught up in the piano roll. As colleague Brian Johnston described the accident, the victim was "gradually being pulled into the pianola and strangled to death."

By 1937 the Superwomen, Jasmine Bligh and Elizabeth Cowell, were both in good health and appeared daily on television in a wider sphere of activities. Jasmine did so many stunts that she became known as the "Pearl White of Television," named after the famous stunt actress of silent movies in "The Perils of Pauline." She went motorcycle riding with the Metropolitan Police and flew an autogiro, an unstable lightweight flying machine similar to today's ultralights. After she was bitten on the arm by a chimpanzee (she kept speaking to the camera and never showed her pain), she was insured against injury by the BBC. The policy was a paltry one thousand pounds. Elizabeth Cowell had her own problems. A speaking cockatoo on the air proclaimed, "Get your cash, you red-headed old cat" and took a piece out of Elizabeth's leg (even though she wasn't a redhead).

Animals of all sizes and shapes were a regular feature on the BBC ever since a celebrated greyhound named Mack the Miller became TV's first animal star in 1936. Two years later producer Desmond Davis had an opera called *The Piper* which required, in addition to the opera singers, a cast of fifty rats. The singers were to be on live and the rats filmed in advance. The script called for the rats to plunge like lemmings into a roaring river. The roaring river was constructed in an old bathtub filled with muddy water. Slabs of mud and turf decorated the bathtub rim and cheese was sprinkled at the very edge. As cameras rolled, and Mr. Davis quietly called for "action," the rats paused on the brink, tested the temperature of the water with their paws, then slowly and deliberately combed their whiskers. Davis screamed "cut" and drained the bathtub. Prop men had to push the reluctant rats over the "precipice."[5]

The Cuban music craze that Desi Arnaz brought to American TV in the 1950s was previewed in London in the late 1930s. Edmundo Ros had a Cuban band that practically camped out at Alexandra Palace. Whenever a show ran short, instead of a "Please Stand By" card, Edmundo Ros would cheerfully bang away on his bongos.

The accidents of early television were never classified as bloopers because it was a miracle when any show aired without a hitch. Finally in 1938, the BBC thought they had a smooth running operation. For *In Town Tonight*, the ultra-smooth hostess, Joan Miller, was interviewing a steelworker named George Brennan. She began, "I believe you are a weild striker"—and since she thought she had said "steel worker" she at first couldn't understand why George began jittering and then roaring with helpless laughter. Then Joan lost it and began laughing. A male announcer tried to take over—and he too started laughing, followed by the stagehands, and then the entire crew.

On "Black Friday," September 1, 1939, Britain declared war on Nazi Germany. BBC television—in the prime of creative and technological achievement—was closed down for the duration. The order came through while the midday broadcast was in progress. The announcer had just introduced an animated cartoon, *Mickey's Birthday Party*, a film that included caricatures of various Hollywood stars: Charles Boyer, Katharine Hepburn, W. C. Fields, Greta Garbo, among others. Just as Garbo uttered the cartoon words, "I tank I go home," the master switch was thrown. The BBC went dark—completely dark—for seven years.

It was a real tragedy to the 190 people who for over three years had been pouring their hearts and minds into TV. Producers, engineers, designers, secretaries—everyone—pledged to each other that when the war was over they would all be back, and with a new and better television service.

On June 7, 1946, with the same equipment that it had used before the war, and without missing a beat, the BBC program schedule picked up where it had left off—in the middle of *Mickey's Birthday Party*. The same announcer from 1939 was then seen on camera, a bit older and a bit grayer, with a classic of British understatement:

"Now, as I was saying when I was so rudely interrupted . . ."

HOORAY
FOR
HOLLYWOOD

1930–1947

Television for Los Angeles began in 1930. Don Lee, a successful inventor and developer of radio, put his experimental TV station for downtown Los Angeles in an eight-story building with an antenna that rose 200 feet in the smogless sky. That station, using technology developed by Philo Farnsworth, was able to telecast to a thirty-mile radius. Miraculously in May 1932, the engineers of W6XAO even broadcast from a tri-motored airplane flying over Los Angeles, the first such remote broadcast.

Don Lee did what every early TV mogul had done. To run his station he hired a whiz kid who was willing to do everything: engineering, programming, even sweeping the studio floor. Such a kid was twenty-five-year-old Harry Lubke. After graduating from the University of California at Berkeley, he had worked for Philo Farnsworth in his San Francisco lab in 1929. Since Harry was experienced with

Farnsworth technology, Los Angeles was spared a false start with the Jenkins mechanical system. The station's first programming was on film: Paramount shorts and Pathe newsreels. Lubke scanned the film with a cathode-ray tube that synchronized with a CRT-equipped receiver. When W6XAO wasn't broadcasting film clips, a typical program consisted of one-camera studio interviews with movie stars like Tom Mix and Jean Harlow.

Full-scale telecasting began on March 10, 1933, and that day, as luck would have it, a major earthquake shook Los Angeles. W6XAO's newsreel crew was dispatched, and the next day films were broadcast of the damaged areas. Since almost no homes yet had television sets, most of these films were seen on sets in department or appliance stores, and subsequent coverage of the broadcast in newspapers gave W6XAO the glow of a major scoop.

Don Lee's Hollywood connections always paid off. W6XAO was the first broadcasting station to show a current full-length motion picture, *The Crooked Circle*, which was followed by Gary Cooper in *The Texan*. During the first three-and-a-half years of operation, Lubke, the station director, estimated he had transmitted 6 million feet of motion picture film. By 1936, W6XAO expanded its schedule to four hours a day; by then its programs were both film and live. Using a tie-in with the University of Southern California and local high schools, the station did a great deal of educational programming.

In 1938, W6XAO telecast four dramatic sketches a week, including TV's first soap opera, *Vine Street*, starring Shirley Thomas and John Berkeley. It was a tragic-comic drama stretching from the hobo jungles of central L.A. to the high life of Hollywood. Fifty-two episodes were telecast, and considering how few receivers existed in the entire city, it was amazing how many people talked about *Vine Street*.[1]

By 1939, W6XAO was ready to expand its operation to a new studio, which Don Lee's son, Thomas S. Lee, built and modestly named "Mount Lee." He was also planning a station in San Francisco, making a west coast "network." In 1940, W6XAO showed itself equal to NBC in its range of programming capability when the station bought an RCA mobile unit and did the first live telecast of the

Tournament of Roses Parade. Then, live from the Hollywood Bowl, W6XAO presented a remote of the Easter Sunrise service, and after a brief foray into boxing at the American Legion stadium, it did the first remote of a beauty pageant. The town that had been built on the movie business had an audience nearly ready for real television.

One of the best remembered faces from the early 1950s and the first Emmy winner for a game show, Mike Stokey was a student at Los Angeles City College in 1939. He was active in the radio club, and when the club members weren't rehearsing, they played charades. Stokey was quite surprised when W6XAO asked him if he would organize two student teams for a charades game. Stokey had never seen a television set, but he sure knew how to play "The Game," a refined version of charades. He brought seven other students to compete, but the Don Lee building at Seventh and Bixel streets was so small that it had room only for Stokey and five others. The two teams of three worked so well that the Don Lee management asked Stokey to repeat the show every Saturday night at 8:00 for two months. No one was paid, but everyone had a great time. TV then was only a passing fancy for young Stokey, and after graduation, he was off to a career in radio. Stokey's real stardom with *Pantomime Quiz* was yet to come.[2]

CBS used the Don Lee station as an outlet for some local television programs they wanted to test. By 1937, CBS presented their own experimental crime series *Take the Witness* from the Columbia Music Box Theatre. Television cameras were installed in the front row and each episode was rehearsed and performed as a play. The Mutual Network's radio programs also had brief TV tryouts on W6XAO. The worst example of this was *The Johnson Family*, a comedy-drama about a Negro family living in Los Angeles. Jimmy Scribner, a white man, was the star, and on radio he performed *all* the characters by changing his voice. Scribner used the same technique on W6XAO, and the show bombed completely. On television there was no way he could play multiple characters, and the public was confused to say the least.[3]

After World War II, W6XAO changed its call letters to KTSL (after the initials of its new owner, Thomas S. Lee). Even though it had bigger and better facilities, KTSL's programming aims became smaller and smaller. Harry Lubke was still in charge, but his programs were a decade old. The competition from Paramount's station, KTLA, didn't make his ideas sharper, it made them duller. Don Lee desperately bought packaged performances from local theater groups. The Pasadena Community Playhouse was first-rate with full-length plays like *Johnny Come Home* and *Hedda Gabler*, but other productions were supplied by amateur groups from hospitals and students enrolled in University of California extension courses. KTSL ended up with canned stuff: short film subjects that were usually classroom films, or worse, home movies. The year of KTSL's death, 1947, was the year KTLA had its "coming out" party.

KTLA, the station that survived, began at Paramount Pictures in 1941 as W6XYZ. During the war, the best of W6XYZ's programming consisted of live, unrehearsed interviews done by a lanky young writer named Franklin Lacey, who became television's first talk-show host, on his own show. As incredible as it may seem with today's proliferation of TV talk shows, in the thirteen years of television development since *The Queen's Messenger*, no one had conceived of an interviewer in a living room chatting with celebrity guests. There was no such show on radio, and as almost all of TV's early programmers were adapted from radio, there was no precedent for a talk show. The uniqueness of Lacey's show was that even though there were a tiny number of set owners watching, week after week Franklin could convince stars like Beatrice Lillie, of Broadway and London musical fame, to join him for an hour of civilized conversation. No prizes. No audience participation. Just talk. And the show was so popular that the forty home viewers would call W6XYZ and invite Franklin and his guests over to their house for dinner afterwards. And Franklin and his guests frequently accepted. Lacey's talk show was a true block party, lasting several years. It is generally accepted knowledge that NBC president Pat Weaver created the talk-show concept in 1952 with the *Tonight Show*. It is generally unknown that during TV's "prehistory," Franklin Lacey beat the *Tonight Show* by ten years.[4]

The boss of W6XYZ was a twenty-five-year-old refugee named Klaus Landsberg. In his native Germany, Landsberg was considered an electronic boy genius. At sixteen he developed the world's most effective short wave radio. In 1936, at age twenty, he was part of the historic broadcast team for the Berlin Olympics. But the political writing was on the wall and he fled Nazi Germany for New York with only two suitcases, both full of electronic equipment. He then worked a short time with NBC as a remote truck engineer on its telecasts from the World's Fair. Vastly overqualified for his NBC work, Klaus quit and headed for Los Angeles, where he convinced Paramount to put him in charge of W6XYZ which debuted in 1941.

He immediately made two important decisions in both technical and programming areas. The W6XYZ transmitter was placed on Mount Wilson (all Los Angeles stations would eventually be on Mount Wilson), giving it a far greater range than the Don Lee station had. Klaus also used his experience in remote telecasts to take the camera out of its designated sound stage on the Paramount lot and onto the sets of motion pictures in production. An early telecast was a scene from *This Gun For Hire* with Alan Ladd and Veronica Lake.[5]

The RKO lot next door to Paramount was busy turning out "Boston Blackie" movies when Landsberg began his TV camera installation. It aroused the curiosity of an actor in the "Blackie" series, Dick Lane, and Lane's interest in the sport of wrestling put W6XYZ on the map.

Dick Lane had already had a variety of jobs. He'd been a silent film actor, a barker in a medicine show, and had even hung by his teeth in a sideshow "Iron Jaw" act. Along the way he befriended some wrestlers and as a hobby managed a Texas beast named "Dangerous Danny McShaine." When Lane approached Landsberg, the latter's idea of a sports remote was certainly not wrestling. Lane convinced him that wrestling could easily be done on the Paramount sound stage. The stage was so small, the "arena" would never look empty and Lane himself could supply the fighters and do the play-by-play.

Wrestling became the most popular program on W6XYZ during the war. Two years later DuMont would be doing it with Dennis James, and NBC would be doing too; but in 1942, it was a video experience unique to southern California. In fact, in 1945, just as DuMont's Jamaica Arena telecasts were starting in New York, Los Angeles wrestling had become so popular that Lane had moved to the ten-thousand-seat Olympic Auditorium where he provided commentary as outrageous as the wrestling acts themselves. Then, as now, TV audiences had no problems with the "fake" aspects of the sport. They were slaphappy as long as the heroes and villains kept coming, and Dick Lane had an endless stable that included the fiendish Mr. Moto, the hulking Tolof Brothers, and Chief Strongbow. Lane programmed interviews with these characters, and their verbal fights were as memorable as the main events. At one point a wrestler grabbed the microphone from Lane and began insulting his opponent as a "pencil-naked geek." Lane's half-serious, half-kidding interviews, along with his overly enthusiastic commentary, set a standard that would be well imitated in Lane's other great contribution to TV sports, Roller Derby.

The name most Americans remember from the early TV era was that of the wrestler Gorgeous George. Texas-born George Weber was truly a creation of television. Lane's luck with Mr. Moto and Chief Strongbow made it clear that a successful wrestler had to have a gimmick. In 1945, Weber was just a slob with no job. He had no gimmick unless you could call wrestling in blue jeans a gimmick. George was such a slob that his wife, Betty, kept nagging him to buy a decent suit. The day that he complied, she screamed out, "You look gorgeous, George!" and a bell went off in George Weber's brain. His audition for Lane a few weeks later was hilarious. Lane and his associates were on the floor, but George never cracked a smile. He had dyed his hair platinum and put it in curls. He wore a flowing satin cape, and his handler moved through the stage with an atomizer spraying what was purported to be Chanel No. 5. Gorgeous George was born.

After the war, Landsberg created more and more remote programming. He sent announcer Bill Welsh to the Pan Pacific Auditorium to do a hockey game, telling him, "You don't have to do a lot of talking. The audience can see the game well enough." Hollywood had its own minor league baseball team, the Hollywood Stars, the only Triple A franchise to wear short pants. Landsberg's W6XYZ did remotes from Gilmore Field almost every night.

On January 22, 1947, W6XYZ became KTLA with its first "commercial" broadcast. It was not a great debut. Bob Hope, Jerry Collona, Dorothy Lamour, and William Bendix appeared in a half-hour show from the Paramount TV stage. Hope had no TV experience, no idea what camera to look into, and flubbed the call letters (he called it "KTL"). Paramount's newsreel department filmed the broadcast but never released the film. In all of Los Angeles there were four hundred viewers. The ho-hum announcement of the event in *Variety* was at the bottom of page six, next to that of the retirement of the head of the Universal commissary. Their review the next day said KTLA's debut "rates low as entertainment."[6]

Though there were only four hundred viewers, it was still the friendly family that Franklin Lacey had found four years earlier. When announcer Stan Chambers broadcast the news with a sniffle, viewers came to the studio with their personal cold remedies.

Now that W6XYZ had gone commercial as KTLA, Landsberg wondered if there could be another kind of programming as quick and cheap as wrestling? Dick Lane remembered seeing a charades show on the Don Lee station during the summer of 1939. Mike Stokey had since become a well-paid radio announcer, but that conflict was worked out, and Stokey united college students from the University of Southern California and the University of California—Los Angeles. On the Paramount stages in the spring of 1947, *Pantomime Quiz* was being broadcast live when Roddy McDowall, in costume and makeup from a nearby sound stage, wandered onto the set. McDowell loved charades and got so animated as an off-camera spectator that Stokey invited him to step up on camera during the live telecast. Roddy joined the students and had such a good time that as the show was about to sign off, he jumped in front of Stokey and shouted, "If this is TV, it's a ball. I want some of my pals in the business to come down next week and join us. Wha'dya say, Mike?"

Stokey was at a loss for words. Then the Paramount phones started ringing. Major movie stars like Lucille Ball were volunteering to play *Pantomime Quiz* for *nothing*. And so they did, week after week and year after year. Stokey went network, and won numerous Emmy awards.

Another show from the same era which Stokey remembers fondly was a minute mystery short called *Armchair Detective*. In keeping with KTLA's pauper budgets, the actors in the sketches were not paid and were usually recruited from colleges—by posting notices for screen extras on campus bulletin boards. One such girl—named Norma—passed her audition largely based on her beauty. Stokey noticed she was very nervous during rehearsals. He kept telling her not to be afraid of the little red lights on the live cameras. The more he talked about the live aspects of the production, the more nervous Norma became. On air she froze completely, bungled the key props, and left Stokey to do some fancy ad libbing to cover the expositional gaps. When the show was over, Norma threw herself into his arms sobbing, "I'll never work again." Stokey assured her that she would indeed survive this debacle, and sure enough the following year, Norma, (or rather "Norma Jean") made a very large impression on movie audiences in *The Asphalt Jungle*, under her new name, Marilyn Monroe.[7]

Landsberg liked Stokey a lot, and it was important to be on Klaus's good side, because he had a short fuse and an imperious manner. Temperamental executives were not usually successful in early television. The hours and working conditions truly demanded a lot of cooperation in the work place. Klaus was not that kind of guy, a fact supported by Judy Dinsdale, a ventriloquist whose puppet show, *The Judy Splinters Show*, was a big hit in 1947 on KTLA. "Judy, the doll, once answered the phone on KTLA when everyone else was busy. Klaus saw the dummy taking messages and went crazy. I guess he never saw us as one big family."[8]

For almost two decades, the Don Lee and Paramount stations had been equal to—and sometimes better than—their better-financed New York rivals. W6XAO did fancy remotes years ahead of RCA. W6XYZ did sports before DuMont and more frequently. Don Lee pioneered fresh newsreel coverage while NBC used "stock" shots. Paramount invented the talk show while the big three cannibalized radio quiz shows. Harry Lubke and Klaus Landsberg, working in an atmosphere of independence and creative freedom, proved that talent and imagination are sometimes more important than money.

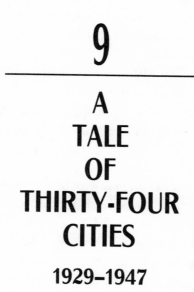

9

A
TALE
OF
THIRTY-FOUR
CITIES

1929–1947

I n 1929, a year after WGY's "The Queen's Messenger," primitive
TV pictures reached across the continent, from as far as Seattle,
Washington, to New York City. Soon the Jenkins mechanical TV
system was everywhere. Cheap to acquire, simple to set up, and wide
in its broadcasting range, the system quickly became a gadgeteer's
dream.

Palmer K. Laberman was a Naval Academy graduate who stood
tall and ramrod straight. A decade later he would be the hugely
successful publisher of *Family Circle* magazine, but in 1927, he was just
another Washington State radio buff tinkering with a home-built rig in
the basement of his home. He had made a few dollars with a small
appliance store in Seattle, and with friend Francis Brott, he founded
TV station KRSC. Its tiny picture—scarcely more than an inch
square—even had color, of a sort. The black-and-white images showed

up red on a white background. Incredibly, Seattle's station was regularly on the air before New York City stations were.

In the next five years, mechanical TV was established in New York, Los Angeles, Boston, Chicago, Schenectady, and Seattle, but who would have thought that in 1933 there would be television in Iowa City, Iowa? Sure enough, twice a week, families in Iowa and all over the Midwest would tune their radio dials to radio station WSVI. Then they would tune their separate mechanical-system TV sets with four-inch, 41-line screens, to W9XK. At 7:30 P.M. the broadcast began:

> Good evening, ladies and gentlemen. Station WSVI now joins facilities with television transmitter W9XK to bring you a program of both sight and sound. WSVI is operating on its regular broadcast frequency of 880 kilocycles while W9XK is transmitting television images on a frequency of 2050 kilocycles with a power of 100 watts.

WSVI was the radio station of the State University of Iowa and W9XK was television's first regularly scheduled educational station. It was seen in Omaha, Nebraska; Duncan, Oklahoma; and Rock Port, Missouri. It often had viewers as far away as Texas. Typical programs, with faculty and student performers, featured musical numbers, college lectures, and dramatic sketches. Regular series included *Iowa Wild Life*, *Spring Birds*, and the inevitable shows for Boy Scouts.[1]

In 1934 Professor Edward Kurtz, the university's head of engineering as well as a frequent performer, played host to the famous radio news commentator H. V. Kaltenborn, who volunteered this pessimistic opinion about television: "There is nothing you have shown me which could not be more definitely shown by lantern slides, or moving pictures. Engineers who have worked on television seem convinced that there is nothing in it."*

In 1934, there were an amazing forty-two stations in operation using the Jenkins mechanical system. Besides those mentioned, there

---

*Ironically fourteen years later, it was this same Kaltenborn whom Harry Truman mocked for incorrectly and stubbornly predicting his defeat by Thomas Dewey.

were broadcasters in Pittsburgh, Milwaukee, Silver Spring, Maryland, and West Lafayette, Indiana, as well as in seven cities in Canada. The most rural of all the Canadian stations was VE9ED owned by a "Dr. J. L. P. Landry" in a Quebec town called Mont Joli.

The groundwork for Chicago television had been literally laid in 1929 when NBC technicians, wiring the Merchandise Mart, added heavy duty cables suitable for TV on the presumption that one day they would be needed. Meanwhile, a twenty-two-year-old inventor, Ulises A. Sanabria, designed a scanning disc that was better than Jenkins's. It had a sharper image and less flicker. His company, Western Television, supplied equipment to Chicago's two stations as well as to the one in Iowa. By 1931, there were three stations in Chicago. In addition to Western Television's WXAO, there was W9XAP, owned by the *Chicago Daily News*, and W9XZV, owned by the Zenith Radio Corporation. But several years later the station that would grow to dominate the Windy City was owned by the Balaban and Katz theater chain, W9XBK. In the 1940s, it would usher in the "Chicago School" of television under its revised call letters WBKB.[2]

The only extant program listing for very early Chicago TV comes from W9XAP, which had a news program ("S. W. Lincoln reads flashes of the day"), a sports news program, the meetings of a model airplane club, lots of cartoons (all featuring host John Mattis), and one big dramatic special—a production by the Goodman Theatre of a play by Louis Parker, *The Minuet.*

In Boston, on a shoestring budget, W1XG had an afternoon schedule featuring "weather forecasts, test patterns, and visual novelties." No one remembers what the visual novelties were, but several programming veterans have fond memories of the big prime-time show on Monday nights, *The Boy Scout Program*, featuring demonstrations of scouting techniques.

The first regular newscaster on TV was John Cameron Swayze, but the show wasn't his 1948 *Camel News Caravan* for NBC. Years earlier, 1937 to be exact, in Kansas City, Kansas, experimental station W9XAC had put on a ten-minute newscast three times a week.

"The work was relatively simple" said Swayze. "I just read the news right out of the paper. I don't think anyone saw me except technical personnel working at the station." Swayze, like everyone in early TV, remembered the horror of burning hot lights. "I started to perspire in the first fifteen seconds; I was a soggy mess when each show was over. For some reason that I can't recall now, I darkened my eyebrows before each telecast. Maybe I was afraid the lights would burn them away if I didn't."

William Parker was a radio engineer in Philadelphia, recruited by Philco in 1934 to run W3XE. At that time, the station had good quality Farnsworth equipment, an electronic system of 345 lines, but a picture that was contaminated with a weird color quality that Parker described as looking like "pink underwear."

The studio was on the fifth floor of the Philco Company where the audio rumble from below was truly intolerable. W3XE telecast with a single iconoscope camera, and amateur groups regularly trooped up to the fifth floor to perform variety shows and dramas. Sometimes it was a group of Girl Scouts, sometimes the wives and children of Philco employees. Everything was on a tight budget. Performers were "paid" with souvenir candid photos taken during the show. Music came from an old reed organ borrowed from Good Will. One day the foot pump broke, so the organ was hooked up to a tank vacuum cleaner in the next room.

In 1937, Parker witnessed a Bell Laboratories demonstration of the first coaxial cable telecast from New York's Radio City to the NBC Empire State Building transmitter to the Philco plant near Philadelphia. This was the longest broadcast yet using electronic equipment, but because there had been so much publicity about long-distance broadcasting with mechanical television—transcontinental and even transatlantic—no one took much notice of this historic New York-to-Philadelphia broadcast. It was indeed the first "network" broadcast, and it was received in a city that had yet to figure out how to do simple remote pickups outside of a studio.

By 1940, W3XE finally had the capability for remote telecasts. It covered Wendell Willkie's nomination at the National Republican Convention, a University of Pennsylvania home football game, the touring Ice Follies, and even professional wrestling, a television first (Dick Lane would get the credit for "discovering" wrestling in Hollywood two years later). The football telecasts from Franklin Field were marred by the unfortunate fact that the video signal from the control room to the relay transmitter atop Convention Hall was parallel to the city's electric commuter trains, which regularly wiped out the video signal.

The Philadelphia video signal was also wiped out in another unexpected way. The FCC had assigned the same frequency and the same channel as W3XE's to another station in New York City. As Parker reported:

> The FCC was under the erroneous assumption that VHF signals do not propagate beyond the line of sight. As I expected, the interference was intolerable, especially about midway between New York and Philadelphia. Not expected, however, were letters from "flat earth" believers who interpreted the results as proving that the earth is not round after all![3]

Bill Parker was everybody's image of a TV engineer, eager and earnest but not a particularly smooth character. At short-staffed W3XE, he was pressed into service as the on-camera interviewer of a remote from backstage at Olson and Johnson's touring musical "Hell's a Poppin'." A troupe of scantily clad show girls were all over Bill, clowning affection for him in order to grab a closeup on Philadelphia television. Bill's wife was not amused.

There was no censorship in early live TV, and nothing profane went deliberately on the air, but there *were* accidents. At Farnsworth's Philadelphia studio, a religious broadcast was underway when one of the engineers bumped his head on a microphone. Certain that the mike was not live, he ran through every expletive he could think of until the panicked control room flipped the right switch.

On July 1, 1941, Philco's experimental W3XE went commercial as WPTZ; then it was quickly shut down for the war effort. By 1946, it was back on the air (still on channel 3) promoting itself with postcards sent using the mailing lists from appliance dealers. There were only 750 sets in all of the city so viewers were easy to track down.

Between 1932 and World War II, the national television picture (not including the mechanical system broadcasters) developed in part like this:

City	Station	Call Name Later	Owner
New York	W2XBS	WNBT	NBC
	W2XWV	WABD	DuMont
	W2XBB	WOR-TV	R. H. Macy
Schenectady	W2XB	WGRB	General Electric
Boston	W1XG		General Television
Kansas City	W9XAC		
Washington, D.C.	W3XWT	WTTG	DuMont
	W3XNB	WRC-TV	NBC
Philadelphia	W3XAV	WCAU	Independent/CBS
	W3XE	WPTZ	Philco
West Lafayette	X9XG		Purdue University
Ft. Wayne	W9XFT		Farnsworth
Milwaukee	W9XMJ	WMTJ	*Milwaukee Journal*
Cincinnati	W8XCT	WLWT	Crosby
Chicago	W9XZV	WTZR	Zenith Radio Corporation
	W9XBK	WBKB	Balaban and Katz
	W9XCB		CBS
Los Angeles	W6XAO	KTSL	Don Lee
	W6XEA	KSEE	Earle Anthony
	W6XKH		Hughes Tool
	W6XYZ	KTLA	Paramount
	W6XCB		CBS
	W6XLJ		LeRoy Jewelers

The only city from this list that could reasonably challenge New York's primacy in TV programming was Chicago, home to a great number of network radio and advertising agencies. The biggest star to emerge from Chicago in the 1940s was Burr Tillstrom. During the early 1940s, Tillstrom went without any regular TV employment for his puppets, the Kuklapolitan Players. Auditioning at one Chicago station after another, he always got the same criticism—his puppet show was too impersonal. Unless he could find his "Edgar Bergen," he would have to do convalescent hospitals and street corners the rest of his life. Ironically it was during one of these dreaded Chicago hospital tours that Tillstrom actually found the warmest, best-loved person in Chicago, perhaps in the whole country—Aunt Fanny.

Aunt Fanny was a character played by Fran Allison on *Don Mac-Neil's Breakfast Club*. In 1947 when Tillstrom proposed they work together in television, although Fran didn't like Tillstrom much, after years as a Don MacNeil supporting player, she liked the idea of being a star with her own name. And so *Kukla, Fran & Ollie* was born. Actually it first was *Junior Jamboree*, but soon everybody referred to it by the name that Tillstrom used when he went network with NBC a year later.

After the war, Chicago's WBKB had offered "sponsorship" of its many programs to advertising agencies and free spots to educational groups. Apparently no viewer accustomed to advertising-free programs of the early 1940s had a problem with the new commercials. However, ad agencies were not happy when WBKB, in its noncommercial mode, showed the drama "Willie Buys a Bond," in which a little boy, planning to buy a new brand-name radio, decided instead to buy a government savings bond. *Billboard*, speaking for the hucksters, summed it up, "In twenty minutes WBKB set (commercial) television programming back ten years."

WBKB was a tiny place. The studio was 30-by-40 feet and had only two cameras. The scenery was frequently painted on brown wrapping paper. To stall for "passage of time," one camera would poke its lens into a toy kaleidoscope which the stagehand slowly turned until the other camera was in place on the new set, and the show could resume.

Hugh Downs had a brief career at Chicago's WBKB during this early commercial phase. In September 1943, he was asked to read the news along with a public-service announcement for the treasury department. Since there were only 400 TV sets in the entire Chicago area, he didn't take the job seriously.

Downs arrived at the station and was greeted by a floor director who gave him thirty-five minutes of news copy and told him he had fifteen minutes to read it on the air. Downs was then taken into a small, windowless room with a desk and chair. It was as cold as a meat locker. It was so cold his breath was condensing as soon as he spoke:

"Boy, this place is chilly."

"Yes" said the floor director. "We keep the air conditioning as cold as we can."

Then a female studio producer came in wearing a fur parka with a hood. Five minutes before air time, "the Eskimo girl" offered to take Downs's sport jacket and told him it was okay to do his broadcast in short sleeves. Hugh was sure she was trying to torture him. His nose was red, his lips were blue, and his hands were numb in this "meat locker." He kept his jacket on.

With a minute to go, the Eskimo girl removed her parka, revealing a halter and shorts about the size of a swimsuit. Downs was shocked, to say the least, that this attractive lady had stripped and was now shouting, "One minute!" and calling for "lights!"

Suddenly the small studio was bathed in banks of spotlights, each of tremendous wattage. More and more lights came on. It felt like an inferno, and for a moment, Downs wondered if this massive sudden use of Chicago's electricity resources might cause a blackout all over the city.

I had never seen light like this in my life. I have never seen it since. Yet I have squinted against giant sun reflectors in making movies. I have looked, momentarily, on the face of the sun itself. Never have I felt such sheer withering force of light as I felt during that tormented quarter-hour. Within seconds my irises had clanked down to pinhole size. Still the light roared in through my eyelids, so that I could see traces of veins in them. I tried to keep my hands away, because if I once covered my eyes I might never have had the courage to uncover them.[5]

Suddenly Downs realized that he wasn't cold anymore. He now knew why he'd been invited to take off his sports jacket. His eyes were squinting. It was hard to read the news copy and harder still to look in the camera. Within five minutes sweat came in buckets. He tried to ignore it, but it began to collect on his nose and chin. Ten minutes into this broadcast his shirt and tie were soaking, which at least alleviated his fear of spontaneous combustion.

As the broadcast ended, the lights were immediately switched off, the air conditioning came back on, heading way back to below freezing, Downs heard the voice of the Eskimo girl over the loud speaker:

"You'd better not sit there long. You've been perspiring."

"Yeah, I know," said Downs weakly. "And it'll freeze me. How do you stand it?"

"You get used to it," she laughed.

"I doubt if I will. I think I'll stick to radio."[6]

Even though the country was marching toward full employment in 1945, not one of the WBKB dramatic actors got paid. Management presumed that an actor's exposure to the Chicago television audience was reward enough. In addition, these slave actors were forced to work with little or no rehearsal. On the horror series *X Marks the Spot*, the lack of rehearsals caused actor Carl Kroenke to accidentally swallow formaldehyde on the set of a photo darkroom. For some reason the prop man, reading the script literally, got a real bottle of the poisonous stuff, instead of putting a formaldehyde label on a prop bottle. Hugh Downs was there.

> Fortunately the poor actor merely touched it to his lips, but it began immediately to embalm the top end of his alimentary tract, and when, on the floor, he began to shriek that he was dying, he thought he was. The other actors were impressed at first by the thoroughness of his suddenly inspired acting, and then annoyed by his obvious upstaging tactics of continuing with his lines, padding his part beyond recognition. 'I'm really dying, he choked. I'm not acting! Get me to a hospital!'[7]

Kroenke was rushed to Wesley Memorial and later recovered, but shock waves reverberated throughout the cast. The next week, most of the actors quit, preferring to work for real money on a competing radio program. The remaining WBKB thespians went to work on a show about "Wamba, King of the Visagoths," a 1680 costume drama with no formaldehyde on the set.

In 1946, WBKB went briefly off the air for a change of frequency and came back with a major talent they had raided from NBC. Captain William C. Eddy, WNBT's special-effects wizard with the hearing aid in his briar pipe, would be WBKB's director of television. He was said to have engaged in *tactical* heroics during the war, and he was back to perform *technical* heroics in the studio. In fact, he'd spent the last four years away from TV helping fight the war in the Pacific. Television was a major part of his top secret work for the Office of Strategic Services (OSS), and Eddy had designed TV guidance systems for plans to send unmanned boats full of explosives into Yokohama harbor.

Hugh Downs described his move from radio into television as "more of a drift than a jump." He wasn't doing television for the money—just for the fun of watching an awkward infant grow up. At WMAQ he met Dave Garroway, whose unique gift of gab had landed him a jazz and commentary show, *The 1160 Club*. This ultimately turned into a popular show of talk and music called *Garroway at Large*, and a few years later, in 1952, Garroway became the first host of NBC's *Today* show.

In 1946, WBKB was producing a soap opera, *Hawkins Falls*, and Downs was approved by Lever Brothers to be the commercial announcer. It was their first soap, and it ran half an hour a day, five days a week, a very ambitious undertaking for a station that had been used to going off the air after a simple newscast.

Downs remembers a special "first" in television history: the first actor to be written out of a soap opera because of a contract dispute. Frank Dane was the star of *Hawkins Falls*, patriarch of the all-American Drewer family. One day when Bill Barrett, the writer, and Ben Park, the producer, gave a reading to their star, Dane blew up. He wanted more money. More respect. More everything. As Downs remembered it:

Don't you guys tell me about my profession! I was acting on the legitimate stage when you were still in knee pants! I don't have to take this! Unless my demands are met, I won't be here for the next episode.[8]

Dane then stormed out of the studio, leaving an embarrassed silence in his wake.

The writer turned to the producer and said, 'Let's kill him.'

And that's exactly what they did. Within three weeks, Dane's character was sent on a long business trip, and his plane was tragically lost over the Irish Sea. His TV wife, after an appropriate period of grief, found a new husband. Chicago soap viewers didn't make a peep of complaint. Hugh Downs was astonished by the original temper tantrum, and in awe of the solution. "I just used to stand around reading the news. True show business was really a shock."

More showbiz reality hit Downs in the face as Burr Tillstrom and his puppets, Kukla and Ollie, became Chicago's biggest TV stars. According to Downs,

Burr was super serious about his work. He never called Kukla and Ollie 'puppets.' They were 'people.' As puppeteer, Tillstrom was kind of schizophrenic. I remember a rare instance of Burr coming to work drunk, and of course on the air Ollie the Dragon was drunk, too. But Kukla was amazingly sober—and chastising Ollie for being drunk![9]

Tillstrom's mind was both compartmentalized and obsessive about his puppets. Absolutely no one was allowed behind his small stage except Beulah Zaccary, his producer. "One time a stagehand clowned around with his hand in Ollie's mouth," remembered Downs. "Tillstrom had him fired."

WBKB had a unique talk show, *Stud's Place*, starring the writer Studs Terkel. It was somewhat like today's Gary Shandling's *Larry Sanders Show*, with real people playing themselves in a semi-fictional setting. Hugh Downs visited the show as did Dave Garroway.

In news, WBKB had the first newscast with two news readers. *Cubberly and Campbell* was set in a typical newsroom to the accompaniment of typewriters and telephones. They would frequently question each other and engage in banter. The first "happy talk" news format was born.

Ann Hunter was Chicago's "first woman commentator," playing solo, and with an unusual combination of memorization and ad libbing, she became the first newscaster to speak memorized material directly into the camera in those pre-teleprompter cue-card days.

Back in Philadelphia, WPTZ tried its first soap opera, *Last Year's Nest*. It wasn't a true soap, since each episode had some new characters, and it was only on weekly. To director Len Valenta, who went on to direct many popular daytime dramas, it was a baptism by fire. As an actor he played the male lead in one episode against a cardboard background so narrow that the slightest camera movement would have revealed the stagehands holding up the set.

Detroit was always a major city in radio broadcasting, thanks to car and cereal manufacturers. Harry Bannister, who had spent thirteen years at WWJ radio, first in sales then as its general manager, was a genial boss who could be easily convinced to do the wildest things, as long as nobody had ever done it before. For example, in the winter, he and several avid croquet fans liked to play croquet in the snow. They were standing in galoshes up to their ankles in snow on December 7, 1941, when they heard the Japanese had attacked Pearl Harbor.

Detroit had a late start in TV, getting its first broadcast equipment in January 1947. Since Bannister's great talent was in sales, he was the natural choice to head WWJ-TV. The studio was still under construction when Harry went live with a forty-five-minute show in which he was the host.

To celebrate the start of regular telecasts, Harry sponsored a contest to find the most beautiful girl in Detroit. For the live crowning of "Miss Television," producer Walter Koste acted as master of ceremonies. The stage set was a floral garden with a rose arbor at the rear, three steps above the stage. Each contestant would pause for a closeup in the arbor and then move downstage in a second camera's wide shot.

As the winner was announced in her arbor-framed closeup, Koste milked the moment: "Now darling, step down with all of the beauty and grace that heaven bestowed upon you." The winning girl took one step, tripped and fell flat on her face; her legs went up and her dress flipped over, revealing her panty-clad bottom. Detroit had officially joined the family of pre-history television broadcasters.

By the end of 1947, with more than 170,000 operating sets in the United States, the several dozen stations outside of New York were on the verge of creating quality programming that would give each community a voice—and a face—that would better represent the diversity of America. But as we will soon see, four broadcasting groups—all centered in New York—had plans to "network" their New York programs. The development of the quick-kinescope or "quick-kine" copy of a telecast, making networks possible without live feeds, was an immediate threat to local broadcasters. By 1948 Madison Avenue was finally ready to buy real network air time at real network prices.

10

THE PLAY'S THE THING

The state of the art in 1939

Thomas Lyne Riley, a young man recently promoted to direct dramatic productions at W2XBS in New York was having a drink with a small group of strangers at the Players Club bar in the spring of 1939. A year later he used this incident to modestly write about his new career.

He bragged about being a director in the exciting new venture called "television." After a lot of puffing and posturing he was interrupted by a simple question:

"How do you direct television?"

Riley thought for a moment.

"Oh, you just do, I suppose."[1]

Before 1939, most television dramas were romantic comedies or turgid melodramas with small casts and low budgets. Some were based on one-act plays, some were adapted from revue sketches. Actors were never paid more than twenty-five dollars and never had a contract. Occasionally a big star like Gertrude Lawrence or Henry Hull had appeared in an excerpt from a current production, but they were the exceptions. In this World's Fair year of heavy publicity and constant promotion, RCA at last decided to pay for better actors and better dramas. Most importantly the content of plays changed—everything was more ambitious. *Good Medicine* dealt with hypochondria. *Emergency Call* was about suspicions of adultery. *Trifles* was about wife beating. Intent on upgrading everything, NBC doubled the $100 budgets. *Dark Eyes Mean Danger* cost an astronomical $237.60. An upper-class drama of infidelity, it began in a "swank London hotel" and finished aboard the style-setting Queen Mary.

NBC Vice-President John Royal decided to do much more. In March 1939, he put Broadway producer Max Gordon in charge of W2XBS programming, largely because Gordon had access to a small catalog of plays he had produced that could be easily adapted to television. Then he doubled NBC's studio space. A second studio was added for dramas, telecast Wednesdays and Fridays. In addition to dramas and comedies, musicals were produced. Since known actors had already tired of the novelty of doing primitive TV, new stars were "created" from the ranks of Broadway hopefuls.

No one in 1939 was more hopeful than Norman Lloyd, the famous character actor who later played the stern headmaster in *Dead Poet's Society* (1989) and was a regular on *St. Elsewhere*.

Norman Lloyd was just another young out-of-work New York actor. One summer night in 1939, he was sitting with his wife, Peggy, in their new apartment, in the Chelsea section of Manhattan, listening to Count Basie on the radio. The phone rang. It was his agent, Audrey Wood, calling. Audrey was with the Leibling-Wood agency which had a stable of young clients, both actors and playwrights. Just a few years later, she shepherded Tennessee Williams to Broadway fame, and for the next two decades she was one of New York's most powerful agents.

"Norman?" she asked. "How about a production of *Missouri Legend*, rehearsing immediately?"

Lloyd knew the play, a moderate hit on Broadway about the life and death of Jesse James. Dean Jagger, Mildred Natwick, and Jose Ferrer had all received splendid notices. There was just one problem. *Missouri Legend* had closed two months earlier.

"Norman, dear, it's not for the stage; it's for television. Since Jose Ferrer's not available, they want you for his part."

Lloyd agreed, forgetting to ask what his salary would be. He'd never seen a TV set much less a broadcast, but the word around the Broadway acting community was that TV pay was pitiful. The real incentive for an actor to do TV was to get a foothold in radio. Radio was a gold mine for actors, and RCA was doing all its experimental television at NBC's Radio City. Broadway actor Ray Collins, making fifty thousand dollars a year doing every radio show he could schedule, was the envy of every Broadway hopeful. Collins even had a "stand-in" for radio rehearsals. The stand-in would mark Collins's script with the director's instructions, and then Collins, fresh from a job three blocks away at CBS, would sprint into Radio City just in time for the NBC live broadcast, "winging" his performance from the notes of the stand-in.

Norman had committed to a fifty-five-dollar-a-month lease on his brownstone apartment. It was luxurious by Broadway actor standards, but he and his wife, Peggy, had never been able to afford more than three pieces of furniture for it. Though only twenty-five, he had been acting since he was eighteen, starting with Eva LeGallienne's theatrical company, and making a hit as Johnny Appleseed in *Everywhere I Roam*. All this made him a good reputation but not much of an income. For now the problem was how to break into radio—and maybe an experimental TV show could be a stepping stone.

Norman rode the subway up to Rockefeller Center. He didn't dare risk being late for the first rehearsal, "but actors had to be very careful with their money." The ride was a nickel.

The rehearsal space was very plain in comparison with the overall Art Deco splendor of Rockefeller Center. Norman's first view was an empty floor lined with chalk marks indicating the sets, and a rehearsal table with a dozen mimeographed scripts. The director was a strong, well-built young man who had come from Broadway and had been a stage manager for other television shows. He had just moved up to the post of director. He introduced himself as "Anthony Bundsmann . . . but call me Tony." Bundsmann would go to Hollywood in a few years where David Selznick got him to change his name to Anthony Mann. He would go on to a successful career as a director of action films including the epic *El Cid*. For now, 1939, he was just nervous and making his debut as a television director.

Very little is known about Tony Bundsmann. His real name may have been Emil Bundsmann or Anton Bundsman (one "n"). His birthdate is "approximately" 1907, in California, maybe in Point Loma, maybe San Diego. His parents are believed to have been two school teachers. His family moved to New York City when he was ten, and Tony dropped out of high school to become a professional actor. On Broadway, the name "Anton Mann" is listed in several playbills, but Tony's real love in the theater was backstage. With the Theatre Guild he got a job as a stage manager. Then he got a chance to direct some WPA plays. All the while he was most fascinated by the movies.

Norman recalled:

> Tony explained to me that he wanted *Missouri Legend* to appear more like a movie than a stage play. I looked over the chalk marks, and remembered the wisecracks I'd heard about television and read in *The Times*. Tony smoked incessantly, chewing gum at the same time. I'll always remember how Tony stood—fairly straight but under so much pressure that his legs bulged out. Of course I was a cocky and brash young actor. I would have been only mildly impressed by the second coming of Gordon Craig.[2]

In a few minutes the rest of the cast began to assemble. Everyone from Dean Jagger on down appeared very serious. "Later I found out that everybody's principal motivation for doing this project was the same as mine . . . to be discovered in radio."

As the rehearsals began—and they would go on for several weeks— the director shaped his "original" version of *Missouri Legend*. He was particularly proud that this would be TV's first western drama. Some of the actors privately expressed a concern that their extravagant stage mannerisms were not being "toned down" the way they would for a movie. Still, no one in the company had seen a TV drama, much less acted in one. The sets didn't look like movie sets and they didn't look like Broadway sets. They looked like high school sets. The flats were very flat indeed. In fact there was a decidedly two-dimensional aspect to the production. During camera blocking, Director Bundsmann was horrified by these amateur looking sets. The chief cameraman pulled him aside and let him look through the camera. He whispered something about the focal length. Sure enough, on the tube, the sets were just a blur.

On July 18, 1939, at 8:30 P.M., W2XBS telecast to a small audience of RCA executives, engineers, several dozen bars, and about a hundred sets in private homes. Because of the show's length, or perhaps the late hour of its conclusion, NBC decided not to relay *Missouri Legend* to the RCA pavilion at the World's Fair. No first-time viewers saw the play or its actors.

The first viewers to greet the actors after the show was off the air were Max Gordon and Guthrie McClintic, Broadway producing legends who had been given fancy titles by NBC in the hopes of bringing in hit plays. Gordon and McClintic were full of praise, but not completely clear about whether they actually had watched the telecast.

For Norman Lloyd, the show didn't lead to offers in radio, but it did lead to another TV drama six weeks later. Tony Bundsmann cast him in *The Streets of New York*, Dion Boucicault's sixty-year-old melodrama. There was irony here since Boucicault had been a major promoter of the first U.S. copyright bill . . . and here was one of his most popular works being done without payment to him or his estate. Public domain was a favorite source in early television.

The Streets of New York is about a banker named Gideon Bloodgood who has stolen some money from the heroine's father in order to trick the leading man, Mark Livingston, into marrying that banker's daughter. It's an old-fashioned melodrama and the day is "saved" by the rescue of some vital papers from a burning tenement.

With Tony Bundsmann directing again, this "original" TV production had a brand-new cast. Norman Lloyd was joined by his friend from the Mercury Theatre, George Coulouris. That theater company, founded by Orson Welles and John Houseman, would soon achieve radio fame with *War of the Worlds* and movie fame with its production of *Citizen Kane*.

Bundsmann's big casting coup was Joyce Arling who had been the lead of most of George Abbott's Broadway shows. Playing a very small part (not even listed in NBC's credits) was then little-known actress named Phyllis Eisley. There was a considerable buzz during rehearsals when her boyfriend, Robert Walker, came to pick her up. Like her director, Tony, she would change her name in Hollywood. She became Jennifer Jones. Walker also became a famous actor starring in many films, such as *Strangers on a Train*.

Norman remembers the studio heat under the lights being worse on *Streets* than it was in *Missouri Legend*:

> On second thought it must have been the same conditions. But in the winter clothes of *Streets*, fur coats and beaver hats, it *seemed* hotter. The toilets were used as dressing rooms and this was the biggest cost yet for an NBC studio drama. Our director would give us a break in the hallway between acts, but the acts were long and the breaks were short. What I remember vividly was the big snow scene. Tony promised us the moon, or at least a realistic snowstorm to be achieved by stagehands with fans in what passed for a lighting grid. Clean up problems being what they were, we didn't dare rehearse the effect. On the air we were sweating, shiny thespians, and as the snow fell it stuck to our faces like the confetti it was. While the program had two cameras, one of them was usually focused on titles or scenic introductions. When something went wrong in the acting Tony had nothing to cut away to. Worse yet, hot-tempered George Coulouris had the snow sticking to his lips during his longest speech.[3]

Through all the technical mistakes both Lloyd and Coulouris thought they'd done decent acting and wished in vain for some validation of their efforts. The director liked it of course, and the actors all patted each other on the back. A few complained that TV was "so constraining." Norman remembers at least one actor saying "this thing will never go." Norman also remembers coming out of one rehearsal for *Streets* and into the NBC elevator:

> Who should walk in but the famous architect Frank Lloyd Wright with his distinctive hat and a beautiful young girl on his arm. He had just been interviewed on W2XBS. Live, of course. The girl was effusive in her compliments. Wright turned to her and said in a very loud voice 'You're wasting your breath. I don't believe *anybody* saw this.'[4]

Fifty-two years later Lloyd was invited to participate in ceremonies honoring New York's Museum of Television & Radio. The museum people had a surprise for him. In 1939, someone had taken a silent home movie of *Streets of New York*. It is the earliest filmed record of dramatic television. And, as Norman says, "It's an embarrassing testimonial to how bad the acting was. Very flamboyant and completely phoney. I was relieved to recall how few people watched it."*

The first full-length modern play of 1939 on NBC was Noël Coward's three-act farce *Hay Fever*. English accents were not attempted, which was fortunate for a very young actor who was making his television debut, Montgomery Clift. Also in May was a comedy *Three Wise Fools* starring Percy Kilbride, who would soon become the movies' *Pa Kettle*.

Props were always backfiring, frequently because the rehearsals never fully prepared the actors for what it would be like on the air.

On May 26, 1939, NBC televised a one-act drama *The Game of Chess* by Kenneth S. Goodman. Eugene Sigaloff played a villainous

---

*At the museum, program #005494 has no special marking in the electronic card catalogue. Since it has no sound and is only five minutes long, it doesn't get played in the museum's popular screening rooms. But for anyone researching the history of television, it is like the Dead Sea Scrolls. Whoever took the motion picture off the tube of "Streets of New York" was far ahead of his time. There are no scanning lines, the picture is clear and it looks remarkably like the early 1948 kinescopes. The film has been edited, it is only the highlights, but the edit includes titles and a "3-minute intermission" card.

character who plotted to poison A. K. Cooper during a game of chess. Both would be drinking the arsenic poison but Sigaloff's character had immunized himself by taking small doses over several months. The prop man used root beer to substitute for the wine, and during rehearsal everything went fine except for a complaint from the director that the drapes made the scene look too gloomy. The solution was to pump up the already hot lights. The root beer sat in the decanter during final preparations. By 8:30 P.M. it was boiling. When Sigaloff reached for the decanter he nearly burned his hand. There was no way he could warn Cooper how hot it was and stay in character. He hoped there would be some telltale steam coming out of the liquid when he poured it; but the rest of the set was so hot that there was no steam. Sigaloff then turned his back to "drink" his glass. He tried to signal Cooper in a mirror to be careful with the root beer. But Cooper was thoroughly into his part and tossed the boiling-hot root beer down his throat. He practically exploded when the hot drink entered his throat and bronchial tubes. He choked, foamed at the mouth, and clutched his throat. The "poisoned" actor had a premature death scene. The director faded to black without Cooper performing his well-rehearsed dying words.

Captain William C. Eddy, the station's special effects man, was very impressed: "As he lay on the floor simulating the throes and agonies of death, he actually steamed at the mouth."

By 1939, a third camera was covering dramatic shows, providing visual variety for the viewer and new hazards for the actors. Earle Latimore was interviewed when he starred on NBC's *The Unexpected* in May 1939. He said, "I think of those cameras as three octopuses with little green eyes blinking on and off." Even though the actors were freer to move with the additional camera, the scenery was always limited, and to avoid forcing the cameras to shoot "off the set," actors had to keep gestures to a microscopic minimum.

Tony Bundsmann, after directing *Missouri Legend* and *The Streets of New York*, used his connections with the prestigious Theatre Guild to try to lure that group into television before the World's Fair ended. In 1939, the Guild was trying out a stage version of *Jane Eyre*, directed by

Worthington Miner, and starring Katharine Hepburn who had already gained great fame in movies.

The try-out was in Philadelphia and the usual out-of-town jitters seized the company. The playwright, Helen Jerome, refused to rewrite and the Theatre Guild closed the show. Tony Bundsmann jumped in and picked up the package for NBC television.

Katharine Hepburn's planned debut on NBC was quite a coup— but it was not to be. She pulled out in favor of a new Broadway play by Philip Barry, *The Philadelphia Story*. Just as Tony was sure the whole deal would collapse, he got Flora Campbell to play Jane Eyre.

On October 12, NBC, using Studio 3H, broadcast a ninety- minute adaptation with two sets, sixteen characters, and no intermis- sion. The production was overambitious and underrehearsed. It was not director Bundsmann's finest hour; he was lucky that David O. Selznick soon whisked him off to Hollywood. That week's *Variety* slammed his direction, complaining that the star spoke too rapidly and never looked in the direction of the actress she was speaking to. The critic faulted everything from the lighting to Campbell's "unflattering" costume. Director Bundsmann's biggest problem had been the very large cast. NBC's new studio was still too small, and cameras could still not back up enough on the action. In every ensemble scene, the actors spilled out of the frame. Tony hoped this look gave the production "*size*." *Variety* simply complained that "principal characters were left out of the picture."

The real problem with pre-war drama on television was similar to the problem with early talking films. Television was not the theater; stage and plays were not being selected for the intimacy that was TV's strong suit. The plays of the 1930s were not adaptable. *Tobacco Road* and *Susan and God* were not slam dunks for TV. Playwrights like William Saroyan and Philip Barry, who would be perfect for TV, were just coming on the Broadway scene. In addition, the problems of television photography with the cheap two-dimensional sets forced directors to shoot every group scene like a police lineup. Nobody liked the visuals of early TV drama, but nobody had time to study or experiment to make them better. With the wartime shutdown at CBS, producer Worthington Miner was assigned to write a study on how to better the techniques of TV drama.

During the two years before NBC's shutdown, in October 1942, W2XBS—now using call letters WNBT—continued to produce dramas. Many actors passed through the revolving doors at Rockefeller Center. Some, like Gertrude Berg, later became TV stars. Actress Eleanor Kilgallen later became a talent agent selling her MCA clients like Paul Newman and Robert Redford to TV while her more famous sister Dorothy gained even more fame on game show *What's My Line*. Actor Robert Mulligan became an important director in television and eventually features (*To Kill a Mockingbird*). Television drama was years away from its "Golden Era" but it really was getting better.

11

A
WORD FROM
OUR
SPONSORS

The earliest commercials: 1937–1947

Television's first commercial was illegal. In 1930 Boston's W1XAV put out a press release headlined "First Chain Commercial Broadcast to go on Air via Television Tonight." They ran a video portion of a CBS radio program, "The Fox Trappers," sponsored by "America's largest manufacturing furrier." Although W1XAV wasn't paid for this rebroadcast from radio, the general counsel of the Federal Radio Commission ruled that even the free rebroadcast of commercials from radio was prohibited.

The FRC's position was that TV's experimental years should be solely for research. All its licensed stations were warned, and the commission's penalty could mean a loss of license. Nevertheless, TV stations were popping up all over the country and the FRC's Depression budget was so poor that their regional supervisors couldn't even afford TV sets. The bottom line was that the government expected TV pioneers to reach an undefined level of *quality* before they could sell products in American homes, much less TV receivers. Before that could happen, advertisers needed to know who was watching television.

Noran ("Nick") Kersta was an NBC statistician working in radio in 1937 when he was asked to develop a ratings system for the infant TV medium. He recalled, "There were several hundred sets in the metropolitan area, and the brass was dying to see what the set owners liked and how much they viewed."[1]

From radio's earliest dates, broadcasters had wondered how many people were listening. The first audience-measuring device for radio was introduced in Kansas City in 1933. The sponsor, a local candy maker, offered a box of chocolate to every listener who wrote a letter to the tiny 1,000-watt station. Within a week, thousands of requests had arrived, and to meet the flood the sponsor had to design a special candy box that only held one piece of chocolate. This promotion nearly pushed that candy maker into bankruptcy, as it proved the drawing power of radio.

In 1937, with no particular need to prove scientific accuracy for his ratings, Kersta sent out four hundred pre-paid-postage-return postcards to the addresses on TV set warranties. An amazing number of people responded, even some of the set-owning bartenders. Armed with "statistics," Kersta approached the advertising agency for Bulova watches. Nick was a forceful salesman, passionate in his belief in television. The agency head threw up his arms in self-defense. This is how Kersta remembers it all:

'What do you want from us?'

'To make Bulova the first advertiser on TV.'

'How many people you got watching?'

'We're working on a technique to determine that. It's getting bigger everyday.'

'How much for one spot?'

'Ten dollars. But for *premiere* sponsors our price is only seven dollars.'

'OK. OK. You write it. We'll buy it.'[2]

Nick's very first commercial was just a Bulova watch face with no announcement. It grossed NBC seven dollars. Kersta's second sponsor, Botany Ties, paid slightly more for a series of still cartoons featuring a wooly lamb. Adam Hats, another client hustled by Nick, paid for a quiet pan shot of a studio hat store window.

Television was still experimental, the call letters of each station were temporary, and by now the FCC did not specifically ban commercials, as long as they were done on a tiny, nonprofit basis. It was, after all, part of an "experiment," and everything about TV was certainly nonprofit.

In mid-1941, the FCC finally approved full-scale commercial television. On NBC, Sunoco Oil bought the *Lowell Thomas News*, a simulcast of the famed reporter's evening radio report. On July 1, 1941, it was transformed to the *Sunoco News*. By contract Thomas had to read the news with a large stack of Sunoco oil cans dominating his desk. It drew a negative notice in *Variety*. "TV is destined to be the mechanized Fuller Brush man of the future." The very same night, Spry Shortening presented *Uncle Jim's Question Bee* and Ivory Soap did business on the TV debut of *Truth or Consequences*.

Commercial TV started so quickly that there wasn't much advertising agency intrusion, and some things slipped onto the air that were embarrassing to sponsors. In the *Question Bee*, a character named Aunt Jenny offered guests to her "dinner party" a chocolate cake freshly baked with Spry. On camera she licked her tongue across the cake knife and then cut slices with the same blade. That week's *Variety* review focused on the unsanitary appearance of the whole business.

Aunt Jenny, like everybody else, had to deal with the heat of the studio lights. Large drops of perspiration kept falling into her cake batter. As the dinner party guests retired from the kitchen to the dining room, hot studio lights melted the candles in a massive candelabra. NBC's effects man Captain William Eddy described the result as a "glorious bonfire." NBC stagehands abruptly joined the dinner party blasting away with extinguishers and the technical director called for the "Please Stand By" card.

In the years to come, TV stations would provide "client rooms" for the advertisers and their agents, but in 1941 there were no such rooms. When ad men came to see a show, they stood in the back of the control booth, creating more pressure for the directors of live telecasts.

Art Hungerford recalled a special prop man, hired by the agency, named Pete Barker. "On one commercial Pete's only job was to blow smoke across a miniature on a table. Camera One was set for the shot. Camera Two was further back with a wide shot planned to go live after a fade out. During the 'black,' the miniature was to be whisked away by Pete. The presence of all those agency men in the booth was too much for our technical director who switched on the wrong camera revealing Pete the prop man in all his smoke-blowing glory."[3]

In the fall of 1943, DuMont's WABD in New York surprised NBC by ending their self-imposed wartime blackout to broadcast a new and improved image. DuMont, at that time, actively courted new sponsors with an attractive offer. DuMont offered all the technical work (today called "below the line") for free, and the airtime was free as well. All the sponsor had to do was pay for the script and the on-camera performers.

In 1943, there were only five thousand TV receivers in New York, and the big ad agencies had mixed feelings about TV. It was not very efficient, even when a lot of it was free. Only a few sponsors could imagine that TV held immediate promise. These few jumped in with the confidence that if they made mistakes not too many people would witness the accidents.

DuMont received considerable backing from Lever Brothers, particularly to promote soap, shortening, and shaving cream. Each product had its share of problems. For example, on radio, famous soap sponsors always trumpeted how much "whiter" their product made white shirts. But on TV shading controls for the picture were always out of adjustment. Two identically white shirts would not look identical when broadcast. The solution was to use a blue shirt alongside a white shirt pretending that the blue one had been washed in a competitor's product.

Miss Mary Stuyvesant, Ponds Face Cream's "beauty expert" held up crudely drawn sketches of the "right and wrong methods of applying make-up." The product was so unappealing on camera that the agency chose to never open the jar. Instead they treated the product like the crown jewels, putting it on a revolving turntable draped in crushed velvet. Lifebuoy Soap got the same royal treatment. When early TV technicians couldn't move the camera, they moved the product.

DuMont was always busy expanding commercial production values. On the *Fred Waring Show*, the director cut away to two sailors on ship sharing a Chesterfield cigarette. The "ship" was, of course, a single porthole with a piece of railing in the foreground.

Many potential sponsors were on the sidelines during the war because their products were rationed and not widely available. Not so for the Vimms Vitamin company. In fact, their commercials patriotically exploited the 1943 rationing laws. Their first vitamin commercial used three sets; the set budget being bigger than the show's. In the first set, a housewife was unsuccessfully trying to order steaks over the telephone. The next scene in a butcher shop had the same woman confronted with a single remaining hot dog. An off-screen announcer then got her attention and told her that even in wartime she could get all the Vimms vitamins she needed. That propelled her to the third set, her local drug store.

Another less successful Vimms commercial showed two women with brooms and mops, housecleaning. One of the women had started her day with a Vimms vitamin, and at the "end of the day" she was fresh as a daisy while the other looked perfectly exhausted. Over a shot of the vitamin-revived housewife, the announcer advised: "Get that *Vimms* feeling."[4]

Wildroot Cream-Oil hair tonic was another early sponsor. The first spot, clocked at three minutes, was a series of silent scenes with an off-camera announcer's voice. This commercial began with two cavemen fighting over a girl. The director then switched to a modern-day scene in which the same two men were trying to win a girl by more subtle means. The hero bribed the girl with nylon stockings.

After the war advertisers chose to exercise full control over the TV, just as they had in radio. This complete stranglehold over a show's contents was best illustrated by a script of *When a Girl Marries* in which Mary Jane Higby, one of the show's star characters, loaned a mink coat to her fictional maid. The sponsor, Prudential Life Insurance, panicked that this would start a stampede of servants borrowing valuable furs—causing personal property insurance rates to rise drastically. Prudential exercised its veto rights. The script was changed; the maid didn't get the coat.

Television was even more quickly produced than radio, and advertising agencies were justly cautious. Those who rushed in often regretted their hasty moves. Every day was a new disaster. A brand-new "automatic" Gillette safety razor refused to open on camera, a refrigerator door hit the announcer's foot, and in a *Tenderleaf* tea commercial the hostess chatted on about the fine taste and quality of *Lipton* tea.

"Tex" McCrary and his wife "Jinx" Falkenburg were a hit on NBC's New York radio station with a celebrity talk show, *At Home with Tex and Jinx*. In April 1947, it was transferred to NBC television on Sunday evenings. Its success led NBC to create for them a daytime show, *The Swift Home Service Club*, a Friday afternoon show for housewives sponsored by Swift's canned-food products. The sponsor had a heavy hand in the show and insisted that the stars prepare and eat Swift products on the air. There was plenty of mayonnaise and other dressings to make the canned meat palatable, but the heat of the studio lights always turned the mayonnaise bad. Tex kept a large off-screen bucket under the food table where he always vomited during or after every show.

In the early days of live TV, very few camera moves were rehearsed even for commercials. A lot was left to the director in the booth, but since he had no way to preview a shot, and with his vision of the set usually obstructed, there was room for error. A lot of error. Ed Herlihy, the smooth-as-cheese voice for Kraft in the 1960s, who had done his first TV announcing at the 1939 World's Fair, was the Kellogg's Corn Flakes spokesman for director Fred Kelly (Gene Kelly's brother). Herlihy was to dip his spoon into a bowl of the sponsor's product and appear to be eating it while he spoke of its goodness. Herlihy knew that his announcement would be terrible if he tried it with his mouth full, so he planned to dispose of each Corn Flakes spoonful off-camera. Somehow the communication between the director and cameraman broke down. On the air the camera panned up after the words, "Kellogg's Corn Flakes are so good, I can't begin the day without them." It panned to a head shot of the announcer tossing spoon after spoon of Corn Flakes over his shoulder.

In Detroit, Harry Bannister produced a commercial for a wall-mounted can opener. Compared to many postwar products, this new one was "state of the art." The can was to be inserted, a lever turned down, and off the top came in a jiffy. Unfortunately, Bannister spent too much time casting a pretty girl for the housewife part, and as the clock approached the 8:15 P.M. airtime, Harry was reminded that no one had produced a can to use in the commercial. The prop man was sent to scour neighborhood for a can. Only bars were open so he returned with a can of salted peanuts, not noticing that such vacuum-packed cans have five times the thickness of ordinary tin cans.

The pretty girl, can in hand, approached the opener. "See how easy the Hudson can opener works. You insert the can here, and with a flip of the wrist you turn the crank. See how easy it works."

Of course the can didn't budge. So the girl took a firmer grip on the handle of the can opener and forcefully repeated her line with a mixture of fear and hope: "See how easy it works."

Station chief Harry Bannister remembered the rest:

> She gave it one hard yank and down tumbled the can; the can opener fell apart, and out of the wall came the panel to which the opener had been attached. . . . Some quick-witted program fellow had the presence of mind to throw a piano player on the air while we signed off the show.

For twenty years television advertising was faced with that infernal chicken-and-egg dilemma. Which should come first, more and better commercials, or more and better shows to bigger and better audiences?

Advertisers were always demanding a cost-per-thousand analysis. Radio delivered. So did magazines, newspapers—even outdoor advertising. My grandfather, Prescott Ritchie, worked in advertising in Wisconsin during the birth pains of television. He remembered making an elaborate presentation to the president of Blatz beer, a crusty old man who resisted radio and print, doing most of his national advertising on the sides of barns. In 1947, the president of Blatz was seeing TV for the first time and was quite impressed with it. My grandfather was convinced he was on the verge of his biggest sale. Then he was asked how many TV sets were in Wisconsin, and he replied, "Only about a thousand. But the greater Chicago area has ten thousand and the number has doubled since the spring. There's no limit to TV's growth potential." The president of Blatz thought for a long time, "I think I'll stick with painting those barns."

12

AND NOW . . .
THE NEWS

1937–1947

The idea of recording news events on film began before World War I when a parachutist named Rodeman Law took a swan dive off the Statue of Liberty. His chute opened late, and he barely survived. The stunt was nevertheless a commercial success because the daredevil had alerted four cameramen to be on hand to photograph the event. The American newsreel was born.

On early live television news breaks were usually accidental. On the BBC, Armistice Day 1937, cameras were televising King George VI in ceremonies to honor Britain's Unknown Soldier when a fanatic broke through police lines attempting to attack the king. Home viewers saw it first. Soon after, an NBC camera crew was experimenting in Queens, New York, when a five-alarm fire broke out on the East River. WNBT carried it "live," of course. Then in Manhattan, NBC cameras were aimed out a studio window at Rockefeller Plaza and happened to capture a young woman as she leaped from a window and fell thirty-six stories to her death. The cameras saw everything, even the crowd running to her body.

The idea for a regular television newsreel was a no-brainer. Every movie theater in the country ran a newsreel, even though the news was always a week old. By the time of the 1939 World's Fair, Sarnoff, Paley, and DuMont knew that the public would want to watch news on television. It just had to be newer news.

After an experimental simulcast of Lowell Thomas's radio news, CBS's first regular news broadcast was in the spring of 1941. Thomas's show was not true TV news; it was a talking head. The only "visual" was the sponsor's product, and the distinguished Lowell Thomas was upstaged by that stack of Sunoco oil cans.

CBS then put on two fifteen-minute TV newscasts twice a week, at 2:30 P.M. and 7:30 P.M. A young writer-producer, Richard Hubbell, read the news with a pointer in his hand and a map behind him. It was a one-camera show, and Hubbell, with no monitor to guide him, frequently pointed to the wrong spots on the map.[1] The CBS broadcast image was so fuzzy no one cared. The day after Pearl Harbor, CBS television broadcast only the sound of President Roosevelt's "day of infamy" speech. The visual was an American flag placed in front of Hubbell's desk with a prop fan to make it wave. On the same day, WRGB in Schenectady tried an ambitious live television analysis of the sneak attack with a large relief model of the Pearl Harbor naval base surrounded by model ships and planes on strings, to be operated like marionettes. Everything went fine in rehearsal but on the air when the Japanese were supposed to "attack," the strings got hopelessly tangled.[2] These very frustrated television news pioneers could hardly have imagined that fifty years later, major wars would appear live on the tube, enhanced by a video technology as impressive as the combat technology.

While World War II was still in progress, NBC hired newsreel specialist Paul Atley of the Hearst-MGM *News of the Day*. With no budget to speak of, Atley mixed free film from the Army Signal Corps with local spot news. When CBS made a similar deal with Telenews,

The RCA Pavilion at the World's Fair attracted most of the young people who would soon "invent" television. The special plastic case for the TRK 660 displayed the inner workings of a set which retailed for $660.00. (COURTESY DAVID SARNOFF RESEARCH CENTER)

In 1937, RCA's first mobile units were forty-feet long. By 1946 DuMont's mobile unit was the back of a station wagon. In cold weather, director Harry Coyle would sit on the equipment to keep warm. (COURTESY GLOBE PHOTOS)

The control room at NBC's 4H. The director and technical director could not see the studio floor, only the the preview monitor. Keys to the studio were fiercely guarded, and technicians were sworn to secrecy. (COURTESY GLOBE PHOTOS)

OPPOSITE: The Empire State Building was topped by WNBC's TV transmitting antenna in 1939. The first RCA broadcast equipment was lower on the building, but when rival CBS's William Paley put a higher antenna on the Chrysler building, Sarnoff moved his to the highest peak in the city. (COURTESY GLOBE PHOTOS)

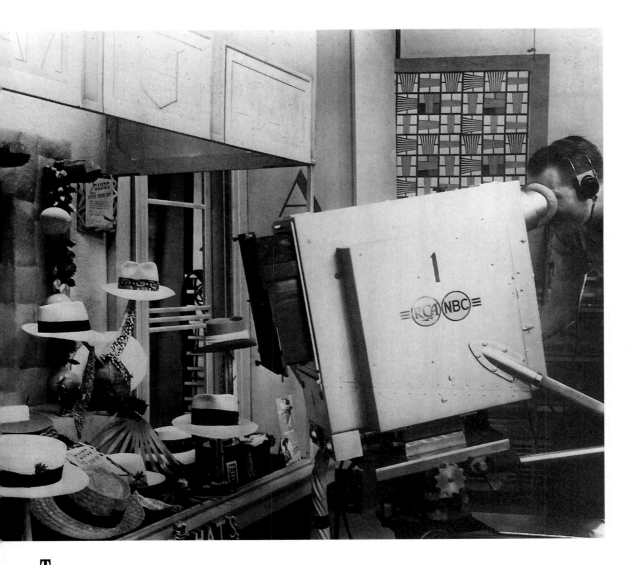

The 1939 RCA-NBC cameras were boxy and their movements were limited by thick wiring. One is shown here shooting a test commercial for Adam Hats. (COURTESY GLOBE PHOTOS)

When W2XBS became WNBT, the weather forecast moved from a talking head to a stylish rear projection. The weatherman turned up his collar and pretended to be cold despite in-studio temperatures that could have fried an egg on his head. (COURTESY GLOBE PHOTOS)

arly experiments often involved projecting a TV image on a movie screen. In 1927, General Electric had a thirty-one inch square screen. In England, at the same time, Baird used a portable theater screen. By 1939 RCA had a large screen projection system in the New Yorker Theater. BELOW: The first televised football game was a narrator's voice over a studio game board resembling a gridiron. The first "live" game was transmitted on September 30, 1939. Fordham defeated Waynesburg State, 34-7. (COURTESY GLOBE PHOTOS)

L owell Thomas was one of TV's first newsmen, but his 1940 NBC show was just a simulcast of his radio broadcast. The only visual was a stack of Sunoco oil cans, a sponsor. The trade press was critical: "TV is destined to be the mechanized Fuller Brush of the future."

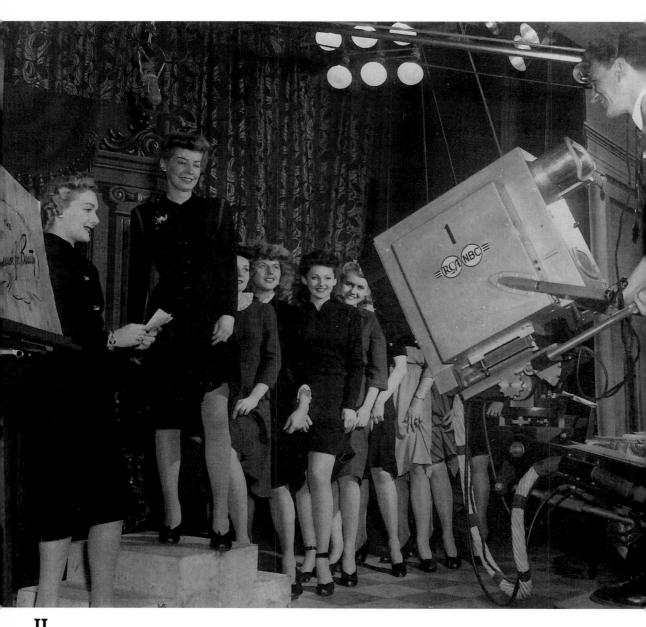

Hosiery commercials were instantly popular after the war—for obvious reasons.

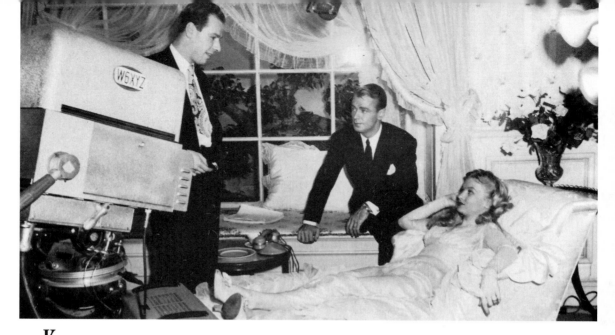

Klaus Landsberg "drops in" with a W6XYZ camera at an adjacent Paramount soundstage to tele-cast Alan Ladd and Veronica Lake in *This Gun for Hire*. BELOW: W6XYZ had a two camera news room in 1944. Since the commentator worked without a monitor, he often pointed to the wrong part of the map. Another camera was fixed on a globe which would cover any obvious mistake.

(COURTESY KTLA PHOTOS)

Magic acts were popular on early TV. At W6XYZ's cramped facilities, the camera on the left focused on the station's ID while the camera on the right alternated with a close up.

(COURTESY KTLA PHOTOS)

BELOW: Klaus Landsberg welcomes a four-legged guest to his studio. Audrey Taylor (now Mrs. Billy Wilder) remembers singing in a variety show followed by the horse. (COURTESY KTLA PHOTOS)

Hollywood's first two camera mobile unit with studio chief Klaus Landsberg on the left. His W6XYZ truck was a third of the size of the one he used with NBC at the 1939 World's Fair.

Dick Lane, the father of wrestling and roller derby, was also a pioneer of beauty pageantry. In KTLA's inaugural year of 1947, he introduced the winner of "Miss Valley Television." BELOW: The end of World War II brought the consumer a surge of kitchen convenience appliances. Here, Keith Heatherington introduces the Ultra-Vac jar opener as Eddie Reznick shoots the insert of a coffee jar manufactured in glass because tin was still in short supply. (COURTESY KTLA PHOTOS)

A Los Angeles culinary tradition, Mama Weiss, in the early 1940s, tried out a TV show called the *Mama Weiss Show*. When she returned in 1951, the station had been rechristened KTLA.

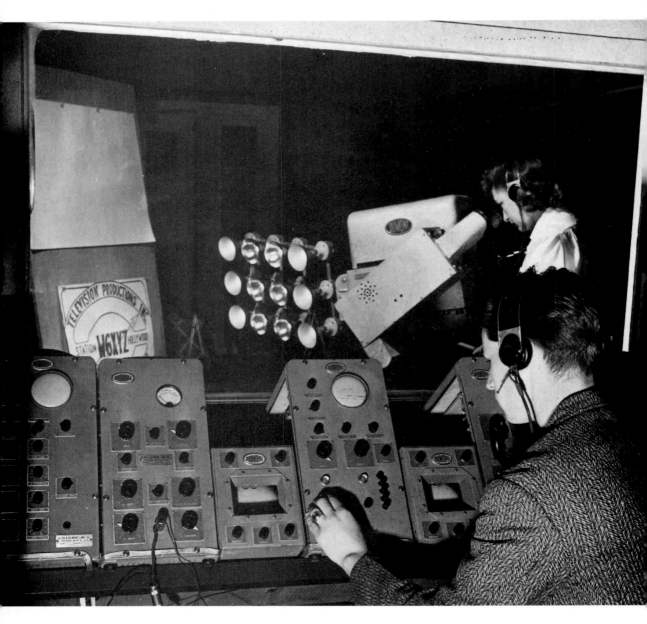

The control rooms of early TV were extremely low tech. Equipment which was often designed for other purposes was crudely patched together, no doubt explaining why each station had to be prepared to quickly switch to the station logo or the "Please Stand By" signal.

(COURTESY KTLA PHOTOS)

an offshoot of Hearst's operation, NBC moved to Fox Movietone. Throughout the early 1940s, newsreel footage ended up being telecast on a sporadic basis.

CBS's first regularly scheduled live television newscast did not come until the end of the war in Europe. It starred Douglas Edwards, who became the second most-famous TV newsman (after Edward R. Murrow) in the first decade of television. Edwards's entrance into TV was reluctant in the extreme. To understand his reluctance, it is necessary to understand the great prestige and respectable salaries that radio newsmen had earned during World War II, particularly under Murrow at CBS. Radio news had been a passion for young Doug from childhood. He was fifteen when he took his first radio job at $2.50 a week in hometown Troy, Alabama. By age twenty, he was a staff announcer at Detroit radio WXYZ, along with another young man with a melodious voice, Mike Wallace. That led to a job with CBS in New York. Doug was so good at the microphone that his bosses didn't want him leaving to join Murrow and the other overseas newsmen. Finally Doug threatened to quit unless CBS sent him to London. It was 1944, and the war was almost over. Veteran CBS correspondent David Schoenbrun remembered Edwards in Paris in November 1944: "I saw a young man in uniform, with a correspondent's identification disk in his lapels, standing in front of a blackboard. His cheeks were puffed up, his lips pursed. I thought he looked like a chipmunk storing nuts in his cheeks."[3]

That chipmunk look should have excluded Edwards from consideration for the job that would someday make him famous. Fortunately radio cared what people *sounded* like, not what they looked like, and Doug sounded so good that Paul White with CBS in New York offered Edwards a job that was more attractive than his European post. He was to anchor the important morning CBS radio "World News Roundup." Back in New York, White told him there were a few other new responsibilities, such as the two-minute news insert on a soap *Wendy Warren and the News*, a daytime drama in which Wendy worked in a fictitious newsroom, but midway through the show there was a break with real news. The catch to the deal was an obligation to announce a television news show. Edwards tried to turn it down.

The twenty-six-year-old Edwards was immediately straightarmed by CBS executive Frank Stanton into taking a job in an area no self respecting newsman would want: television.

Stanton gave him a visionary pep talk about the future of television, but to Edwards and his colleagues this was not a plum assignment. Stanton knew exactly what he was doing when he promised a raise in Edwards's staff salary to make up for the radio fees he would lose. It clinched the deal.[4]

Doug's TV producer, Henry Cassirer, gave him a tour of the facilities. It was a few floors above Grand Central Station and to get to it Edwards was led down steel-lined corridors under overhead iron beams. Later, Schoenbrun, visiting Edwards's studio said, "I felt like the Hunchback in the towers of Notre Dame."[5]

The studio had reopened in May 1944 for an intellectual quiz show featuring essayist Gilbert Seldes and guests like literary critic Stanley Kauffman (still covering television today for *The New Republic*). It was there that Worthington Miner began directing "experimental" drama with *Women in Wartime* sketches from *Mademoiselle* magazine. There were no well-known artists in those shows, just young people on the way up. One such show featured Betty Furness still trying to find her way to Hollywood as an aspiring starlet.[6]

A year later a few props and sets were left over from these shows, but for the new shows there was almost nothing. It was producer Henry Cassirer's job to find visual aids for the nightly newscast, and of course he hoped for as many film clips as possible. The problem was that CBS had no film lab on the premises. All film, new or old, had to be processed in Liederkranz Hall, a former German glee club center. The "rushes" were indeed *rushed*, often on foot, though one late-breaking segment was pulled out of the developer, still wet and spread out on the floor of a speeding taxicab to dry.[7]

Initially Edwards's show was once a week on Saturdays. On week-days Doug was still doing radio work, and the news stars of CBS were still their *radio* stars: Murrow, Robert Trout, and Charles Collingwood. After Edwards had been doing double duty for a year, Stanton again called the young man into his office.

"We're dropping your Saturday night newscast."

Doug had mixed feelings about this. He'd grown fond of television.

"Instead," continued Stanton, "We want you Monday through Friday five times a week. Fifteen minutes every night."

Edwards thought out loud: "I'm earning $400 a week on my radio shows. TV can't match that." Edwards then asked an evasive but leading question, "Why me?"

Stanton told him that Murrow, Trout, and the others didn't have the right chemistry for television. TV was a different medium. He warned the twenty-eight-year-old Edwards that if he passed up television he would live to regret it. "In a year or two you'll be the most famous name in America and earn three times as much. TV will be a bonanza."[8]

When Doug's boss, Edward R. Murrow, read the news of Edwards's assignment, he offered sincere sympathy. In 1945, Murrow had no faith in television.

Every local television station of course had news. In the 1930s, Los Angeles earthquakes and fires were covered on the Don Lee station and in the mid-forties the Paramount station, under Klaus Landsberg, was doing many news remotes, usually with young Stan Chambers. Inside the studio, newsmen had to deal with the heat, outside they were at the mercy of the elements. Chambers was at the Santa Monica seashore reporting on a beached whale when a fly flew into his open mouth. Stan kept his live report going despite coughing and choking. The next day the station received a complimentary letter from a woman who appreciated the announcer's emotional involvement with the story: "Mr. Chambers was so moved by the plight of the whale that he was in tears, God bless him."[9]

NBC's television news film department wasn't open for regular business until 1946, when they offered *Your Esso Reporter* twice a week. Eighteen months later NBC created television's second news anchorman.

John Cameron Swayze, who had sweated through dozens of shirts in the broiling heat of Kansas City's experimental station W9XAC, was picked by NBC to be the announcer for a NBC news show that was still just twice a week. Swayze seemed like such a natural for television. His appearance was men's shop perfect; his refined diction the result of his Kansas City mother insisting that he take elocution lessons. It's astonishing that he had to audition to get the NBC job. Swayze remembered it as more like an interview for a modeling job than for news announcing. He sat along side four other men in the WNBT studio. No one was asked to say a word as the camera panned their faces. Then a voice from the control room told them all that they could go home. Six days later, Swayze was hired for a new twice-a-week program. God forbid something newsworthy should happen on one of the other five days of the week. It was retitled the *Camel Newsreel Theatre* in February 1948 and ultimately became NBC's first nightly newscast, the *Camel News Caravan*.

CBS radio journalists were not alone in their disdain for television. At NBC, broadcasters and writers avoided TV except when ordered. Years earlier executives of the NBC news department tried to keep TV at arms length by subcontracting a theater newsreel firm to photograph news events for them. The newsreel company turned them down, so NBC hired two recently unemployed newsreel makers to do the dirty work. Until 1948, NBC news films were shot without sound on 35-mm film, just like the theater newsreels. Background music from a "mood library" was added on the air. The subjects were the dreariest aspects of theater newsreels: pie eating contests, women's fashions, movie openings, and pretty girls on water skis.

All this would change with the gavel-to-gavel coverage of the Democratic and Republican conventions. That event galvanized audiences and newsmen alike. It inspired the networks to get serious about the possibility of news reporting on television. But it didn't happen until 1948.

The extraordinary fact of the slow development of television news was that it took a long time for everybody—programmers, advertisers, and viewers—to realize the full impact of a statement of "fact" by a face on a television tube.

Radio had conditioned its listeners to use their imaginations with shows like *I Can Hear It Now*, which recreated historic events as if they were news events. Orson Welles's *War of the Worlds* used a news format to present science fiction. The line between radio fact and fiction was blurred every day. This is still the great advantage that radio has over television. But in 1946, *real news* on *television* was a grabber. Even if it was just the talking head of Douglas Edwards, it was more real, more immediate and more important than a fact on radio. Frank Stanton of CBS knew it even though Murrow didn't. It took years for David Sarnoff to learn it.

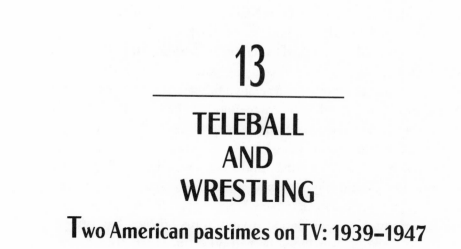

13

TELEBALL
AND
WRESTLING

Two American pastimes on TV: 1939–1947

By 1939, television finally had the capability for extended remote sports telecasts. Up to then, every football game had been presented as a radio broadcast with a studio-based football game board and anonymous hands moving wooden players up and down the board. Now, in the year of the World's Fair, the medium was ready, the national pastime of baseball was ready, and two sports-casters, Bill Stern and Red Barber, both wanted to sit at the NBC microphone.

Three years earlier, Bill Stern was working at Radio City Music Hall with a burning desire to announce on radio. He was then stage manager of the Rockette Show, and producer Leon Leonidoff kept him so busy that lunch hour was the only time he could go across the street to pester NBC for a job. John Royal was NBC programming chief and young Stern impressed him with his play-by-play skills in a two-minute tryout, which landed a job as an NBC sportscaster for college football. He was told he would start work in two weeks.

Stern immediately called his family and friends and asked them to send telegrams to Mr. Royal praising young Bill's play-by-play skills during a Princeton football game. Two things upset this clever scheme. First, Royal rescheduled Stern to another game. Second, many of Stern's shills sent their telegrams several weeks early. John Royal was not amused. Stern was fired.

Stern then moved to the southwest where he did local football sportscasting. One night he was struck by a speeding automobile, smashing his left leg. Back in New York, doctors found a deep infection and recommended amputation. Lying in his hospital bed, Stern was deeply depressed, convinced he had no future in anything, certainly not in sportscasting. John Royal heard about Stern's condition, visited the hospital and promised Bill a job when he was recovered. And he kept his word. Bill Stern became NBC's first chair of football.

Rival Red Barber remembered Stern's style, "He never admitted he made a mistake. When Stern would do a football game and name the wrong ball carrier, he would simply pretend the wrong man lateralled the ball to the right man. College football never had so many single and double and triple laterals as when Stern had the mike."

May 11, 1939, marked the first baseball telecast in America. It was not the major leagues. Princeton was playing Columbia, and NBC thought enough of the event, or at least of the telecast itself, to assign Bill Stern. This in fact was not the first "sport on TV" as was claimed, but it was the first *complete* game. *The New Yorker* was slightly snotty, as could be expected, in its "Talk of the Town" item headlined *Teleball*:

> If you follow television closely, you probably know that the first telecast of a sporting event in this country took place last week, the subject being the second game of a doubleheader between Princeton and Columbia at Baker Field.[1]

The audience, for what Stern described as a "televised broadcast" instead of a "telecast," was an invited crowd of press reporters and broadcasters watching at Rockefeller Center, along with an undetermined number of the two thousand set owners in the greater New York City area covered by W2XBS.

What the *New Yorker* didn't know was that this broadcast almost went on the air without its broadcasting voice, Bill Stern. Stern was bald, and while this condition had been no cause for alarm on radio, that particular day Stern forgot he needed to appear on camera. He arrived at the ballpark without his toupee and insisted on going home to retrieve it.

The program was scheduled to start at 4:00 in the afternoon which, since it was the second game of a doubleheader, was a gutsy bit of scheduling. Fortunately, Stern was able to get back from his home wearing the toupee before the second game began. There is a story, perhaps apocryphal, that Stern, speeding to get back in time, was stopped by a policeman who coincidentally recognized Bill's voice and happily waved him off to the stadium.

Stern had not rehearsed anything. How could he? All his rehearsal plans went down the drain when he had to drive home for that damn toupee. So his stage manager frantically ad libbed instructions to him behind the camera while Stern interviewed rival coaches and captains. "Stand over here or you'll lick the focal-plane idea," said the stage manager, or at least that's what the *New Yorker* reported Stern had said even though it didn't make a lot of sense then or now. "This is one of the best ball diamonds in college parks today," beamed Stern, "holding roughly five thousand people. If you're seeing this, you're seeing history being made."

While Stern made his way to his assigned broadcast seat on the wooden bleachers along the third-base line, the Princeton coach took a header, stumbling and rolling down the hill under the first-base bleachers. But most of the crowd missed this, because they were preoccupied with Stern and the single TV camera, a bulky gray machine on a platform behind home plate. Cables connected Stern's mike and the camera to two square blue trucks several yards away. Signs marked them as NBC "telemobile units."

Two camera operators took turns at the panhandle of the camera following—or attempting to follow—the action of the baseball around the diamond. The first ball ever thrown on television was bunted down the third-base line by Frank Murphy, the Columbia second baseman. It went foul, and a Princeton infielder lost his cap racing for it. By this time, Stern was getting comfortable with the new medium. Instead of keeping his eye on the camera and where it was pointing he just reported the game as if he were on radio. On radio Stern could take it easy. If he made a mistake, he could easily rectify it. In football there was refuge in his famous "lateral" trick. Frequently, in radio, he had just let a mistake stand. TV marked the end of this kind of lazy reporting. The television audience watching the Columbia-Princeton game saw the ball caroming off the first baseman's glove, while Stern reported it going through his legs. Frequently Stern would get bogged down in an anecdote and would catch up to the game by reporting a batter on the way to the plate when, in fact, he was already at bat.

Stern was unfamiliar with college baseball teams and players, so ad libbing did not come easily. He always relied on a spotter, someone who knew the players well and could slip him a steady stream of notes that would be the basis of his running commentary. The spotter from Columbia was well equipped with knowledge but had no experience in the specifics of spotting. Instead of writing notes on the players, the spotter would get emotionally involved in the game, handing slips to Stern that read "Go Columbia!" or "Roar, Lion, Roar." Finally Stern stopped this with a killer stare. Frantically trying to atone, the collegiate spotter began writing an extensive biography of the Columbia coach, Lou Little.

After reporting endlessly on the coach, Stern read the next note verbatim.

"Lou Little is in back of us!"

And then the next note.

"And he'll be right over."

Pause. Lou didn't show up. Fortunately there was some activity on the field. The spotter passed a new note.

"He's coming soon."

Stern ignored him and went on with the game. The spotter passed a new note.

"You can't push *him*. The publicity man will bring him over when he's ready."²

Stern rolled his eyes and continued.

The game ended with a second Princeton victory. Stern breathed a sigh of relief, but still in some confusion, he announced erroneously that Princeton and Columbia had just split a double header. This was probably of no consequence to the already confused or irritated television audience. One camera was no way to photograph baseball. Panning a small white ball made it totally disappear on the screen, and frequently the camera missed the action anyway.

The *New York Times* review the next day did not give any particular praise to Stern or his toupee. Instead they concentrated on the visual disappointments. Players looked like "white flies," and the "single camera panned and jerked around in a desperate search for the ball." Stern remembered that particular horror and years later confided to a sports reporter that he and his NBC crew had been praying for nothing but strikeouts.

Even in radio broadcasting baseball was not a sure thing. Three years earlier, the Ford Motor Company had tried broadcasting the World Series. They hired top announcer Graham McNamme, who pitched his heart out for Ford's Model A. The cars didn't move. Ford dropped baseball sponsorship, and Madison Avenue wondered if the national pastime could ever lure a major sponsor.

In July 1939, Fred Weber of the Mutual Broadcasting System scheduled lunch at Manhattan's Ritz Carlton to try to talk the Gillette safety razor company into the future of major league baseball on radio and TV. His luncheon guest, a young man named A. Craig Smith, had not cleared the meeting with the boss Joseph P. Spang, Jr., the president of Gillette. Weber was either a great salesman or Smith had vision, because at that luncheon the two men closed a deal that would cost Gillette $203,000. When the deal was fully consummated at the office of the commissioner of baseball, Keneson Mountain Landis, Mutual Radio Network had the radio rights to the upcoming World Series, and NBC was given the smallest of bones. One that Gillette didn't want. NBC got the *television* rights to whatever games were of interest, not including the World Series. NBC accepted, mainly because of its promotional activities at the World's Fair.

NBC scheduled the first TV Major League game on August 26, 1939, at Ebbets Field, the first game of a doubleheader between the Brooklyn Dodgers and the Cincinnati Reds. Alfred (Doc) Morton, NBC's chief of programming, had a choice between his two premier baseball announcers Bill Stern and Red Barber. Remembering Stern's toupee crisis at Baker Field, he chose Barber.

Walter Lanier Barber, called "Red" most of his life, was the son of a railroad engineer for the Atlantic Coastline in Florida. When Walter was thirteen he would often ride in the cab, helping at the throttle. He wanted to follow in his dad's footsteps but his father discouraged him: "Don't break your heart by going into a drying up industry." Some years later, when young Barber got his first radio job at a Gainesville, Florida, station, his father's eyes lit up with pleasure. His son would never have to be a railroad man.

Red asked NBC's chief Morton, "Do you think there's a chance of televising a game in Brooklyn?" Barber not only had to agree to announce, he also had to get the Dodgers to agree to television. Dodger owner Larry MacPhail was buttered up with the promise that he would be "the first owner to have his team televised." He took the bait but without much enthusiasm. On broadcast day, the Dodgers forced the NBC crew to pay for their own admission to the ballpark and put broadcaster Barber in the stands, among the fans, up in the second deck on the third-base side.

On August 26, 1939, there were 35,525 people in the stands to watch the fourth-place Dodgers try to stop the pennant-bound Reds. There were no portable radios then. People who wanted sports news usually got it from New York's daily newspapers, several of which published special Ebbets Field's editions with box scores on the front page. On this day Hitler boasted he would conquer Europe, Chamberlain was warning the British people of an imminent peril of war, and the French government was warning citizens to evacuate Paris.

Up in the second deck, Red's earphones didn't work; he had lost contact with the director in the remote truck. On the positive side, this game had the technical improvement of *two* cameras, one next to Red in the second deck, and one high above home plate. The broadcaster had no idea which camera was "on" but that didn't matter much since the wild camera panning of the Columbia-Princeton game now escalated to the wild panning of *two* cameras. Between innings, Barber did "spot" commercials. One each for Ivory Soap, Wheaties, and Mobil Gas.

> My three radio sponsors insisted on TV commercials, too. For the gasoline sponsor, I put on a filling station man's hat and spieled about gas. For the breakfast cereal spot, I poured some of the stuff into a bowl. There wasn't much I could do for the soap sponsor. I just held up a soap bar and extolled its virtues.

Barber had already appeared on television a few times. He looked forward to this assignment because it was outdoors, in the blazing sun, and no matter how hot an August day in Brooklyn, it was more pleasant than the heat of the lights inside a 1939 television studio.

Red's telecast was seen by very few, but it was a huge publicity boost for the Dodgers. "The three New York teams," remembers Barber, "had a radio ban through most of 1938. So in 1939 I was the first announcer to tell the Brooklyn people about their ball club." TV made it official as well as historic. Several times during the afternoon, he reminded his small collection of viewers that they were watching "an historic first." To make sure he didn't forget to announce the score with regularity, Red brought an egg timer to the park, announcing the score with each inversion of the timer.

Baseball on TV still had big technical problems. At central control, the director gave his cues to the technical director in the remote truck. The players still looked like "white flies" buzzing around the screen. It was impossible to identify individual players. Even the opposing team identities were unclear. Red saved the day. Barely. He relayed the umpire calls and did as much play-by-play as if he were on radio.

Proud of his achievement, he wrote to NBC and asked for a memento of this broadcasting first. The network sent him a silver cigarette box engraved "in grateful appreciation, National Broadcasting

Company." To Red's astonishment, NBC enclosed a bill for the "gift," charging him thirty-five dollars.

Sports on television needed more than a celebrity narrator borrowed from radio. It needed talented directors who could solve the technical complexities of presenting sports on television. Such a director was an Irishman named Harry Coyle from Patterson, New Jersey, who came from the ranks of journeyman technicians at DuMont to become the dean of television's sports directors.

Harry Coyle was only seventeen when, with friend Bob Jameson, he visited the 1939 World's Fair. They were too poor to consider paying extra money to see the naked Amazon Women and not in the least interested in the RCA television exhibit—even though it was free.

Both were tough kids from New Jersey, interested in anything with a military slant. The gathering storm in Europe was tantalizing to many of their age. In several short years, Harry would be flying thirty-five bomber missions for the Air Force over Germany. Bob tried to enlist, but he was declared 4F and sent packing for a job. Bob found one at nearby Passaic, making electronic parts for radar and television at the DuMont laboratory. When the war ended, Harry married and landed a good job at Wright Aeronautical in hometown Patterson. The job paid $150 a week, a terrific salary for 1946, but for someone who'd been risking his life under enemy fire, the job was pure tedium. Harry envied Bob's job at DuMont. Jameson wasn't stuck in place; he was in fact, all over the place, helping develop technology for remote and sports telecasts. One night in Bob's living room, Harry saw his first TV receiver. It was playing the Army-Navy football game, and there were problems with the reception—only the middle of the tube showed a picture, and the corners were black. Harry didn't care; this looked like fun. Then Jameson's phone started ringing. Radio owners over a five block radius were calling to complain about Bob's TV, which was jamming each and every radio in the neighborhood. Harry sensed that television needed a lot of help.

One day there was an opening at DuMont for a cable pusher, and Harry grabbed it. His pay unfortunately dropped from $150 a week to $41. Harry's wife was supportive, but his mother wouldn't speak to him for over a year. "In fact," said Harry, "it was ten years before my parents could figure out who I worked for."

Harry remembers the DuMont studios at 550 Madison Avenue with a mixture of nostalgia and horror:

> It was just a couple of business offices with the wall knocked out. The ceilings weren't more than 8 feet. All the lights were really close to the performers. There were banks of lights, 150 watts each, six to a row, twenty-four in each set—the same bulbs you'd use for sunlamps. The flats were just that— flat. And Rudy, our painter, didn't take his job very seriously. Since the cameras had no depth of focus, the set detail was never noticed anyway.
>
> Once we had a star of the Metropolitan Opera making her TV debut. She insisted on wearing her original Wagnerian costume, which was largely metallic. The metal conducted too much heat from the lamps, of course, and by the end of the fifteen-minute show, the poor gal was covered with blisters.[3]

Harry was relieved and excited when DuMont moved to a real studio space newly built in the Wanamaker department store on April 15, 1946. At first Harry's job was listed as cable pusher, but since he was doing every job in the place he was labeled "studio assistant." The worst job was climbing up to the grid and cleaning the kleig lights by hand. Harry had to join a union, but the International Alliance of Theatrical & Stage Employees (IATSE) had no foothold in TV, and Harry's stretches of work went on and on, without any overtime.

The three air-conditioned studios had a more than adequate lighting grid, audience risers, four cameras, and the best in DuMont facilities. Gala celebrity-packed festivities were telecast—the grand opening night along with two new productions, a game show *Let's Have Fun* and an original drama, written especially for TV by George Lowther and directed by Louis Sposa.

The good news was that DuMont had successfully connected its New York and Washington, D.C., transmitters by coaxial cable. It had been six war-rationed years since NBC had connected New York and Philadelphia. The technology was the same but this time there was more publicity. DuMont claimed it was TV's first "network" broadcast.

The bad news at Wanamaker was that despite the high ceilings and air conditioning, the heat from the studio lights was still unbearable. In the booth, director Sposa kept complaining about all the noise from the studio floor. No one could figure out where it was coming from. Finally the cause was determined. The crew members had collected enough perspiration in their shoes that just walking around the studio floor created an enormous "slushing" sound.

Florence Monroe, one of the three women on DuMont's staff, remembered the debut show from Wanamaker's, "It was really corn-ball, but the evening was spectacular."[4]

In the accident-prone weeks that followed, nobody griped, and nobody got mad when sets fell down, and the mikes on camera went dead. It was all in a day's work. The first big panic came with DuMont's first regular sponsor, Longine. The watch company insisted that their commercials appear exactly on the hour and half hour. Prior to this, if a thirty-minute show ran thirty-three minutes—nobody cared, and pre-1946 shows often ended later and later. Under the new edict, shows ended when they were scheduled to end.

"The first two weeks, it was scary," Harry Coyle remembered. "Variety shows ended in the middle of a song, mystery stories in the middle of the plot. Finally, we got it together."

Harry worked on a lot of audience-participation shows in 1946; today they would be called "game shows." Big-shot announcers from radio acted like they were slumming in the small bucks arena of TV. John Reed King, Johnny Olsen, Lew Lehr—as Harry saw it from behind the cables—were self-annointed kings. "They did anything they wanted to do, and if you were the director, you'd be subjugated to them. If you fought them you were out of a job." Harry reflected, "They were all assholes."[5]

During his DuMont studio days, Harry worked in every capacity, frequently doing work that later became the exclusive domain of either the director, associate director, or the technical director. There were no credits on any shows except for the performers.

The boss of the Wanamaker DuMont Studio was Louis Sposa. His brother had been a staff announcer for five years—Dennis Sposa, who performed under the name Dennis James. Dennis did cooking shows, ping pong demonstrations, and the DuMont "man on the street" show. The last was an accident of sorts. When a regular program fell through, Louis dropped a microphone out a window to brother Dennis on the street. The camera was trained on the passersby, almost all of whom thought they were on radio, not TV.

Harry Coyle loved the craziness of improvised television, but working conditions—and his associates—were far from perfect.

> There was another guy who started when I did. His name was Barry Shear, and I suppose that if you threw any fifteen guys together and worked them the hours we worked, at least one guy's going to turn out to be a pain in the ass. That was Barry Shear. Of course, he was a Jewish guy who thought he knew everything— and I was an Irish guy who thought he knew everything. He probably thought I was a pain in the ass too.[6]

Whatever the differences, everybody who worked the long impossible hours ended up at McSorley's Ale House, which was across the street and so traditional that "it hadn't been dusted for a hundred years." The things that drove the DuMont men to drink were not the programs but the commercials. On one show, a "semi-Hollywood star" had been signed by the ad agency. He finished his rehearsal at three in the afternoon and was told to take a break. He went home, and thinking he was finished, never came back. WABD went on the air live with the ad agency man reading the copy.

Sometimes an entire show was one long commercial (much like today's "infomercials"). On October 30, 1946, WABD scheduled such a show, budgeted at an unheard of four thousand dollars. Supposedly a comedy sketch starring Jerry Colonna, it was in fact a fifteen-minute commercial for a Westinghouse electric blanket. Colonna arrived at the last minute, thinking that he could just "wing it." He should have been pleased that his part was short and in pantomime. On the contrary, Colonna had a temper tantrum about his part being too small and quit on the spot. *Billboard* reviewed the remains of this corpse a week later and kindly dismissed it as "a very bad job."

One of Harry's many jobs was that of a wardrobe censor. In 1946, Jane Russell was fast becoming America's biggest movie star "in two ways more than one." Cleavage was in. But not on TV. In fact DuMont mandated that a large sign hang in the studio where all could read: "DON'T FORGET THAT YOU ARE A GUEST IN THEIR LIVING ROOMS. BEHAVE ACCORDINGLY."*

Harry always carried a half-dozen silk handkerchiefs, and any female guest with a low neckline had to be decorated with a hankie in the appropriate place.

Harry had now worked almost a year for DuMont. Kowtowing to Johnny Olsen on *Ladies Be Seated* was not why he quit Wright Aeronautical. He began to lobby for work with the remote truck. He knew the director Jack Murphy had been cooking up a sports remote from Jamaica Arena.

In 1946, professional wrestling was a sport known to a few wrestling fanatics, and it was as fake as it is today, maybe more so. Lou Sposa had heard of the success that Los Angeles W6XYZ was having with wrestling, and the Jamaica Arena across the river in Queens had regular wrestling bouts every week.

Once DuMont solved the technical problem of broadcasting from the arena, wrestling programs quickly dropped into the weekly schedule. In fact, since there was no *TV Guide* before 1950, and newspapers rarely carried program logs, scheduling was left to Lou Sposa, who was free to make last-minute changes.

DuMont's Dr. Tom Goldsmith designed a location transmitter that could take the signal from Jamaica to the 550 Madison broadcast antenna forty-two stories high. The very first transmission worked like

---

*It was just a few years later that Ernie Kovacs came up with the proper response to his premise: "Thank you for inviting me into your house—but couldn't you have cleaned it up a bit?

a charm, and Sposa told his brother Dennis to get out to the arena for that night's bout. Dennis protested that he knew very little about boxing.

"It's not boxing," his brother corrected him. "It's *wrestling*."

". . . And I know *nothing* about wrestling."

"Then find out about it!"

Dennis made a beeline for the New York Public Library where he took out six books about the manly art of wrestling. He spread them across the back of a taxi for quick study, and hoped his brother would reimburse the $2.10 for the ride. On the way to Jamaica, he passed a butcher shop and ordered the cab to stop. With the meter running, he bought a bag of chicken bones, and, as an afterthought, gave a dime to a kid for a rubber dog toy he was carrying. Meanwhile Harry Coyle and director Jack Murphy prepped the "mobile truck" which, in fact was a station wagon. Harry asked Jack how he planned to "direct" wrestling. Jack laughed and pointed out that they only had one camera. They would either point it at the wrestlers or at Dennis James. "Any idiot can direct TV in those circumstances. I could be a hero if I just stay on the air."[7]

The first DuMont wrestling remote telecast was in the dead of winter, 1946. Inside the Jamaica Arena, Dennis James continued to "bone up" on his terminology, carefully placing the chicken bones and doggie toy on the table beside his microphone. Outside, young Harry, vaguely realizing that he'd been promoted to associate director by default, tried to keep warm. "I didn't freeze my ass off because my ass was sitting on the equipment."

Dennis hadn't told anybody what he was planning to do. Outside, Harry followed the show with his earphones and a tiny monitor and began to laugh. His announcer was doing "sound effects." Everytime a wrestler got in a bone crashing hold Dennis would crack a chicken bone. "Ouch!" he'd moan. "That musta hurt!" Then he'd slap the dog toy into his palm in perfect sync with a splattering punch. Back at 550 Madison, Lou Sposa knew that this was a turning point in television history. DuMont immediately became New York's number one sports station.

Week after week, Dennis James, Jack Murphy, and Harry Coyle improved the "art" of wrestling on TV. Or, rather two of the three did. Basically Jack Murphy abdicated. Harry Coyle remembers:

> Murphy is dead now, and I hate to speak ill, etc.—but Jack was a very lazy person. I'd direct four nights, he'd do one, and then say 'My wife and I have to go to dinner tonight. You do it.' For a while nobody knew what was going on. Then it was spring and we had our first screwup when 550 Madison didn't get the transmission. Doctor Goldsmith came out to check and realized that all the leaves of all the trees from Jamaica to Manhattan, now in good bloom, were blocking the signal from the remote truck.[8]

Harry was amazed at the solution. Goldsmith directed the signal *away* from Manhattan and into a relay dish that he placed on top of the Jamaica subway station. The broadcast could now work in any weather. In Jack Murphy's absence, Coyle was retitled "Director Harry Coyle."

Then *Wrestling at the Jamaica Arena* added an intermission segment. Harry got in trouble. The second wrestler Dennis interviewed used the word "hell." Nobody working behind the scenes thought twice about it, but the phone lines were lighting up at 550 Madison. A hundred letters of complaint followed—an extraordinary number considering how few sets were in houses in 1946. "It was a catastrophe" remembers Harry. "As director I had to take full responsibility in letters I wrote to all the executives. When I got back to the studio, friends kept steering me in the direction of the sign that read 'Don't forget you are a guest in their living rooms.' "

With spring 1947 came TV's first full baseball season. DuMont scored a major coup with a deal to supply the equipment and manpower to broadcast many of the Yankee home games from the stadium. Harry did a lot of the directing, but Frank Murphy was still taking credit.

The baseball team owners were often suspicious that TV might encourage people to stay home, emptying the ballparks. "I wanted to put a TV camera behind home plate, looking down from the press box," said Harry. "Organized baseball was against this. At Wrigley Field they held out until 1952. Originally at Yankee Stadium we were restricted to the upper deck. No chance they'd let us take cameras onto the field." This was part of a constant conflict between the baseball management and the young broadcasters. When a TV camera shot into a Yankee dugout, team executive Tom Gallery, came out to the mobile truck to complain.

"It's invasion of privacy."

"Privacy?" Harry exploded. "Fifty thousand people in the stadium can see into both dugouts! What are we talking about?"

The only "fifty thousand" that organized baseball cared about was the fifty thousand dollars that Gillette had paid for the rights to the first World Series.* That, along with the production cost, brought each game's broadcast cost to $10,000. Before 1947 the most expensive studio show had cost only $4,500.

The Gillette company was powerfully sitting in what announcer Red Barber used to call "the catbird's seat." This sponsor dictated everything. Even though the Gillette shows were all done on NBC, that network's staff had very little baseball experience. That's why Harry Coyle and his DuMont crew did all the broadcast work on the first World Series. NBC squawked but Gillette had the last word.

Gillette paid so much for the broadcast rights, they decided to crack down on salaries. Harry didn't care; his check was peanuts. But Red Barber, who'd done the whole season with Harry and who had "one of the greatest voices of all time" was offered scale, about thirty dollars a game. Barber turned down Gillette's offer and sat out the series.

Red was great with commercials, and maybe he was lucky to sit this one out, because opening game marked the last commercial that Gillette ever did "live." Gillette was proudly introducing an "automatic" safety razor. The debut commercial was more rehearsed than anything connected with the series. Hand models were carefully

---

*A Brooklyn brewery offered a lot more but at the last minute the czar of baseball, Albert B. "Happy" Chandler, decided that "it would not be good public relations for baseball to have a series sponsored by the producer of an alcoholic beverage."

auditioned and the winning hands were rehearsed by Gillette's ad agency man over and over. The script was simple. The left hand held the neck of the razor, the right hand twisted the bottom. The top of the razor magically opened like a two petalled flower, the left hand dropped in a Gillette blue blade which practically floated into its slot as the right hand deftly twisted the mechanism closed. Everything was timed to a golden-voiced announcement, while recorded music from the truck was ready to back it up. When people ask Harry Coyle about his worst moment in a lifetime of sports broadcasting, the premiere Gillette commercial leads all.

Naturally the razor refused to open on the air. The carefully auditioned right hand twisted with all its might, the cosmetically perfect left hand tugged and pulled at the top. The golden-voiced announcer paused for what seemed an eternity, and the music played on and on. The baseball game resumed at the top of the second inning with the "automatic" Gillette razor completely stuck. From that "live" moment on, the Gillette company did all its commercials on film.

Harry summed up the prehistory of television with words that are echoed by his contemporaries in other interviews with broadcasting pioneers:

> Nobody ever thought TV would have the importance it had. We were all young, and working for peanuts. We all would rather have been in radio earning more money and in less chaos. Of course, on TV we sometimes got a chance to make up our own shows, and because job titles were meaningless, the chances for advancement were everywhere. Of course in the early days you never got credit for what you did, and most of the time you didn't want it. We were happy nonetheless.[9]

14

ALLEN DUMONT AND THE FOURTH NETWORK

1938–1947

I n 1949 Allen B. DuMont, early manufacturer of the cathode-ray tube and founder of the DuMont Television Network, financed a "docudrama" about his scientific achievements. While Lee De Forest and other pioneer inventors were played by actors, DuMont elected to play himself. A fascinating piece of history, *The Miracle of Passaic* is in the collection of New York's Museum of Broadcasting. It shows how DuMont became a major competitor to RCA, manufacturing sets that were bigger and better at a competitive price.

In the late 1920s, after DuMont had been an engineer in charge of tube manufacture at the Westinghouse Lamp Company, he worked as chief engineer for the De Forest Radio Company. Working out of his own garage in Passaic, New Jersey, he started DuMont Laboratories with an initial capital of only $12,000. By 1931, he had, on his own, made major improvements in picture-tube technology and produced TV receivers that were better than RCA's.

When DuMont decided to tackle RCA, the rest of the industry took notice. Radio pioneer Lee De Forest saw it in a mythic context:

> The history of invention is replete with instances where the old fable of David and Goliath has been reenacted in bloodless disguise. The slingshot of youth, equipped with courage, daring and an inborn skill at invention, has frequently outwitted the cumbersome sword and armor of gigantic capitalization. Thus we find the really great, epoch-making inventions wrought by individuals working almost alone and unaided, equipped only with their genius and resistless determination. Witness Eli Whitney, of the cotton gin; Jacquard of the loom; Charles Goodyear and rubber, Alexander Graham Bell and his telephone, Thomas Edison and his incandescent lamp; Lee De Forest and his radio tube.[1]

It was, of course, typical of De Forest to cast himself as another David, but he was generous to praise DuMont for his fight against RCA's 441-line picture and its flickering picture. If America had listened to DuMont instead of RCA, today we would have a sharp 567-line picture with less flicker and even better reception than the PAL system in Europe. DuMont's system, demonstrated in 1940, would have made sets cheaper for the public and less subject to obsolescence. Indeed his demonstration for the FCC from the NBC transmitter on top of the Empire State Building to the DuMont Laboratories had been "astonishing to visiting engineers."

Actually two Davids were up against Sarnoff's Goliath. Early on, Philo Farnsworth had made a deal with Goliath by licensing his patents. Allen DuMont thought that slow and sure would win the race. They both were wrong. Neither had sufficient capital assets to create enough quality programming.

In 1938, DuMont surprised RCA Chairman Sarnoff with an announcement that he was moving into TV programming, applying for as many stations as the government would allow, and affiliating with others. It was a bold gesture that didn't cost much money; some licenses were bought for as little as five hundred dollars each.

Ironically Sarnoff's own priority in 1938 was neither TV sales nor programming. It was politics, and his chief "political" foes were CBS and the FCC. As far as Sarnoff was concerned, DuMont was cash poor, and television was a kind of high-stakes poker. However, DuMont had two aces up his sleeve: money and manpower. He had borrowed $200,000 to start a flagship station in Manhattan, putting the people who were building sets in New Jersey to work in New York programming on a volunteer basis. Paramount Pictures provided $56,000 of the seed money in return for 25 percent of DuMont television. Years later it proved to be a very bad deal, since Paramount had its own TV stations and the FCC totalled them in with DuMont's and limited their expansion. W2XWV wasn't licensed commercially but it "cheated" the same way W2XBS did. DuMont tried out commercials on his regular Sunday night variety shows.

In May 1941, the FCC approved "commercial status" for any TV station that could stay on the air for fifteen hours a week. Was commercial approval a financial bonanza? Hardly. The flagship NBC station, rechristened WNBT, was the first to set rates—an entire hour's program in prime time (there was no other time) was $120. DuMont's sponsors paid even less.

On those early TV sets, it was extremely difficult to tune from one channel to another. DuMont had been assigned Channel One by the FCC but he wanted his W2XWV (soon to be WABD) to be on Channel Four, because of rumors that the first channel might be usurped for military purposes (it was). After Pearl Harbor, the TV programming of NBC, CBS, and DuMont ended, and for the first year of the war, there was no programming in Manhattan at all. Then it slowly resumed in 1943. On Channel One on your fourteen-inch DuMont set, called "The Clifton," you could have seen DuMont programs four nights a week. On Sunday WABD resembled real television with a modest variety show.* Later that year, WNBT carried an air warden's course. A newly renamed CBS station filled out Thursday and Friday with Red Cross demonstrations, news read from a

---

*Sunday DuMont variety shows would remain a staple through the original *Jackie Gleason Show*.

teletype machine, and a quiz show, the details of which are permanently lost. That same year NBC boldly expanded its civil defense program, adding two more cameras but limiting itself to volunteer actors. The brief skits were on such lively civil defense subjects as "Gas Warfare" and "Bombs and Fire Protection."

By the end of the year there were a few better programs. On Sundays there was *Irwin Shanes' Television Workshop*, a regular live dramatic series. It won some critical praise for its hour version of Shakespeare's *Romeo and Juliet*. Also on Sunday was *Thrills and Chills*, an uninspired series of travel films narrated by Doug Allan and the tourists who took them. Its host, celebrating in early 1946 that *Thrills and Chills* had been running over two years, boasted, "We consistently held top place."

There was attempt at comedy with ventriloquist Paul Winchell and his dummy Jerry Mahoney. The multitalented Winchell probably winces today that he will be best remembered as the voice of Tigger in the *Pooh* cartoons. In 1943 Winchell was considered a better ventriloquist than Edgar Bergen, but his recent radio show had failed because his material was inferior to the creator of Charlie McCarthy. Winchell's initial TV appearances on DuMont were brief and unimpressive, but he'd be back—a few years later—with the dawn of the "Golden Age." DuMont's low point in the war years was 1944's "The Peanut Is a Serious Guy." Designed and supplied by the J. Walter Thompson agency, it was simply a fifteen-minute commercial for Planter's Peanuts.

There has always been some confusion regarding the exact role of ABC, the American Broadcasting Company, during television's prehistory. ABC radio began in 1943 when the Supreme Court upheld the FCC ruling that NBC had to sell its second radio network, the Blue Network, to Edward J. Noble, the founder of Life Savers candy. From the day of his radio "debut," Noble was determined to be a force in television. The trouble was that while he had bought dozens of radio stations, no TV frequencies were available New York City. So Paul Mowey, the new ABC television boss, made a deal with Allen DuMont for WABD to air a certain number of ABC shows a week. DuMont's technical personnel would do the work, though the shows would technically be produced by ABC, and necessarily aired on DuMont. DuMont received the princely sum of $625 for each half hour. In November 1946, Mowey increased ABC's leased airtime to nine-and-a-half hours. ABC's own channel wasn't assigned until 1948.

Clearly, if Alan DuMont aspired to beat NBC in the programming game, he would have to expand to larger quarters, so he leased an unused wing of the John Wanamaker Department Store. The bare bones resembled a warehouse, and its high ceilings kept the intensely hot lighting equipment slightly above the performers' heads. With room for more than one studio at Wanamaker's, DuMont never had to go off the air to set up a new show. Of course, in live television, solving one problem just led to another.

Lots of young men, fresh from wartime service, were getting a break in the new industry. At DuMont, Harry Coyle worked long hours on the Wanamaker studio floor. Jobs seemed to be available to any young man like Coyle, willing to work for very little money.

In 1946, as we saw Harry Coyle describe it, DuMont accomplished what many consider the very *first network commercial broadcast*. It was a four-camera show from the Wanamaker Studio carried by coaxial cable to the Mayflower Hotel in Washington, D.C., then relayed to the several hundred set owners of DuMont's WTTG in Washington. The special program had several parts. First, New York's mayor William O'Dwyer gave a warm welcome, followed by a cooking demonstration of the sponsor's macaroni, in which the mayor took part. Then there was a game show called "Let's Have Fun" and finally a one-act drama called "Experience," which concerned the erotic wanderings of a dental patient under the influence of laughing gas.[2]

Jack Gould, making his debut as a television critic for the *New York Times*, declared the entire, much-ballyhooed event "an astonishing evening of ineptitude . . . a major disappointment."

DuMont's first soap opera, *Faraway Hill*, was created by David P. Lewis, who had been working in Omaha producing radio shows. He noticed a story in *Life* magazine about the commercial viability of TV and persuaded his Omaha bosses to establish a TV department in New York. Making himself the boss of his own creation, he "sold" *Faraway*

Hill to DuMont, and it debuted from DuMont's Wanamaker Studios on October 2, 1946. The ten programs were budgeted at three hundred dollars each, and starred Flora Campbell and Mel Brandt in a drama involving "love, heartbreak, death, and gossip." At the beginning of each episode, an off-camera narrator revealed the thoughts of widow Karen St. John, a rich Park Avenue lady who, trying to escape the memory of her late husband, falls in love with a poor wretch living in the country. When it was clear that the tenth episode would be the last, writer-producer Lewis matter-of-factly wrote the death of Karen St. John. There was a savage outcry from the show's four hundred fans, a surprising early warning of the power of TV soap opera.[3]

With material for the production of postwar TV receivers in short supply, and with CBS sniping at RCA over color TV, Allen DuMont tried to seize a postwar competitive edge. He faced three obstacles. First, there wasn't enough money to extend the length of the broadcast day. Second, the American Federation of Musicians had been on strike for almost two years to prohibit the broadcasting of live instrumental music. At NBC, musical shows got around the ban the same way they did with many musical radio shows: they used pre-1944 records. On TV they either lip-synched records or they performed a cappella. As with the 1940 American Society of Composers, Authors and Publishers (ASCAP) boycott to protest the rival organization, Broadcast Music Inc. (BMI), Steven Foster's music was everywhere. Spike Jones later parodied the problem with "I Dream of Brownie with the Light Blue Jeans." Finally, fully staged dramas and musical productions were just too expensive for DuMont. This left programmers with no choice except to fill up most of their airtime with panel shows and audience-participation game shows.

DuMont tried to copy the stunts of *Truth or Consequences* with a Dennis James show called *Cash and Carry*, sponsored by Libby Foods. The "cash" was a top prize of $15 and "carry" was the stunt side of the show. For example, one early show featured a blindfolded housewife trying to spoon feed ice cream to her husband.[4]

Not all radio game shows were easily transferred to the screen. *Detect and Collect* had actress Wendy Barrie as its radio emcee. The

DuMont brass didn't think TV was ready for a female emcee and recast with comedian Lew Lehr. A woman's place was in the house or out shopping; only men should do the selling. Prior to that, Wendy had been on only a few Dumont shows, most which had been poorly received. One day in the mail, she received the anonymous gift of a chain saw. "What is this fan trying to tell me?" Wendy asked, "That I should slit my wrists?"

Before moving into the Wanamaker Studio, the DuMont broadcast center was in an office on Madison Avenue and 53rd Street. One of the more ambitious dramatic shows from its Madison Avenue studio had the institutional title *Products for War and Peace*. On July 12, 1945, director John Hewlett ambitiously turned the tiny studio into a storm at sea. One remaining photo shows how it was done. The script called for two men in rags on a floating hatch cover while waves lapped over them and drowning seemed imminent. The studio set was only about ten-by-twelve feet and looked like a large waterbed covered by a dark blue rubber blanket. Here's a sample of the dialogue:

> YOUNG MAN: A good skipper. A brave man. He sure pulled us out of this. But—water? What kind of water? Would you ever think it would happen to me? And my first trip out. Water, water, every-where, and not a drop to drink.
>
> SKIPPER: Poor lad. We're going to die, boy.
>
> YOUNG MAN: Die? We're not going to die. I come from trout-fishing country. Let's catch a fish.
>
> SKIPPER: You're delirious. It's too late.
>
> YOUNG MAN: You don't know what I mean. Let's go fishing, I tell you—let's go fishing!
>
> SKIPPER: How?
>
> YOUNG MAN: Sock me in the jaw.
>
> SKIPPER: I know you're crazy now. You're a good lad; you're young enough to be my own son, and I don't want to see you suffer. Roll off the raft—and go to heaven.

During all this, studio manager Frank Burnette and studio assistant Barry Shear threw buckets of water on the actors, simulating passing waves. Sometimes the volume of the dialogue was lowered so that announcer Al Henderson could say, "Men have fought the oceans of the globe from time immemorial. But today the U.S. Rubber Company has provided the modern mariner with new weapons to fight and conquer the sea."

Remember Betty Furness passing up the TV exhibit at the 1939 World's Fair because she thought "television" was an invention for telephones? Out of work, she was now living with her husband and child on East 85th Street. After a brief stop at CBS, she landed at DuMont. She recalled,

> I've always believed that when you needed a job you should take the first one that came along. Any job is better than no job. So when F. Wesley McKee, who'd directed me in summer stock, called with an offer to appear for thirty minutes on television I quickly accepted. The pay was $20.
>
> I've worked in show business for sixty years, and I've often been in the eye of the hurricane, not always aware of the hurricane itself. In President Johnson's administration when people predicted the dawn of a new age of consumer power, I scoffed. It was the same with television. I didn't think it was any big thing; I never guessed its future. In fact, I didn't even own a TV set until 1949.[5]

Betty appeared in a new series of weekly fashion shows, *Fashions: Coming and Becoming*, filmed in the Madison studio.

> The show was sponsored by the Sanforizing Institute, promoting pre-shrunk clothing. I was to be 'Nancy Dixon' their corporate spokeslady, much like Betty Crocker. I would introduce three or four models each having two costume changes. Talking about the fashions and working without cue cards, I never shut my yap for a full fifteen minutes.

The size of the studio had a lot to do with the show. DuMont's "stages" were just normal Madison Avenue offices with eight-foot-high ceilings. This meant that the overhead lights were right on top of the performers and the side lights almost as close. Performing a fifteen-minute show in such broiling heat gave Betty an insane headache. She rushed home to bed after every show, exhausted and dehydrated:

> The second week I took a room thermometer onto the set and secreted it on my office desk. In five minutes the temperature was 130 degrees. I had combs in my hair with bits of metal in the clips. I accidentally touched one during the show and burned my hand. From then on whenever I had to be in the studio, but not on camera, I dressed like a fireman entering a burning building.

The show was not as ad libbed as Betty remembered. The advertising agency Young and Rubicam kept a part of a 1945 script in its files. The show, directed by Wes McKee, began with as long a long shot as the cramped DuMont studio allowed "on a fairly plump girl, extremely badly dressed." She walked up to the single camera and recited a pastiche nursery rhyme:

> "Hickory dickory, dock!
> I ran up this frock.
> I pinned it and sewed it,
> Basted and gored it.
> I'm the pin-up girl of my block."

Then Betty, as Nancy Dixon, intercepted her with "And I'm the voice of the turtle, yuck, yuck!" Nancy, still offstage, introduced herself to Miss Pin-up and delicately suggested that "Help is coming. Mother is sending Madame Lyolene out there to help." The strange use of "offstage" technique was necessitated by the one-camera limitation of the DuMont studio.

This mini-melodrama finished with the still offstage Nancy reading Madame Lyolene's Parisian couture credits. The intro finished as follows:

GIRL: Ou-la-la!

NANCY (offstage): Oui-oui!

GIRL: OK. Bring her on. Anything for Sanforized.

While Betty Furness was busy frying her hair combs, production meetings filled the adjoining DuMont offices. One of the executives kept arguing the need for a quality children's show. Bob Emery, who had been narrating *Movies for Small Fry*, a series of not-so-classic kiddie films, proposed a new live kiddie show with humans in costume. In an entertaining way, he proposed to educate youngsters in manners, self-discipline, health, and nutrition. Emery had created Buffalo Bob Smith's *Triple B Ranch* on radio and clearly knew what entertained kids. For DuMont, he stuck his neck out and suggested that he himself emcee his new idea, *The Small Fry Club*.

The show turned out to be an instant hit: New York citizens and celebrities fought tooth and nail to get spectator tickets for their kids. All this happened nine months before the first *Howdy Doody* and it showed how quickly TV could now create its own stars. By 1947, *The Small Fry Club* was on Monday through Friday at 7:00 P.M. Emery's hit show ran on DuMont for five years.

Of course no live show for children was without peril. *The Small Fry Club* had a large set, and DuMont's state-of-the-art overhead lights were not powerful enough. So the technicians added "cherry lights," smaller lights mounted on a panel that could be wheeled around next to the camera. On one show, a floor electrician was so concentrated on listening to his technical director over his headphones that he didn't notice the camera operator dolly backing up. The operator's bottom was rammed by the blazing hot cherry lights, producing history's first televised broadcast of the word "fuck." It was accompanied by a bloodcurdling scream, which Big Brother Bob quickly covered with an extra big laugh.[6]

A Woman to Remember (1947) was the second soap opera presented on DuMont. In the debut episode, John Raby had a terrifying experience unlike anything that had ever happened to him during his many years of radio soaps. In front of live cameras for the first time, an actress who appeared with Raby in the opening scene panicked and tried to run off the set. Raby grabbed her, pushed her into the nearest chair and recited her lines, interspersed with his own. The plot of this scene made no sense, but the flabbergasted director moved on to the next act. Raby rushed offstage and promptly threw up. *A Woman to Remember* lasted less than three months.

DuMont's greatest year was perhaps 1947, and it was also his worst. He had founded a true network, and several of his programs, particularly *Wrestling from the Jamaica Arena*, were winning their time slots. Waiting in the wings were three more DuMont future successes: *Ted Mack's Amateur Hour*, *Bishop Sheen*, and *Jackie Gleason*. Then, almost without warning, CBS television returned to full programming, gobbling up stations, five as its own and the rest as affiliates. DuMont, because of his ten-year-old contract with Paramount, was stymied. He couldn't add any more stations in the key Eastern markets he needed, and his lack of available cash made the new independent stations reluctant to affiliate with him. Sarnoff and Paley on the other hand had cash reserves that insured their domination of television for more than a decade.

15

BRINGING GOOD THINGS TO LIGHT

GE broadcasts through the war: 1942–1945

D r. Ernst Alexanderson's WGY in Schenectady had been General Electric's pioneer effort in mechanical television. It was abandoned in 1934. Its chief distinction was being the first television station in 1927, and constant innovation helped it outlast all the mechanical television systems in New York, including CBS.

General Electric's ambitions in television were dimmed but not diminished, and in 1940, WRGB, an all-electronic station, rose from the ashes of WGY. Once the FCC had approved the use of commercials, WRGB, nestled quietly away from the competition in Schenectady, felt free to make mistakes without embarrassment. And they made some big ones.

GE, then best known as a light bulb company, did not advertise on its own station. It settled for tie-ins and educational plugs. *Death on Flight Forty* was a good example of the seamless connection between the commercial and the program. It began with GE's announcer giving a two-minute history of light bulbs, culminating with the modern GE Mazda bulb. Just as he finished his pitch, a uniformed stewardess came into the commercial to remind him that their plane was about to take off. The camera followed them both into the airplane mock-up and the drama began. The teleplay, by the agency ad writer from Batton, Barton, Durstin and Osborn (BBDO) Harry Larewn, took place entirely aboard a transport plane in flight and featured an undercover Nazi spy and a U.S. Army private. After the opening commercial everything went smoothly. The airplane mock-up was elevated three feet off the ground. One camera could easily pan while another took close-ups. Then the director cut to stock footage of a plane in flight. The climax of the hour drama came when the hero had to force the murderous Nazi out the open airplane door to fall to a certain and well-deserved death. Everything was rehearsed, even the moment when the stagehand was to turn on a high-powered fan as the plane door opened, with appropriate sound effects of wind and engine noise to disguise it. The recorded music was cued to make the most of this spectacular ending. All Schenectady—or at least all of its eighty-four television sets—were probably tuned in as the Nazi moved toward the door, his left hand on the door handle. Then the door stuck. The actor frantically ad libbed. The stagehand dropped the fan. The director in the booth put both cameras on the reactions of the now genuinely horrified passengers, while the stage manager leaped like Douglas Fairbanks onto the wing of the plane and yanked the door out of its socket. After a few more reaction shots, the set was "clear" for the rest of the play to go on.

WRGB did not have a pool of professional actors like the New York City stations. For larger productions, particularly drama, they had to rely on local amateurs. WRGB was conveniently close to Russell Sage College, an all-girls school, and many of these young ladies assembled in November for a performance of Sheridan's restoration classic *The Rivals*. Most of the roles in that play belong to mature men, but on November 18, 1942, all the parts were played by these college girls, who insisted on innumerable costume changes, stretching the playing time by over an hour.

With its production of *Uncle Tom's Cabin*, that station showed what better preparation could achieve. Robert B. Stone was in charge, insisting on five weeks of rehearsal and a complete camera blocking followed by a full dress rehearsal. Everything went perfectly on air until Uncle Tom's death scene. Carefully rehearsed week after week, a commercial recording of *The Battle Hymn of the Republic* was to be played while Uncle Tom's body was slowly lowered into the open grave. Then on the air a careless sound man played the wrong side of the disc and *Yankee Doodle* almost rose Uncle Tom from the dead.

Public service took many forms in Schenectady. *The Art of Glass Blowing* was followed with *The History of Tea*. *How to Prepare Banana Dishes* and even a *Bridge Demonstration* were considered public service. Unfortunately for that one, neither the director nor the cameramen knew anything about bridge. The cards were hard to read on TV, and the cameras were always on the wrong cards.

WRGB considered it a public service again when they sponsored what they claimed was the first bathing-beauty contest. The "Electronics Queen" was selected, along with two runners-up, on a specially raised stage set with a throne against draped curtains. Background music accentuated the ascension of the Electronics Queen to her throne. She tripped on the last step and fell to the studio floor.

Vaudeville circuits were still alive in 1943, and WRGB showed almost every vaudevillian on the planet. Milton Sabotsky, "the Demon Mathematician," was a natural. Don Tranger was a one-man band with a twist; he could wrap his mouth around four trumpets and a clarinet, playing them all at the same time while he quick-stepped a Russian dance. A lady magician, Sandra Landi, did fancy dance routines. At each finish, she landed on the studio floor, her legs in a split, as she pulled a rabbit out of her top hat. Hal Vine, another magician, was so popular on the vaudeville circuit that he earned his own show on WRGB. The debut show was poorly planned, however, and his biggest trick—using his tongue to thread twelve razor blades together—was a bomb with the home viewers. Vine assumed everybody knew his famous act, so he refused to describe in advance what he planned to do, and the blades, thread, and background were all the same color. The audience had no idea what he was doing.

From 1931 to 1947, vaudeville, theatrical, and some radio acts, were an essential part of every TV variety show. NBC and CBS could pull out the stops and hire well-known acts such as Hildegarde or Ed Wynn. Programs of the smaller stations like WRGB often looked like amateur shows. A typical night included a ventriloquist, a girl's trio, and a small boy playing a miniature organ. *Novelty Night* (1943) had a weight lifter, a roller skater, and a human pretzel. To seem less of a hodgepodge, there were theme nights. *Scottish Night* had performers in kilts speaking in brogue. *Polish Night* was followed by *Russian Night*, but *Ebony Escapades*, *Sepia Tones*, the *WRGB Minstrels*, and the *Mauve Revue* are best left undescribed. It is sufficient to say that an inner-studio memo suggested: "The camera is particularly favorable to Negro performers, catching and projecting their natural rhythm." The biggest variety show mistake was the *Phone In Variety Show* (1943), in which viewers were encouraged to call in with requests for encores. The phone almost never rang and there was a lot of dead air. Clearly the public was not ready for two-way TV.

At WRGB disasters were a way of life. *The Hawaiian Variety Show*'s debut broadcast had a set with palm trees and a sandy beach. While Schenectady was close to General Electric's headquarters, it was at least a half-hour away from the nearest talent booking agent in Albany. When producer Douglas McMullen telephoned for Hawaiian acts, the Albany agent offered a man who played the ukelele and a hula dancer-singer. The act that arrived just in time for air was a Brooklyn-born radio disc jockey and his girlfriend, a blonde who sang *Aloha* in a grass skirt with a southern accent.

When the war ended, General Electric and WRGB were uncertain about what to do with their little pioneer station that had been broadcasting for so many hours on such a provincial basis. With Madison Avenue moving in a big way to sponsor shows on NBC, CBS, and DuMont, there was no room, even in Schenectady, for bumbling vaudevillians and collegiate thespians.

The writing was on the wall. WRGB was scrambling unsuc- cessfully with limited funds to compete with the big guys. Like today's public-access television, WRGB offered some of its time to anyone who would pay the minimal air costs and provide a program. They even advertised: "The station is particularly interested in any new, unusual, unorthodox programs with real viewer interest."

The Russell Sage College players were back on the air, this time producing and directing themselves. If *The Rivals* (1942) had been sickly under WRGB staff supervision, the Russell Sage 1946 production of *The Shadow Passes* was death itself. Soon after that, WRGB provided the Mount Pleasant High School airtime, and the results were even worse.

By September 1946, *Billboard* was declaring WRGB extinct. Using some local radio actors and without a script, WRGB had attempted "The Ad Lib Theatre of the Air." The trade magazine's review declared, "This show proves once and for all that radio actors are not for television." The parent company, General Electric pulled the plug on WRGB and decided to sit out the earliest years of TV's "Golden Age." It did not seriously invest in television again until 1953's *General Electric Theatre*, with host Ronald Reagan.

16

SARNOFF
OUT
IN FRONT

1946–1947

General David Sarnoff, "the father of television," also claimed to be "the father of television programming." Throughout 1946, the general "sold" the idea of network television to radio manufacturers in Chicago and to broadcasters in Atlantic City. He promised that the success of the NBC television network would exceed that of his radio network. He vowed to spend millions to do it, with no prospect of an immediate return on his money.

NBC's postwar television operation was modest by any of today's standards. A young Bob Keeshan, long before he gained fame as Captain Kangaroo, went to Rockefeller Center to interview for a job as page boy. This is what he saw:

> The whole NBC building was devoted to radio. There was a little office up on the sixth floor where the television department

comprised a staff of no more than four or five. Nobody believed that television would ever become a major force for a long time to come—their most optimistic projection was 1956 or so.

Sarnoff was TV's great salesman to the press and public. His enthusiasm was principally to promote RCA's television set sales and to fight CBS's negative publicity about the incompatibility of color and black-and-white systems. CBS had released a comprehensive study of the potential of television. The study said that TV faced "seven lean years" with huge expenses and small income. Sarnoff responded, "No one can retard TV's advance, any more than carriage makers could stop the automobile, the cable the wireless, or silent pictures the talkies."

It may be unfair to criticize Sarnoff for failing to plunge unlimited funds into programming. The standard procedure in radio and early television was for advertising agencies to package complete shows for their clients (the advertisers) and for a radio or TV station to broadcast these shows, collecting money for the airtime. In early TV, unpackaged advertisers were never willing to cough up more than a few hundred dollars for a show.

As long as CBS was producing TV shows at WCBW in Manhattan, Sarnoff would have to keep spending more than his rival, even if it meant losing more and more money. In 1945, CBS was ahead of NBC in news and drama. That year CBS staff producer Worthington Miner introduced the first "nonexperimental" postwar piece of television theater, *The Favor*. The show was written by Lawrence M. Klee and starred three well-known radio actors: Joseph Julian, Leslie Woods, and Edith Tachna. Though it was a tawdry tear-jerker with a sledge-hammer message for U.S. Savings Bonds, it was an important training ground for talents like Miner.

General Sarnoff, who frequently called his opponents "parasites," was willing to compete on every level with CBS. But he hoped to find someone to share the costs. In 1946, the general received a "gift" from Standard Brands. The company, makers of Chase and Sanborn coffee and Tender Leaf tea, committed $200,000 for a variety show, enough money to keep it on the air ten months. The show was called *Hour*

Glass, and everything about it was expensive and more complicated than anything previously done on TV. When it first aired on June 14, 1946, NBC assumed that almost every one of the twenty thousand set owners in New York City would be watching.

The opening show began at 8:00 P.M., immediately after the Esso newsreel. Broadway star Paul Douglas appeared in a seriocomic sketch, followed by comedian Joe Besser, a monologue by Doodles Weaver, and a ballroom dancing sequence. The show's biggest novelties were its two commercials. The first was two-and-a-half minutes long, and the second was a full five minutes. Standard Brands was paying big money, and it wanted its money's worth.

In the weeks that followed, hostess Evelyn Eaton was replaced by Helen Parrish, a pretty young actress who became America's first celebrity created mainly by appearing on television. *Hour Glass* also introduced TV's first regular chorus line as well as the concept of the expensive "guest" star. Bert Lahr, Dennis Day, Jerry Colonna, Peggy Lee, and Edgar Bergen and Charlie McCarthy all made their television debuts on *Hour Glass*. Thanks to the faith which Standard Brands showed in the potential of TV, NBC's *Hour Glass* paved the way for Berle, Sullivan, Gleason and the rest.[1]

NBC also made a heavy commitment to sports at this time, since sponsorship for sports TV was easy to come by. Throughout 1945, and much of 1946, most people saw television in public places—bars, hotel public rooms, and appliance salesrooms. These viewers favored sports programs. Bar owners needed the largest television screens possible and were the first to shell out thousands of dollars for twelve-inch pictures. Of course every TV paid for itself almost immediately with increased patronage. Sarnoff boasted of the first "network" telecast with the Lewis-Conn fight in 1946, but the "network" which broadcast this fight was hardly an NBC network, since its farthest flung station (in Washington, D.C.) was owned by DuMont. DuMont did its own true network telecast in 1946, a debut production from its new Wanamaker's Studio at the John Wanamaker department store.

Most of NBC's "sustaining" programming was low-cost, simple stuff, barely a step up from the test pattern. Amazingly, NBC convinced

Gulf Oil to pay sixty dollars a week for their first show, which could only be seen in New York and Schenectady. *You Are an Artist* was a weekly fifteen-minute instructional program. John Gnagy, the star of the show, wore a plaid shirt and sported a beret to go with his goatee. For fifteen minutes he would draw a simple picture and explain his technique. *You Are an Artist* lasted four years, though its time slot changed every few months, ending up in daytime. Almost every Gnagy program had a regular segment featuring a painting lent by the Museum of Modern Art, accompanied onstage by two armed guards.

A few months later, Borden's milk products agreed to sponsor a cooking show with the twenty-six-year-old James Beard. Beard had performed cooking demonstrations alongside John Gnagy's art talks in an earlier show, *Radio City Matinee*. Both were spun off as separate fifteen-minute shows—with Gnagy's popularity surpassing Beard's.

NBC stuck Bristol-Meyers with an eighty-dollar price tag to sponsor *Geographically Speaking*, a fifteen-minute show starring Mrs. Carreth Wells, who showed and narrated her own travel films. The show ended in less than three months when Mrs. Wells ran out of film.

Television Screen Magazine began in November 1946. It was a low-budget attempt as a "magazine" format news operation. Opening programs featured the Police Athletic League Chorus and Walter Law, an NBC employee who showed his stamp collection on the air.

NBC's best show of this early period was probably the *Kraft Television Theatre*. It was created by Kraft's advertising agency in a direct deal with Kraft's top executives. The first play on May 2, 1947, was called *Double Door* and starred John Baragrey. No script or kinescope survives from that landmark production. Only the budget. But at $3,000—a huge budget for its day—it set a pattern for Kraft that would last two decades: large casts, elaborate sets and first-rate scripts and directors. During the lifetime of the *Kraft Television Theatre*, it commissioned 18,845 scripts. The concerns of Moss Hart's Dramatists Guild ("Where was it ever decreed that man had to have so much entertainment?") were well founded.

General Sarnoff hoped that in these early years it would be possible to present on TV the jewel of NBC Radio's cultural crown, namely

Arturo Toscanini and his NBC Symphony. To seduce the maestro, Sarnoff installed in Toscanini's Manhattan apartment one of the first RCA television receivers, a TRK660. Toscanini was, however, not interested in any of NBC's "cultural" shows. After a dinner party in his home, he would usher his guests into the library for telecasts of wrestling on DuMont's WABD, offering his own commentary on the unique talents of George Weber, the wrestling showman known as Gorgeous George.[2]

For a long time NBC held a firm corporate policy against nepotism—which Sarnoff began while his own children were young. It was no skin off his own nose since his relatives were all in obscure towns in Russia and his in-laws lived in France. But after the war, his oldest son, Robert, was twenty-six and had no job prospects. Nick Kersta, the numbers man in NBC's statistic department, was discussing with Frank Boal the problems of selling TV time to Madison Avenue without a strong liaison. Kersta recalls:

'I think I've solved the problem. I hired Bobby.'

'You hired the General's son? The old man is adamant about nepotism, you know.'[3]

A short while later Kersta's phone rang. It was a summons to see Sarnoff.

Nick remembers an elevator ride to the fifty-second floor that seemed to take forever. Then the long walk into the enormous art deco office. He found Sarnoff sitting behind his desk, theatrically spotlighted by the overhead track lights.

'Do you understand our policy on nepotism?'

'Yes, sir.'

'And you went ahead and hired Robert?'[4]

Nick began to carefully explain that his decision was already paying off. Advertising agency doors that had been previously closed were now opening. In less than a week, Robert had earned the company fifty times his salary. As Nick spoke, Sarnoff rose from behind his office desk, coming forward and sitting in an informal friendly way on the edge of it.

"I explained everything I could," recalls Kersta. "It was a simple but important business decision. The general agreed and that was that."

In the 1920s, Sarnoff had been approached by Vladimir K. Zworykin, a fellow Russian émigré, with a proposal to develop electronic television for RCA. Philo Farnsworth had been experimenting with electronic television for several years, but if Sarnoff agreed to authorize a small budget for research and development, Zworykin promised to perfect the iconoscope and kinescope for RCA. Sarnoff, who'd been cautious about Armstrong's superheterodyne in 1923, was instantly in favor of the television idea and approved it without consulting his RCA partners. Vladimir went to work in the Camden, New Jersey, laboratory with four assistants. He told his friend Sarnoff that it would take one hundred thousand dollars to perfect electronic television. Sarnoff ended up spending fifty million dollars. Thanks to the RCA publicity machine, Zworykin would get most of the attention as "the inventor of television" —though years later at the age of eighty-four, when he was asked what part he liked the most about television, Zworykin answered, "the off switch."

Did Sarnoff build a monopoly? For decades NBC continued to run a network, own stations, and produce shows in which it had a financial interest. By tying up Edwin Armstrong in litigation, Sarnoff had delayed the entrance of competitors into the FM and UHF frequencies. By outmaneuvering William Paley, Sarnoff had set the broadcast and manufacturing standards for color television. With excessive RCA influence, he had pushed the FCC to the sidelines. A few years later he was the first to break up the programming controls long held by advertisers and their agencies by selling commercial time instead of program time. Over the years TV programming became obsessed with reaching the widest possible audience. Ratings finally dictated program content. Executives said that they were just giving the people what the people wanted.

When prizes were given out for programming, Toscanini, or the NBC opera, Sarnoff quickly took credit. When attacked for the low-brow slant of the rest of NBC programming, the general would blame sponsors, ratings, and the general public. For those occasions, he would only present NBC in its network role: "We're in the same position as a plumber laying a pipe. We're not responsible for what goes through the pipe."

17

THE
MINER
LEAGUES

1939–1947

The television pioneers were all kids. Philo Farnsworth was in his teens, Dennis James, and Harry Coyle were in their twenties. The exception to this rule was Worthington Miner, who began working for CBS television in New York in 1939. By the standards of early TV he was "one of the old guys." He was thirty-nine.

The son of a prosperous clothing importer and a graduate of Kent, Yale, and Cambridge, Miner was a charter member of New York's Theatre Guild, which transformed the face of Broadway in the 1920s with fourteen hits out of fifteen tries. Miner was busy in the 1920s and 1930s as an actor, producer, and director; he did thirty productions between 1929 and 1939.

In the spring of 1938, he had dinner with Joe Wharton, a BBC executive who was an adviser to Philo Farnsworth. Wharton filled Miner with dreams of the infant industry but suggested that American television, while feeling the heat of British competition, wasn't yet ready to begin. Miner recalled the bug Wharton placed in his ear:

> "So what do I do?" asked Miner.
>
> "Give it a year."
>
> "OK. But will you let me know?"
>
> "You have my word."[1]

Miner's next Theatre Guild production *Jeremiah*, starring Kent Smith, was an unmitigated disaster. This catastrophe forced Miner to "take stock of my whole career." *Jeremiah* was his final impetus to get out of theater to see what he could do in TV. One Friday evening in late August 1939, there was a phone call from his friend from London, Joe Wharton. Joe came right to the point:

> "Tony, you remember a year ago you asked me to let you know when I thought television was going to take off? Well, I think it's here."

A week later Worthington cleared out of his Theatre Guild office and began working for author-producer Gilbert Seldes at the CBS Grand Central Studios, 15 Vanderbilt Avenue. He was flushed with excitement; in on "The Creation," or so he thought, because William Paley's big return to TV may have only been window dressing. Years later one of Paley's main lieutenants, Frank Stanton, confirmed this had been a possibility:

> Bill did not want television. He thought it would hurt radio. It was also a question of money. He didn't see any profit in TV at all. Bill was concerned about the bottom line, that we couldn't afford television, that it was too costly.[2]

Whatever his real strategy was, William Paley directed Gilbert Seldes, Worthington Miner, and a new creative team to focus their efforts on July 1, 1941, the date the FCC had approved for commercial licensing. CBS planned to schedule fifteen hours a week. As Miner recalled it:

> Our first show was a fairy story read by a mother to her child (the child was Anne Francis) while a cartoonist illustrated the narration. Then there were discussions, interviews, and quiz shows. Everyone who was anyone in theater, the arts, business, and government, was sooner or later to be seen on one of our CBS quiz shows. Conservatively speaking, I did everything. I produced and directed the entire fifteen hours for the first ten weeks that CBS was on the air.

Miner had grand schemes in his mind for TV musical productions, until Seldes reminded him of the ongoing dispute between all broadcasting owners and ASCAP. Since November 1940, the entire ASCAP catalogue had been banned for broadcast. It constituted almost every song written since 1888, so Miner and his associates and competitors were limited to songs by Stephen Foster or none at all. They chose none at all.

On December 7, 1941, Miner was fixing a drain pipe in his Connecticut home when news reached him of the Japanese attack on Pearl Harbor. He put down his plumbing materials, drove to New York, and even though it was supposed to be a dark weekend for broadcasting, the station went on the air at 8:00 P.M. that night with a news announcer on the audio and a video picture of an American flag slowly waving under the influence of the studio prop fan.

A few weeks later Gilbert Seldes, who was Miner's creative boss, heard a rumor that German planes were about to attack Manhattan. He directed Miner to set up a camera at one of the few windows at 15 Vanderbilt. "Then it occurred to us," recalled Miner, "that a transmitter is like a beacon. The German bombers could use our camera as a beacon to zero in and raid New York." Seldes cancelled his plan twenty minutes before air.

Paley closed down his CBS experiment in television within months. Nevertheless he took the remarkable step of offering Miner a continuation of his job, at $250 a week, even though CBS had no TV shows to produce. Either Paley had foresight or Miner had talent. Worthington kept busy with an assignment to write a "History of Television (1932–1942)." Proof it was a "make-work project" was that CBS quickly announced it had *lost* its only copy of the 450-page manuscript.

Those quiet years of nonproduction gave Worthington Miner opportunities to speculate and postulate his theories of television, unique approaches on everything from scripts to camera work. Many of these theories he actually put into practice when CBS went back on the air. In *Billy the Kid* (1945), which Worthington directed, he photographed that western like a ballet, keeping the camera as low as possible and showing full figures at all times. Miner had been scornful of the flat "line up look" that NBC dramas had featured throughout the 1930s. Of course a lot of that flat look was the result of the iconoscope TV lens, which required tons of light and had no depth of field.

Miner's aesthetics were helped immensely by the invention of the image orthicon tube. In 1944, industry representatives were invited one afternoon to a demonstration at Madison Square Garden. Miner remembered the event.

> First we were shown a man on horseback using the customary iconoscope camera. Then, at an appointed moment, all lights in the Garden were extinguished. We were left in total darkness. Suddenly the man on horseback struck a match and lit a candle, after which he started moving slowly around the arena. And all of this we had been able to see by the light of that single candle.*

The image orthicon tube was not quickly ready for production, but when directors finally were able to take advantage of the lower lighting bills, they often *added* to the banks of studio lights for the new visual

---

*This was done with an experimental camera with an image orthicon tube. NBC held the patent and CBS and DuMont were deprived of its benefits for years.

effects that had become possible. For the rest of the decade, performers still complained about the heat from the lights.

Before CBS lost the manuscript of Miner's "History of Television (1932–1942)," it was read in 1945 by CBS senior executive Paul Kesten, who suffered from chronic insomnia and had probably hoped the lengthy treatise would put him to sleep. On the contrary, it aroused his curiosity about Miner. Kesten asked to meet him.

The meeting went famously for Miner, who was so flattered by Kesten that he thought sure he was on the fast track for a major executive position in the corporation. Furthermore, Miner was completely unaware of Paley's strategy to slow down television. Only a few of Paley's closest aides knew about his true foot-dragging intentions. One was William Fineshriber, who years later described his marching orders "to slow down the progress of television" and subtly "to indicate the virtues which were uniquely those of radio."[3]

Miner was Paley's point man to fight for a freeze on industry development until compatible standards could be agreed on. Everybody else, including the public, wanted TV to get off the ground. As "Paul Kesten's boy," Miner's job was to keep TV grounded, but he became more and more unhappy in his "role as spoiler."

In 1946, at an industry-wide meeting in Schenectady, Miner spoke out of hand, without clearing what he had to say with his CBS bosses. He proposed, hypothetically, that all of television be moved from VHF to UHF, which had enough band widths for black-and-white, RCA color, and any other future developments." Before Miner could catch a breath, DuMont moved in like a Sherman tank, treated the hypothetical question as a formal motion, and got the group to vote on it and pass it.

Miner, in horror, abstained. It was too late. He had broken, for the moment, the logjam he was supposed to keep in place. His mentor, Kesten, was furious and never spoke to his protege again.

> Television was taken out of my hands by noon the following day. A short time later I was moved from my courtly offices at 15 Vanderbilt to a dust closet on the top floor of a building opposite

CBS. I was given the meaningless title of Director of Program De-velopment, but others were hired to take over all my prior activities, and I was forgotten.

By the end of 1947, Paley realized that television could not be stopped. He would make up for all his foot-dragging in 1948. It would be easy because he had hired smart, talented people like Miner and Seldes—even though he hadn't really wanted them to succeed. It was an irony not lost on his rival, Sarnoff, who noted, "Bill likes to surround himself with geniuses. I don't want anyone around as smart as I am."

18

TELEVISION AROUND THE WORLD

From New York to Argentina to Russia to Iceland, television spread quickly all over the globe. The Danish government in 1938, for reasons undisclosed, even planned a transmitter in Reykjavik, Iceland.

In the earlier 1930s, working parallel to the BBC, the Baird Company had cooperated in the development of mechanical TV in France and Sweden. Holland and Russia used electronic equipment, provided by Phillips and RCA. In Germany, Farnsworth's system beat out Baird's mechanical system in 1935, and on April 27 of that year the Associated Press filed this dispatch from Berlin:

> The Nazi government hopes to use television widely to cement further its grip on Germany, a grip whose strength is the huge propaganda machinery, with the powerful German broadcasting system as one of its main instruments.[1]

A few years later, the Berlin correspondent for the BBC publication *World-Radio* reported watching a telecast of Hitler from Nuremberg via cable:

> It is only when watching Nuremberg street scenes, in a Berlin television room, that one realizes the real achievement of the cable. Here I was just off a busy Berlin thoroughfare, watching Herr Hitler drive up to his hotel, walk out on to the balcony and salute the people in Nuremberg, over three hundred miles away. Unfortunately for the Post Office, the engineers did not seem in tune with their apparatus. Their "sidechat," which was partly audible, made us realize that, and results were poor. They will undoubtedly improve as the relays continue; but the people in my television room were greatly disappointed when the picture deteriorated just at the moment the Fuhrer appeared on the balcony.

Germany's propaganda machine insisted that German television was technically superior to British TV but that was not the case. The Nazis just did a better job covering their mistakes. In all their publicity stills, even in their newsreels about television, the TV picture itself was "matted in," faked with a still photo or movie film inserts, to give the appearance of the "highest quality" German picture. The most popular "insert face" belonged to Ursula Patzschke, an announcer who began on German TV in 1935, when there were only 180 scanning lines in the broadcast picture. Ursula's career was all off camera until the day she brought her dog to the studio and got him to bark on camera. From that day on, Ursula and her dog were "regulars" on German TV.

Soviet television also exaggerated its technology for press releases, but haphazard reality always seemed to leak out. For instance, Soviet technicians suffered the same infrared problems as early BBC experiments. When Olga Vysotskaya, presenting her own TV gymnastics class in 1938, appeared to be nude, Russian viewers flooded the broadcasters with letters.

The Soviet government radio-TV system often had problems with letters from confused radio listeners. To promote TV, the radio station ran an ad: "Attention: Radio Viewers." Thousands took the ad literally and stared at their radio receivers trying to see a picture. Letters from them always began plaintively, "Tell us where we should look?"

The beginnings of French television were very much imported from England. A French industrialist named Ernest Chamond was attending a British soccer match in 1928, when he just happened to drop into John Baird's lab and witnessed a TV demonstration. Returning to Paris, Chamond ordered the director of his own laboratory, Rene Barthelemy, to develop a similar system. Some sources claim that Barthelemy was already at work developing his own mechanical television system, but would never have had the means to pursue his research were it not for Chamond's fortuitous visit to England.

Barthelemy, the son of a tailor, had originally wanted to make his career in agriculture but had gotten sidetracked into broadcasting. A quiet and unassuming man, he was destined to play a pivotal role in the development of television in France, but he would never accept the title "Father of French Television," which the public-relations apparatus of the government repeatedly tried to bestow upon him. Perhaps his reluctance was simple honesty. The development of television in France and in every other country was a collaborative process.

Barthelemy assiduously began work in a well-furnished laboratory in Montrouge and by April 1931, he was able to transmit a 30-line signal to a school of engineering in Paris. The following year, the French government mandated the National Laboratory of Radio Electricity to study the available television technologies from all over the world in order to propose the best system for France. Following its "exhaustive" study, the laboratory conveniently concluded that the French system—Barthelemy's system—was the best. Of course it wasn't. No mechanical system could compare with the electronic systems of Farnsworth and Zworykin. In comparison with mechanical systems, the French system was several years behind the Baird's English system and Jenkins' American system, and by 1932 the French were just beginning to "marry" sound and picture. One of Barthelemy's French rivals was Henri de France, whose system was probably better but lacked any political clout behind it.

In 1933 French television went on the air with regular programming. Variety shows were the order of the day. Mademoiselle Tony Rico demonstrated her ability to perform on a half-dozen musical instruments, while an actress named Lucienne Peguy sang "Le Temps des Cerises" and contemplated a handful of cherries. The cherries appeared white on TV screens, so no viewer knew what she was gazing so melodramatically at.

Since there were virtually no commercially manufactured television receivers in France at that time, only a few Parisians watched on their mostly homemade contraptions. Reception difficulties were compounded by the fact that there was no standard form of electricity. Some outlets delivered alternating current, others provided direct current. To make things even worse, the signals themselves were changing rapidly, from 30 lines to 60 lines to 180 lines.

In 1934, the French government decided to create an "Inter-Ministerial Television Commission." This commission decided that television should be commercialized in France, and with that aim it adopted a plan to cooperate with industry to produce television receivers as well as shows. On April 17, 1935, the minister of the Postal, Telephone, and Telegraphic Services (PTT) decreed into existence a full-fledged production studio and a 500-watt broadcasting facility for mechanical television. Television images were to be transmitted by cable, with radio simulcasts for sound. (The French still hadn't caught up to Philo Farnsworth's electronic television.) A large crowd attended the televised opening ceremonies. For that event, actress Beatrice Bretty had the honor of recounting a recent trip to Italy. Her lips and eyebrows were painted black for contrast, she ad libbed travel anecdotes for a full twenty minutes.

Following this event, French television screens were regularly visited by circus performers, cabaret singers, dancers, and actors. The heat, of course, was no less stifling than in other television studios of the day. Despite the discomfort, well-known talents such as Harry Baur, Gaby Morlay, Serge Lifar, and Elvire Popesco all put in appearances. Even the most famous writer, actor, and director of his time, Sacha Guitry, showed up and read a poem on the air.

Each artist was presented by a woman by the name of Suzanne Bridoux, the first *speakerine*. To this day, the tradition of the *speakerine*— a pretty woman who announces television shows—continues to be cherished in France.

That the icons of French culture would lend their names to the fledgling enterprise that was television begs the question: What was so different about early television in France than its counterpart in America, which assuredly was not taken seriously at all? It seems that the most salient difference in the two approaches is that television in France (and in virtually every country except the United States) was given the stamp of approval by the government—the same government whose Ministry of Culture had a very important role to play in deciding which plays would be performed on French stages and which movies should be funded. The participation of the arbiters of culture lent television an aura of prestige from the beginning. There were few institutions in America that could do the same, and those institutions (such as the major museums and universities) had no interest in the vaudeville known as television. Only today, for that matter, is the serious study of television programming becoming acceptable (and still only marginally so) in American universities.

Despite the symbolic power of the French Postal, Telegraphic, and Telephone service, French television was not immediately able to realize its grand ambitions in 1938. They had finally converted to electronic television, but when they asked for a 500-watt transmitter, they got only a 10-watt station.

As befitted a properly reared child of bureaucracy, the early French television shows were utterly devoid of spontaneity. The *speakerine* read from a piece of paper—always, it appeared, the same piece of paper—which she held in her hand. The terms she used to describe the talent acts were almost always the same. She always exited in the same direction. Then came the opening shot of the performer. If the bottom of the television frame cut him or her off at the waist, the audience could expect a song or a reading. If his or her feet were visible, there would be a dance.

Private television broadcasting in France was briefly approved in 1937. Unlike the government television, private TV was designed to make a profit. Among the shows planned by the would-be producers were aerial views of Paris, cartoon footage, and film clips starring the singer/dancer Mistinguett. Unfortunately for those involved, a new French government came into power, and permission for private TV broadcasting was quickly retracted.

In 1937, Paris had its largest World's Fair ever—dedicated to the arts and technical developments of modern life. It stretched from the Champ de Mars to the Place des Invalides and even spilled across the Seine onto the Right Bank. The new Palais de Chaillot at Trocadéro, with gardens, fountains, and a wide-open terrace, provided a stunning view of the fairgrounds. Other buildings erected for the occasion included the Musée del'Art Modern and a German pavillion designed by Albert Speer. The Italian pavillion vaunted the advantages of tourism and life in Mussolini's Italy. There were special constructions just to display modern building and manufacturing materials, aluminum, plastic, and even linoleum. The Eiffel Tower, adorned with six miles of fluorescent tubes, was the launching-pad for a fireworks display over the river every night.

In the pavillion of French Radio, a 455-line, all-electronic television was on display. Bear in mind that this was 1937, two years before the World's Fair in New York, where RCA was to promote their own invention to the world. On French television, fair visitors watched magic shows, plays, gymnastics, and a wide variety of other performances, as well as live interviews from a roaming cameraman who dragged an enormous cable along the banks of the Seine. The size of the audience at this attraction greatly exceeded the most optimistic expectations of its designers.

Following the Paris World's Fair, all television equipment was moved to the station where Barthelemy and Cahen had been working, making it the most powerful television broadcasting facility in the world, pumping 455 lines of resolution over a fifteen-kilometer area (about ten square miles). The government and the press now saw in television a new opportunity to disseminate France's proudest propaganda: *la culture*. Not, of course, the culture of the people, but that of aristocrats (just by coincidence, the same culture that was taught in the elite schools attended by the ministers of France's successive governments). Piano recitals were performed by bewigged musicians on eighteenth-century sets. A mime artist interpreted a poem by Alfred de Musset while the verse was read offscreen. A series entitled "When Paintings Come Alive" featured re-enactments of scenes from famous paintings by Antoine Watteau and Jean-François Millet.

Projection television in theaters was almost ten years old in England and America when the French triumphantly unveiled theirs in a prestigious Champs-Elysees theater on March 1939, to an audience composed exclusively of dignitaries from the Académie Française and other official institutions of French culture. Its screen was smaller than its English and American rivals. It measured less than two meters (about six feet) in width and 1.5 meters (about four-and-a-half feet) in height. On this screen, the assembled notables solemnly watched a star of the Paris Opera Ballet Company perform a new dance by André Messager and the actor Louis Jouvet bring to life a scene by the popular playwright Jules Romain.

In the years that followed, the French government kept changing in the most dramatic ways: from a succession of middle-of-the-road and socialistic governments to Nazi occupation (beginning in 1940), and then to Charles DeGaulle's near-autocracy following France's liberation. Each ruling party had a different opinion about television and its uses.

These cataclysmic political changes profoundly affected the infancy of French television, and the French even sabotaged their own television transmitter (located in the Eiffel Tower) in 1940 so that their occupiers would not be able to use it to spread propaganda. It took the Nazis three years to get the transmitter up and running again. When they left in 1944, the Nazis again sabotaged the transmitter; but the officer in charge of this demolition left his job half completed.

During the occupation—from 1940 until 1944—Rene Barthelemy virtually hid in a basement, where he pursued the experiments that would lead to a thousand-line TV screen. The Nazis, who were broadcasting exclusively on closed-circuit during the first years of the occupation, never learned of his research—or simply didn't care about it. They preferred to import their own engineers to Paris, along with extensive electronic equipment, and to appropriate extensive studio space in the heart of the city for their productions. Since French technicians were intensively trained and employed in the new Nazi television studio, the experience turned out to be very beneficial for French television.

It wasn't until 1943 that the Nazis, having repaired the Eiffel Tower antenna, began broadcasting over the air in France. The narrowly defined purpose of their shows, which included clown acts, marionettes, films, and cabaret performances, was to entertain and distract wounded soldiers who lay recuperating in Parisian hospitals. To this effect, they brought five hundred television receivers from Germany and installed them all in hospital rooms.

The Nazis found their greatest French television star not in a French citizen, but in a Swiss man with an English-sounding name, Howard Vernon. Vernon's resume fit the bill perfectly: he was a tap-dancing instructor, and he could speak both German and French with no detectable accent in either. Vernon appeared ubiquitously on the recently named "Paris Television" as an actor, translator, and news reporter. The attitude of the French themselves toward him becomes abundantly clear as soon as one attempts to look him up in any biographical reference work. Even the "Grand Larousse" biographical encyclopedia contains no mention of the biggest French TV star of 1943.

Since soldiers tended to move out of the hospitals rapidly, the same shows were repeated over and over again, at intervals of a week or two. This was fine for the hospital-bound; but the ordinary French citizens who had paid good money for French television sets (about five hundred Parisians in 1944) soon found themselves with nothing they wanted to see.

After the liberation, the French gave the name Radio Diffusion Française (RDF) to their television and radio company, which now had more equipment and space than ever before. The studio that it inherited from the Germans, on Rue Cognacq-Jay, remains to this day one of the most important television studios in France. The first postwar French production, "The Dance of the Feather Dress," was directed by Pierre Gout, whose assistant was the future film director Alain Resnais. Among the earliest TV performers was a young mime artist named Marcel Marceau. Within a year or so, the French began broadcasting from 4:30 P.M. to 5:30 P.M., Monday through Friday. On Tuesdays and Fridays, there was also an evening broadcast—often a performance of a play or an opera such as *The Barber of Seville*. Weather reports were introduced in 1946. The weatherman would stand in front of the camera and actually draw a map of France, together with indications of rain, sun, etc. Full-blown news shows followed shortly thereafter. Those who didn't own television sets could watch on receivers that the government set up in public places.

Since it was still much more difficult to televise shows from remote locations, everything that could be brought into the studio was shot there. For a sports show, four swimmers were lined up on a big wooden board, and went through a waterless demonstration of swimming. Concerned that their intent wasn't getting across, the producers decided to cut to a film clip showing what swimming actually looks like when a body is placed in real water.

The French version of the talk show, *Paris Cocktail* was soon renamed *Tele-Paris*. Five or six guests would discuss whatever came to mind with hosts Jacques Chabannes and Roger Feral. Francois Babault played piano. The show was an instant hit.

Of course, in a country where the government holds a TV monopoly and where there is only one channel, the word "hit" has quite a different meaning than it has in the United States. The French had no Nielson ratings, for the simple reason that they had no use for them. The purpose of television, in the French mind, was only partially to entertain. Far more important, to those making programming and other decisions, was the vital task of preserving and propagating French culture.

The postwar French public were wary about investing in a TV receiver while technical standards were in a worldwide flux. In 1947, the government issued a formal promise that the standards then in effect would remain in effect for ten years. This meant that consumers could purchase 441-line television receivers without having to worry that they would be obsolete the following year. In 1948 a young secretary of information named François Mitterand abruptly decreed a new French broadcasting standard of 819 lines. Because of the promise the government had made to owners of 441-line receivers, it maintained a 441-line transmitter on the Eiffel Tower, right next to the 819-line transmitter, until 1958. Finally on election night of 1956, the 441-line transmitter mysteriously burned. It was never restored.

RIGHT: The flight attendant for the drama *Death on Flight Forty* does a commercial for G.E. light bulbs and then walks straight into the dramatic action. (COURTESY HALL OF HISTORY)

BELOW: A Nazi spy is looking already suspect in the first row. Midway through *Death on Flight Forty* a crucial cabin door can't be opened and the control booth is turned to panic.

(COURTESY HALL OF HISTORY)

Studios were small and cameras had a narrow depth of field. WRGB tried a dance line of eight girls but some were cropped out and the dance line remained at six until after the war. BELOW: Bridge on TV was a disaster. The cards were too small to read and the technical crew knew nothing about the game. It didn't last, even in Schenectady. (COURTESY HALL OF HISTORY)

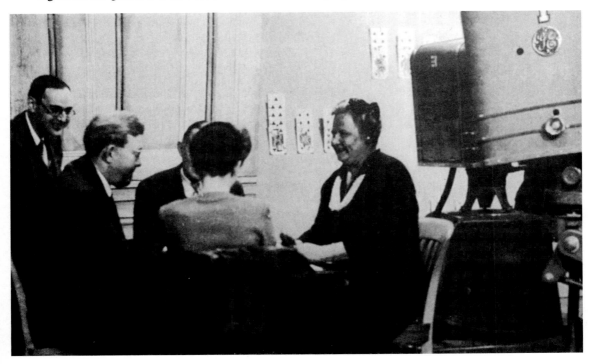

WRGB's dog show debut was nearly ruined when the star animal would only present his back side to the single live TV camera.

General Electric used every opportunity to plug its products. This "War Bonds" public service spot featured the newest G.E. fluorescent desk lamp.

One of the most popular television shows of 1944 was WRGB's broadcast with Andrew Ponzi, world pocket billiards champion. The stage was so small, the fire marshall refused to let the set block the emergency exit.

ABOVE: **W**RGB, General Electric's Schenectady station did its first dramatic rerun in 1928 of *The Queen's Messenger*. Its second was in 1944, *Op-o'-Me-Thumb* which viewers rated higher than televised plays by Anton Chekhov and Noel Coward.

(COURTESY HALL OF HISTORY)

LEFT: **T**wo Schenectady families competed on *Photoquiz* with host Col. Lemuel Q. Stoopnagel. The escalating scores were handwritten on cue cards. Everything was fine until the teams ended in a tie. The host tried to ad-lib a new, unrehearsed question and the whole show ran five minutes overtime. (COURTESY HALL OF HISTORY)

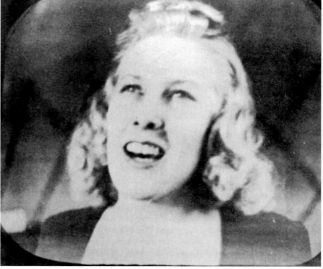

Singer Marie Rogndahl, winner of the 1944 *Hour of Charm* contest on WRGB, is telecast from the General Electric Studios in Schenectady to a relay tower in Manhattan, and then into dozens of set owner's homes.

(COURTESY HALL OF HISTORY)

ABOVE LEFT: **W**ild Wig Charlie was a WRGB commercial character created for Wildroot Cream-Oil. Each commercial was a complete comedy sketch, often running as long as five minutes. RIGHT: Vaudeville was dying but television gave it a brief resuscitation. Putnam and Slate did their "Fleegpoop" routine on WRGB. In this sketch, they portrayed two girls on a skiing trip. BELOW: Sandra Laudni finishes her "rabbit out of a hat" magic routine with a dance ending in the splits.

(COURTESY HALL OF HISTORY)

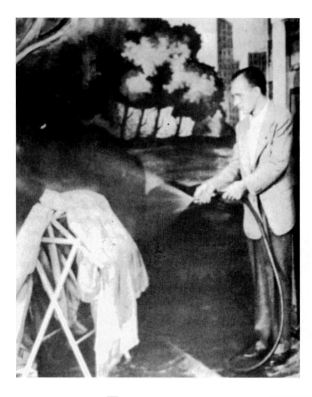

TOP LEFT: **E**arly television demonstrated every form of "how-to" known to mankind. Here, for example, is a show demonstrating "how to wash curtains."

(COURTESY HALL OF HISTORY)

TOP RIGHT: **T**he "first" Mr. Science was a puppet promoting a popular magazine. He gave lots of wartime household hints, including how to make cupcakes without butter.

(COURTESY HALL OF HISTORY)

RIGHT: **H**oe-Down Night was big in Schenectady. One night during the "Kerry Dance" the main performer had a leg spasm, and finished his solo writhing on the studio floor.

(COURTESY HALL OF HISTORY)

TOP RIGHT: On *Faraway Hill*, TV's third soap opera, Flora Campbell abandoned Park Avenue riches to find true happiness with poor farmer, Mel Brandt. The backdrop left something to be desired but at least it didn't burst into flames like the one on *The Boys from Boise*. RIGHT: Two housewives compare their victory gardens in a wartime Vimms commercial. The housewife who took her vitamins has, of course, a more successful garden. BELOW: 1943's *Phone-in Variety Show* was an all-request-for-encores concept whose time had not yet come. Nobody called. No pictures remain for WRGB's unique *Milton Sabotsky: Demon Mathematician.* (COURTESY HALL OF HISTORY)

DuMont's Wanamaker Studio opening with fanfare in 1946. Everything was state-of-the-art except for the heat from the lights. It was still an oven. After an hour of the debut broadcast it was determined that the "strange noise" picked up by the microphones was the "sloshing" from sweat in the technician's shoes. (COURTESY HALL OF HISTORY)

At DuMont, Dennis James created a very successful audience participation show called *O.K. Mother* that starred real life mothers of all ages in a club called "Mothers, Incorporated." BELOW: The audience sat in a cramped Madison Avenue studio which was simply a converted office space with low ceilings. The heat was intense, but not as bad as it was for the performers. (COURTESY DENNIS JAMES)

ABOVE: **P**rizes for *O.K. Mother* were donated by Gertz Department Stores. Top prize was never worth more than a few dollars.

(COURTESY DENNIS JAMES)

LEFT: **A**BC rented DuMont airwaves before they had their own stations. Using Dennis James and Buffalo Bob Smith, they did the first Macy's Thanksgiving Day Parade in 1947.

(COURTESY DENNIS JAMES)

MEMO TO: Mr. A. B. Du Mont

FROM: Will Baltin

For the first week of the experiments, we can flash
the bulletins without sound. On the following week,
if our sound unit is connected, I should like to have
recorded musical accompaniment while the bulletins
are being shown. I can supply recordings from my
home, and I think we can economize for the present by
obtaining a small electric phonograph (on rental)
through which the records might be played into the
microphone. I don't know how good the pick-up would
be, but it would be a temporary set-up and might en-
liven the transmission. ASCAP (musical union) will
give us clearance on the recordings without compen-
sation, I feel certain.

Early news broadcasts stalled for time with typewritten "Bulletins" and musical accompaniments. Notice the request to RENT a small electric phonograph. (COURTESY BROADCAST PIONEERS MUSEUM)

TELEVISION SCOREBOARD TO FOLLOW PLAY-BY-PLAY OF GRIDIRON GAME

Football enthusiasts in the metropolitan area
who cannot travel to the nation's capital on Sunday to see the
championship professional football game between the Chicago Bears
and the Washington Redskins, may follow a play-by-play account of
the contest on the screens of television receivers.

Since no facilities exist at present to televise
the actual game between New York city and Washington, D. C., Du Mont engineers and production men have devised a means of indicating a play-by-
play account of the contest through the use of a mechanically operated
scoreboard.

The board shows the full sweep of the gridiron
with a miniature football moving simultaneously as the plays occur.
Numerals are flashed immediately revealing the number of downs, yards
to gain and other pertinent data.

This press release celebrates the first pro-football broadcast. The operation was so primitive that the sound could only be picked up by listening to it on the radio! (COURTESY BROADCAST PIONEERS MUSEUM)

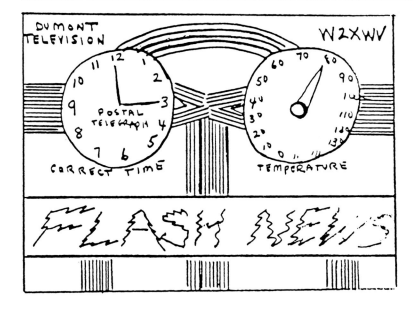

ALLEN B. DU MONT LABORATORIES, INC.

INTER-OFFICE CORRESPONDENCE

S. R. Patremio   DATE 10-9-47

Dr. A. B. DuMont   LOCATION Passaic

Program interruptions covering July, August, September
and October 1st.

    The following is a list of interruptions to regular programs
over WABD:

                    LIST OF INTERRUPTIONS

Date   Time   Loss-Brs:min.   Reason

7-10-47   6:46 to   14 minutes   Breakdown of audio equip-
            7:00 PM   ment in our Washington Studios

7-14-47   6:45 to   15 minutes   Failure of Washington Coax.
            7:00 PM

7-16-47   10:50 to   6 minutes   Video transmitter off due to
            10:56 PM   loss of GL 8002,IPA water-
                                      cooled tube. Lost 1½ rounds
                                      of final bout.

Breakdowns were still a way of life as late as 1947. Notice that a single tube failure prematurely terminated a boxing match broadcast. (COURTESY BROADCAST PIONEERS MUSEUM)

DUMONT TELEVISION   W2XWV

POSTAL TELEGRAPH

CORRECT TIME   TEMPERATURE

FLASH NEWS

Early television's state-of-the-art time and temperature bulletins. . . (COURTESY BROADCAST PIONEERS MUSEUM)

In order to assist us in the development of home television we would
appreciate your frank comments on the program you have just witnessed. These
will be used solely for research purposes. Please give your candid opinions
whether they be complimentary or otherwise.

Name _Ethelbert Furlong_

Address _605 Valley Road Montclair N.J._

Occupation _Landscape Architect_

1. Did the program have entertainment value?   Yes ✓ No ____

2. Was the picture clear enough?   Yes ✓ No ____

3. Do you think the picture was large enough?   Yes ✓ No ____

4. If not how large would you like it? The present screen is
8 inches high by 10 inches wide. My dimensions would be
_____ inches high by_____ inches wide.

5. Would you consider a television set like the one on which
you saw the pictures satisfactory for home use without
further improvement?   Yes ____ ✓ No ____

6. What kind of programs would you enjoy most on television
   No News events
   ✓ Films
   ✓ Sports
   ✓ Educational
   ✓ Plays

7. Have you any comments or suggestions to make on the
television set or the program? _Amazing Advancement.
Enjoyed it very much. Consider screen
size ample. Certain programs may better be
enjoyed by Radio, which requires less concentration_

Thank you

ALLEN B. DU MONT LABORATORIES, INC.
Passaic   New Jersey

DuMont surveys his audience. Note that this landscape architect with enough money to buy a television set has "no" interest in news events. He likes radio because it requires "less concentration."
(COURTESY BROADCAST PIONEERS MUSEUM)

Ralph Edwards had created a big success with radio's *Truth or Consequences* (which had a brief pre-war TV debut). When DuMont was back in full swing in 1944, Dennis James was host of a similar "consequence" quiz show called *Cash and Carry*. BELOW: This "losing" contestant is mounted onto a bucking bronco. On later shows the stunts included a man putting on a woman's girdle.

(COURTESY DENNIS JAMES)

In-studio wrestling began almost simultaneously across the continent. Dick Lane in Los Angeles was first, WRGB in Schenectady was second, but DuMont's Dennis James made it a household word. Telecasting live from the Jamaica Arena, James came with chicken bones to simulate breaking legs. He rubbed balloons to simulate groans, and with his harmonica he accompanied the "zip" of a wrestler flying out of the ring. (COURTESY: TOP, HALL OF HISTORY; BELOW, DENNIS JAMES)

The interaction between wrestler and commentator was often as fake as the sport itself. The fighters would frequently plan to land on the announcer's table at ringside. (COURTESY DENNIS JAMES)

19

THE
DAY
THE
MUSIC DIED

Many reasons are given for establishing 1948 as the official birth year of television. Clearly, a panicked reaction from William Paley to NBC's success with the 1947 baseball World's Series forced CBS on a fast track. Nevertheless, Sarnoff at NBC was determined to stay ahead of his rival. DuMont's three-city network had beaten the other two to the punch, and thanks to a long list of receiver manufacturers, the price of owning a television set in 1948 was within the reach of many middle-class Americans.

But another reason that television did not take off until 1948 is the least reported, and least understood. It was embodied in the stubborn character and dogged perseverance of one man, James C. Petrillo, president of the American Federation of Musicians (AFM). In 1944, his union had prohibited its members from performing live music for *any* television station. This "strike" lasted until 1948, and the date of its conclusion is almost simultaneous with the date given for the official birth of television. Without union musicians, there could never have been a Milton Berle or an Ed Sullivan show, much less a Toscanini.

Labor unions had great influence in the 1940s, so today it is hard to imagine the power which the AFM held over broadcasters. The story of James C. Petrillo is unique even in its time. Here was a union leader who could force singing stars to lip-synch to their old records and who gained enormous support by enrolling into his union a piano-playing president. Harry Truman was a card-carrying member of the AFM.

James Caesar Petrillo was born in Chicago on March 16, 1892. His father was an Italian immigrant who worked for the city as a sewer digger. Jimmy was not considered to be a bright boy. He languished in elementary school for nine years, and never went beyond the fourth grade.

"They bounced me around," remembered Petrillo years later, in one of his few quotations not peppered with vulgarity. "One year I would be in the fourth grade and the next year in the third. They drove me nuts! After nine years I gave it up."[1]

When Jimmy was five, his father bought him a trumpet. He practiced a lot, but never played it well. He was too busy fighting with the other boys in the neighborhood. He once beat up nine boys, one at a time, in two hours of continuous fighting.

This was the background of the man who was to become America's feistiest labor leader. He was always spoiling for a fight. While a teenager, he became active in the politics of the Chicago local of the AFM, and he won enough fights to become president of that local by age twenty-two. In the fifteen years that followed, he fought with everyone from the vice-president of the United States to Benito Mussolini.

Five-feet-six-inches tall and weighing 190 pounds, Petrillo was the prime bull of American labor negotiations. He was the highest-paid labor leader in the country, with a lavish expense account that included full-time body guards.

In the 1940s, when I was a boy addicted to radio, I always wondered about a strange credit that was often heard at the end of broadcasts. Performances were always brought to us "through the courtesy of the American Federation of Musicians, James C. Petrillo, President." Who, I wondered, was this courteous president who was always being thanked. In fact, he wasn't being thanked out of any emotion other than fear. For almost two decades, the man whose middle name was Caesar was a true emperor of his labor union, leaving movie studios, recording companies, and radio networks trembling in his wake.

In 1944, he took on the infant industry of television. No one, least of all James C. Petrillo, knew what to make of the medium. That year, no one could predict when people would start buying sets or when advertisers would start buying time. But Petrillo knew that once both these things happened, program producers might begin trying to save money by replacing live musicians with recorded music. As a young Chicago union leader, Petrillo had seen this happen in the movie industry. When sound films replaced silents, thousands of musicians in major city cinemas were thrown out of work—and this had occurred right at the start of the Depression. Petrillo decided he would nip television in the bud.

He had already won a major concession from the record companies after he had banned all AFM members from making records in 1942. Even a personal appeal from President Roosevelt could not break Petrillo's resolve. In 1944, the record companies capitulated and agreed to give the musicians royalties on every record sold or broadcast on radio, with the monies to be deposited in a union pension fund. It was a milestone in labor relations.

Early television, as we have seen, could broadcast anything— Broadway plays, sporting events, and popular songs—with little or no payment to the artists. Audiences were smaller than those that attended most high school plays. By 1945, with the widespread availability of TV sets in bars, there was a potential national audience of a million people for TV, and that was enough for Petrillo. In February 1945, the AFM international executive board prohibited musicians from playing on any kind of television program. This immediately affected studio productions and mobile pickups. A remaining loophole—filmed television—was soon closed so that no motion picture containing music could ever be televised.

This strike, and particularly the banning of television films, was a great comfort to the Hollywood power elite, who worried even in 1945 about TV displacing movies. Perversely, however, there were unfounded rumors that the whole point of the ban was to help the movie industry take control of television away from the radio industry.

It was a bizarre strike. At first glance it resembles the attempts in the 1970s to block the sale of video recorders to ensure that copyright holders received royalties from the sale of blank tapes. But Petrillo's strike had no stated objective. He didn't want standby musicians, and he didn't want royalties for the pension fund. *He didn't know what he wanted.* He just knew that someday live musicians might be unemployed, sitting at home listening to their old work being played on TV. Petrillo would only say that he wanted a clearer idea of the direction in which television was heading. He pointed out to his union that they had received $23 million from radio. Maybe they could earn even more from television.

James C. Petrillo's American Federation of Musicians did not end their total ban on live television music until March 20, 1948, over two years after it began. The strike solved none of the union's problems, but the ending was long awaited, and NBC and CBS rushed to be the first to bring back live music. As it happened on March 20, Eugene Ormandy conducted the Philadelphia Orchestra on CBS at 5:00 in the afternoon, and NBC's Toscanini came on at 6:30 P.M. CBS beat out NBC by ninety minutes.

Another part of the drama occurred in the middle of 1947. While TV executives were scrambling to find a way to get around the AFM ban, DuMont found *one* small loophole: *amateur* music. Someone remembered that Major Edward Bowes's *The Original Amateur Hour* had been a big hit on radio. It had ended with the Major's death, but his assistant, Ted Mack, still held the rights to the show's name. Working hard to convince Mack to go on television, DuMont cleared its Sunday night variety time slot for the new show, which began in January 1948.

  The Original Amateur Hour was a big hit. So NBC set about stealing the show from DuMont for their own network. CBS began to scramble for a Sunday night variety show to schedule against it the moment the AFM ban could be ended. Sunday night was about to become the battleground of Ed Sullivan, Ted Mack and Jackie Gleason.

20

LADIES' DAY

1944–1947

At the end of 1944, Allen DuMont was having a problem selling his technology to the industry as well as to the public. His own studio equipment was better than RCA's product in almost every respect. It produced much sharper pictures using studio cameras with electronic viewfinders. Moreover, the equipment was simpler to use and lighter in weight. Even the "tea tray" camera dollies were better designed by DuMont. It didn't take a fellow built like a linebacker to operate the stuff. In fact, thought DuMont, even a *girl* could do it.

Five women were recruited by program director Lou Sposa. Three of them, Florence Monroe, Eulalia Turner and Ina Mae Commadelli, would last more than a year. They were all in their early twenties. Florence had just graduated from New York University and Eulalia was fresh out of a finishing school. Sposa told them they would have to begin as simple production assistants, but that DuMont's master plan was to eventually promote them to major technical roles—even operating the cameras. DuMont intended to release photos industry wide showing these dainty gals (none were over 5-foot 5-inches) doing big-time jobs with superior DuMont equipment. Each was offered $25 for a seven-day week, which came to about 35 cents an hour.

All five girls reported to work at DuMont studio at 515 Madison Avenue at the same time on the same day. They were stared at by a sullen group of men wearing the new DuMont uniforms.[1]

"Who are you?" someone asked them.

"We're starting today as production assistants," the girls replied.

The DuMont regulars—to a man—rose up and walked out of the studio.

Lou Sposa raced after them and lied through his teeth.

"These gals are just P.A.s. They're not going to replace any of you."

When peace was made, Florence and the other women were given their uniforms. Since the men had overalls with the DuMont logo on the back, the ladies wore slacks with a jacket top that had the same logo. On the front was a smaller version of the DuMont insignia with each name inscribed. "Florence" was too long for the pocket so Monroe became "Flo"—a nickname she hated but couldn't avoid.

Florence Monroe was only twenty. During her senior year at New York University, majoring in theater, she had her first experience with television. Her father was a friend of DuMont executive Tom Hutchinson, and Florence was sent to him to discuss her ambitions for a career in radio. "Mr. Hutchinson immediately said 'Young lady, you should look into television.' He moved me into the DuMont control room, and I almost went bananas with excitement."

Before summer had even started, Florence became a volunteer prop assistant during her after-school hours. Her first job was working a primitive "special effect." On a cooking show, the host wanted to talk about a cake that was "lighter than air." Florence's job was to make the cake fly up out of the set. "I rigged up a cardboard platter with four black strings against a black background. The maiden flight was about five feet and it got right out of camera range before it crumbled. After the show the P.A.s got to eat the leftovers."

Flo had a head start on the other new production assistants. For one thing, she was prepared for the infernal studio heat. She remembers Betty Furness and the thermometer test vividly. According to Florence, Betty actually put the test thermometer on her head and not on the prop desk. Florence also remembers strict instructions to avoid sudden gulps of water in all that heat. One of the new girls was so hot she disregarded orders and downed a whole glass of water. She promptly passed out. "When I finally got to be a camera operator I was less aware of the ceiling lights. Dollying in for a close-up, those lights got so hot that my hair began to smoke. An alert P.A. quickly smothered by burning hair with a wet scarf."

Florence and her squad of female technicians could always brave the heat better than the actors and models who appeared on camera. On a fashion show, she once had to take off her DuMont uniform and wear the fur coat of a model who had passed out in the heat. But Florence had no interest in being a performer; she loved her role as DuMont's first female camera operator. But when the war ended, men like Harry Coyle and Barry Shear were joining DuMont. They too started as P.A.s and had the same high ambitions as the women. The new men were told they would be given preference—that they quickly would be "moved up to camera." According to Florence,

> Barry was slick. If he could get what he wanted by being tricky, that's the way he'd work it. Once while I was working camera, I had to leave during a meal break to get to my dentist for a tooth extraction. The dentist used gas and when I got back to my job, I wasn't feeling too good. That day's show was accurately titled *Stories in One Camera*, and Barry was pushing the dolly for me. When I saw I was getting dizzy, he only made matters worse by whispering in my ear during the show, 'You look awful. How sick are you? Feel like you want to throw up? Are you sure you don't want to lie down? Maybe I should take over for you?' I may have had a pain in my jaw, but Barry was a real pain in the neck.

Soon after that, Florence heard a rumor that Barry would be moving up to camera replacing her. She got so upset she called the office of the station manager, Sam Cuff. She pointed out that while there were no complaints about how she was doing her job, she was about to be passed over in favor of a man. While she was talking, Cuff's secretary received a call from DuMont, who was accidentally patched through and by chance eavesdropped on Florence's call. After hearing Florence's complaints DuMont exploded: "This Monroe girl who wants to keep working camera. Does she have seniority? If she has seniority, she keeps the job."

Soon after that Bob Emery came in to run the station, and the studio moved from 515 Madison Avenue to Wanamaker Studios. By then "DuMont's girls" were more accepted by the men, but as DuMont expanded, new expansion jobs always went to the men. The ladies were put to "more suitable work." If Betty Furness needed a desk chair for her *Fashions, Coming and Becoming* set, Florence was sent to Bloomingdales to try to borrow one (there was no budget for *purchasing* set dressing). While working in the Wanamaker Studio, Florence was always appropriating things from that department store—even small children to sit on Santa's lap.

Things never got monotonous. The women used to play tricks on announcer Dennis James. Once they put bricks in an empty sack the announcer was supposed to toss over his shoulder. Later they instigated an unscripted studio snowball fight with artificial snowballs. Florence remembers a slew of accidents—on and off camera. Records played at the wrong speed all the time, and Botany clothing was justifiably furious when the Botany Wooly Lamb sounded like a jungle predator.

By her twenty-third birthday, Florence Monroe had had enough of TV. She had learned a great deal, but the career possibilities for a woman were limited. She was ready to do something else. It was 1947, and some of the DuMont performers were leaving as well as the staff people. One day Florence got a bad cold. She called Lou Sposa.

"When are you coming back, Flo?"

"Maybe never."

21

FULL
SPEED
AHEAD

1944–1947

N one of the major competitors in commercial television, NBC, CBS, or DuMont waited for the war to be over to begin broadcasting again. They were all broadcasting many hours a week before the victories in both Europe and Japan. Major advertising agencies by 1944 had established television departments and were busy at every station. The future of television now rested with the FCC. The actions of that government agency regarding the availability of frequencies and the standards for receivers would determine the destiny of American television.

The first important decision was, in reviewing broadcast spectrum allocations, to move Edwin Armstrong's FM radio into another part of the broadcast band. This had two results. It made all existing FM radio sets practically worthless, which was a victory for Sarnoff. Second, it opened new spectrum space for the development of television, followed by an okay for the mass production of receivers using RCA existing designs.

Paley and CBS were furious. They had already developed a scheme for color television that was completely incompatible with RCA's receivers. Their system was silly by today's standards, using a rotating color wheel, but within closed-circuit laboratory control, CBS was capable of giving stunning demonstrations far superior to RCA's early demonstrations of electronic color system, which was at that time incompatible with its own existing receivers. What is unclear, even to this day, is how serious CBS was with its pinwheel color system. Was it their best shot or a devious scheme to stop RCA's momentum in both broadcasting and the production of television sets? The research was headed by Peter Goldmark, CBS's in-house genius and ultimately the inventor of the long-playing record. But if CBS was so intent on developing commercial TV, why in preceding years did it give up so many of its valuable TV channel assignments?

Whatever CBS's real intentions, (since in radio it was secretly planning a raid on NBC's major talents, like Jack Benny, and shows, like *Amos and Andy*), the FCC took the dilemma of competing color systems seriously and declared a "brown light" (a system shut down, like a "brown out") rather than a "green light" for new broadcasting technology, set manufacturers, stations, and systems. This was actually good news for NBC, since by the fall of 1946 it had demonstrated to the FCC an electronic color system compatible with its black and white receivers.

The real casualty of the "brown light"—and a later freeze—was Allen DuMont and his DuMont stations. All along he sought to be a partner in all the scientific discussions. He was developing his own color system with a receiving tube called the trichromoscope. DuMont TV sets could actually pick up both the RCA and CBS color signals. DuMont was candid with the FCC, preferring the RCA systems, but the practical effect of the FCC's policy of no more than five stations to a network was to help RCA and stop DuMont from acquiring enough stations and owning a real network. (The FCC counted Paramount's two stations in Chicago and Los Angeles as two of DuMont's five, because of Paramount's stock ownership in DuMont.) In 1946 there were about a million sets in the country. The cost of a receiver had dropped below $500, and some manufacturers like Earle "Madman" Muntz would, within a year, get the price down to $170. Most were made by RCA with the remaining share split by GE and DuMont. Thirty-four stations were now broadcasting in twenty-one cities. Of these, the ones controlled by NBC would be the big money makers for decades to come. It was certainly no coincidence that in October 1947, when the freeze ended, FCC chairman Charles Denny resigned from the FCC to become RCA's vice-president and general counsel.

Hollywood film studios, which had cooperated with television during its experimental stages, used the freeze as an excuse to put a freeze on their own participation. While no high-level conspiracies can be documented, it is safe to assume that the studio chiefs collectively realized that this "toy" could, after the freeze, become a drain on movie theater attendance. A wait-and-see attitude for TV benefited all the studios.

While Hollywood tried to shrink the potential of TV during the FCC freeze, Madison Avenue made money in television by taking advantage of a loophole in the tax laws. During the war, there was a heavy excess-profit tax on wartime industries to discourage profiteering on war contracts. The advertising industry was exempt, taxed at normal rates. During the war, companies were quick to take advantage of this loophole, but paper shortages actually limited the amount of advertising in newspapers and magazines. By 1945 radio was taking 40 percent of all national and local advertising expenditures, and radio was fully booked. There was no more advertising time available; advertising dollars *had* to go to TV. Once again television achieved an early success by simple default.

This necessary diversion of advertisers to television led to quick schedule expansions among the existing thirty-four stations. By 1946 WNBT had a six-day weekly schedule broadcasting twenty-eight hours a week. Since television sets were expensive, advertisers assumed that TV shows were playing to an affluent, well-educated audience.

This was a prime period for everything from Lincoln automobiles to Kraft's Imperial Cheese.

Programmers assumed that affluent big-city viewers preferred news (which went into full-scale production at both CBS and NBC), sports (baseball, football, and boxing were taking off), and drama. Indeed the first plans were being made for what would ultimately become the "Golden Age of Television." While the programs were more sophisticated than *The Three Garridebs* or *The Streets of New York*, by today's standards they were still charmingly primitive. It was inevitable that the programmers who did the inept stuff in 1946 and 1947, would be the same people credited for the "Golden Age" starting in 1948.

In 1945, for example, Worthington Miner, who later would gain fame as producer of the CBS prestigious dramatic anthology *Studio One*, was a director churning out episodes of *Big Sister*, WCBW's first commercial drama, sponsored by Rinso detergent. Episodes were at oddball times. One week it would be a half-hour long, starting at 8:15 P.M., a month later it started at 8:24 and only lasted twenty-one minutes. Miner's next assignment as a director was for Spry shortening, *Aunt Jenny's Real Life Stories*. This show ranged from nineteen minutes to twenty-three minutes. On December 12, 1946, Paley mercifully pulled the plug on all these shows. CBS wasn't back in the drama business until 1948.

Frederick Coe was a lanky, young, sandy-haired man from Mississippi who had spent his early years in Nashville where he worked as an actor, writer, and director, first at his church and then at the Nashville Community Playhouse. His local draftboard gave him a 4F deferment, and he spent the war years first at Yale Drama school and then directing theater in South Carolina. His success there took him to Broadway where he was just successful enough to be spotted by NBC's Warren Wade and given a contract at WNBT. In 1945, Coe produced his first television drama, *Ring on Her Finger*, a forgettable melodrama about a woman in love with two men at the same time. Comedy was Coe's next shot: *Petticoat Fever*, set in a wireless station in Labrador. A month later he was doing *The Strange Christmas Dinner*. NBC producer Edward

Sobol gave him nothing but raves, but Coe had taken nothing but lumps from the press. Then in mid-1946, his *Homelife of a Buffalo* was greeted by *Billboard* as "perfect proof that Coe has put on his directorial long pants to stay." By the end of 1946, Coe produced one of the first "originals" on NBC since its primitive experiment with Eddie Albert almost ten years earlier.

Just as Worthington Miner worked at CBS under the aegis of Gilbert Seldes, Coe worked at NBC under Owen Davis, Jr. Davis and Seldes got most of the praise and attention until Seldes got tired of television, and Davis was killed in a boating accident. Then industry attention focused on Worthington Miner and Fred Coe.

In the summer of 1947, CBS closed their cavernous studios in Grand Central, and began a few months of "all location" telecasts. The idea was to catch up to NBC with an entirely "new look" freed from the limitations of the studio walls. Television on NBC and DuMont, they claimed, was just "radio with pictures." The CBS experiment began with sports events. Dramas were added from Broadway theaters, cooking shows from Manhattan restaurants, and children's shows from Central Park. Everything was remote, except the Douglas Edwards newscast. Poor Doug was just a "voice-over" narrator for the news, since he no longer had a studio.

Throughout that year Worthington Miner lobbied for CBS to get serious about drama designed for the home tube and variety shows that could be broadcast the moment the Petrillo ban ended. Miner was stockpiling programs in his mind when one night he had to fulfill an obligation to attend a charity dinner—"The Harvest Moon Ball." The emcee was newspaper columnist Ed Sullivan, who did that sort of thing better than anybody else—even if it meant a straight-faced introduction for "Peg Leg" Bates, a one-legged acrobat and tap dancer. Sullivan had been given a chance at his own radio show, but radio didn't seem to take to a man like Ed. Miner had a hunch Sullivan could be perfect for television, and so did Marlo Lewis, a promoter-producer who also "discovered" Sullivan at the same "Harvest Moon Ball." Miner later summed up the quality that defined what he thought television needed: "Sullivan comes off just like the guy next door. The viewer can identify with him. . . . His performance is *good enough*."[1]

Both Miner and Lewis began planning a variety show designed to the unique talents of Sullivan for early 1948, just as soon as the Petrillo ban ended.

Other organizations were expanding studio space and technical capabilities. ABC and WOR knew that they would outgrow the DuMont studio they rented. Cable hookups were uniting more and more East Coast cities, and the kids who had manufactured camera parts right after the war were now in the control booth. Announcers who in 1945 were broadcasting from studio toilets while the scenery got changed were now the stars of their own shows. Producers like Worthington Miner and Fred Coe had shown what could be done with *no* money. In 1948 they would prove what they could do with a *little* money.

Hollywood movies were no closer to getting back on television. In fact, many powerful stars were writing into their contracts specific exclusions of TV exhibition for their movies.

Some thought that filmed shows should be made expressly for TV. During the summer of 1947, a Paramount-based Hollywood producer of short films, Jerry Fairbanks, announced he was setting up a unit to produce TV films for syndication. He filmed seventeen episodes of *Public Prosecutor*, each twenty minutes long. Since the "networks" hadn't figured out a way to broadcast coast to coast, Fairbanks had a hot idea. However, the big guys strong-armed the independent stations. TV, they insisted, should be *live*, not filmed. They were influenced by DuMont's new plan to make quickie films of live TV shows off the kinescope monitor, and fly them west from Chicago. "Quick-Kines," as they were called, were ready for massive use in early 1948. They were grainy and hard to hear, but they were what the public needed. Poor Fairbanks couldn't sell *Public Prosecutor* to anybody. TV syndication was certainly a dynamic idea. But not yet.

In 1947 the first baseball World Series was televised, and credit was shared by both NBC and DuMont. It was far from perfect, but it achieved what was still the main goal of both DuMont and RCA—to get people to buy TV sets. The baseball series was seen in four cities by an estimated 3.9 million people— 3.5 million of them had watched in local bars. Even though there were only 100,000 sets in New York City, newspapers reported that one out of every five people in Manhattan saw Tommy Henrich's R.B.I. single that won the series for the Yankees. The success of the series as an NBC-DuMont co-production scared the pants off CBS's Bill Paley. Television was ready for prime time.

Six manufacturers tried to keep up with the growing demand for receivers. Despite competition among the three biggest, RCA, DuMont, and Philco, the average price was far above three hundred dollars, and out of reach for most 1947 consumers. Someone had to break the price barrier so TV could at last reach its adolescence—and its audience.

That man was Earle "Madman" Muntz, a Los Angeles dealer in cars and appliances who liked to offer at discount anything he could lay his hands on. Since New York had four operating channels in 1947, Muntz decided to check into a suite at New York's Warwick Hotel, where he ordered delivery of three TV sets; an RCA, a DuMont, and a Philco. He turned them all to the same channel and than systematically removed tube after tube, noting when the picture failed on each one. Then he repeated the process with the other New York stations. Finally he substituted RCA parts for DuMont parts one by one, repeating each test. At the end of the day he had what he needed: a suitcase full of TV parts to take back to Los Angeles where he could put together and market the *cheapest possible television set*: "The Muntz TV." As "Madman" Muntz left the Warwick, he gave an extra large tip to the chambermaid who could only stare dumbly at the mess of TV parts and broken cabinets.

Muntz returned to California ready to break the price barrier. His singing jingle all over California radio began, "There's something about a Muntz TV . . ." His set, priced at $170, cost $10 an inch. Muntz was also the first to measure TV width diagonally across the tube, ignoring the very round corners.

Applications for stations at the FCC, which averaged about two a month, climbed to three a week by the end of 1947. Sales of sets were climbing into the hundreds of thousands. Every New York station was ready to broadcast seven days a week from 7:00 P.M. to 11:00 P.M., and some afternoon time slots were being filled as well. Everything that had been tried out in the experimental era was back in new packaging. *Charades* with Mike Stokey was back as *Pantomime Quiz*. Situation comedy, begun in 1937 with Eddie Albert's *Love Nest*, had emerged as *Mary Kay and Johnny*, starring a real-life married couple in their "humorous trials and tribulations." The "talk show," started in Hollywood by Franklin Lacey, now had new versions, first with *Stud's Place* and *Garroway at Large* in Chicago and later with CBS's *At Home*, which featured as its regular singer-guitarist, someone who went on to be a successful TV director and then a movie star: Yul Brynner.

By June 1947, the BBC had completed its first year of postwar television. The original Super woman Jasmine Bligh retired, replaced by just an ordinary mortal, Gillian Webb. Television sets were selling five times as fast as in prewar days, and if it hadn't been for parts shortages, sets would have sold even faster. In November 1947, the BBC televised the marriage of Princess Elizabeth to Lieutenant Phillip Mountbatten and scored its biggest TV audience ever.

As the experimental era of television came to a close, broadcasting people got more serious. Despite all the "disasters" in the early days of television, there was always time for fun. When only a few people were watching TV, studio crews could have a lot of fun. Bored engineers would sometimes alternate the WNBT test pattern with a card reading, "NBC unfair to television engineers."

Part-time actors were not allowed to be prima donnas. If they "acted up" the stagehands could always handle them. An obnoxious English actor made a big deal in an NBC drama about his need to smoke a meerschaum pipe. Before airtime, the prop man replaced the contents of the irritating actor's humidor with a ground-up mixture of rubber bands, horsehair, and tobacco. As Captain William Eddy, the dean of early TV special effects, remembered it: "The actor's lines and action both tapered to a dismal end to the surprise of all . . . except the prop man."[2]

Eddy's favorite bit of horseplay was on a mystery show in which the hero was scripted to reach into a wall safe, pretending to pull out the valuable jewels demanded by the villain. Of course the script called for him instead to pull out a pistol surprising the scoundrel. Since the "wall safe" had been built into a studio flat, there was no depth to it. The actor naturally expected to be handed the pistol by the prop man, hiding on the other side of the flat. According to Eddy,

> The actor backed across the set and, as rehearsed, opened the vault and stuck in his hand, but instead of receiving a pistol as he expected, he found that the prop man handed him a peeled banana. The look that crossed the actor's face in response to this bit of horseplay would have alone done credit to any actor. Necessarily, the gun was finally delivered and the play went on, but only after several more technicians backstage had seen the fun and insisted on shaking hands through the vault door with the already shaking hand.[3]

As the dawn of the golden age began to rise, technicians were blissfully unaware that TV would have to be treated seriously. During the summer of 1947 in New York, a station's crew was setting up for an afternoon remote from a swimming pool for men only. Everything was in place on a very hot day, so the crew broke for a swim and then began horsing around. In Manhattan an unknown engineer threw the wrong switch, and for several minutes the airwaves were full of naked men climbing in and out of the swimming pool—even doing mock "strip" routines for the cameras.

Back in the 1930s, when everything was unpaid and obviously experimental, big name stars were happy to get on the tube. From Kate Smith and Tom Mix to Ed Wynn and Helen Hayes. Edgar Bergen made a brief volunteer appearance at the height of his popularity in 1946, as did Jimmy Durante. In 1947, with real commercial TV almost a reality, there was a sudden chill in the relations between TV and its guest stars. DuMont had to present a "fifteen-minute talk show" with unknown Jack Eigan in a nightclub setting, and the only way that stars Frank Sinatra and Fred Allen would agree to be guests on the show was by telephone hookup. In 1948, TV would have to create its own stars.

By 1947, the noble experiment of Allen DuMont—putting women in important television jobs—was in eclipse. Two of the five women had quit, and Florence Monroe was thinking of leaving as well, so DuMont put her to work in audience research. It was more than a year since DuMont's Washington station, WTIG, had used a map full of push-pins to determine its viewers. DuMont needed to know more about his audience, so he lent his new black Cadillac to the twenty-two-year-old Monroe, instructing her to drive around northern New Jersey and interview any person living in a house with a TV antenna. Monroe remembered,

> I made a wrong turn and found myself at the edge of an enormous marsh. To my surprise I saw a house almost in the middle of this swamp and on top of that house was a brand new TV antenna. I drove down the muddy road to see a middle-aged negro woman sitting on the porch. I asked her about the antenna and she cheerfully answered 'Oh, yes. I have a TV. Please come in.' Sure enough, inside this sparsely furnished shack was DuMont's biggest floor model—a humongous set. The woman said she wasn't married and said she had to work very hard to support her three children. Then she pointed to the television set 'And this is a wonderful way for them to learn about the world.'[4]

There was one more cloud over the TV industry in 1947, indeed over the entire entertainment industry. The start of the Cold War had produced an anti-communist paranoia that led to a Hollywood witch-hunt by the House UnAmerican Activities Committee. Some of those Washington hearings were televised on coaxial cable between the Capitol and New York, and brought wide exposure for first-term California Congressman Richard Nixon. While most of the film community was in a panic, television producers and performers viewed the witchhunt from a calm distance. None of them had been called to testify, largely because the investigators were sure that television in 1947 couldn't possibly be worthy of Communist infiltration.*

*In less than two years the witchhunt would engulf TV as well.

Meanwhile in Chicago, at WBKB, Dave Garroway was assigned to narrate a series of old silent movies. Garroway read the subtitles and then poked fun and ridicule at the old-fashioned quality of these movies that were made thirty years earlier. One Chicago critic wondered if one day, "Won't we be doing the same thing to 1947 television?"

22

A CLOSING CHAPTER: THE CURTAIN RISES (ALMOST)

As every history of television programming begins in 1948, it is fitting that this book should close with a story from the last week of 1947—the week that featured the debut of *Howdy Doody* . . . almost.

It's a story that sums up earliest television, full of ambition and struggle, still waiting for public acceptance, still waiting for a series that would last more than a few weeks.

None of the people connected with *Howdy Doody* thought they were making television history. Not Bob Keeshan, who had been recruited from the NBC page staff to wear a clown suit. Not Frank Paris, the master marionette maker who was determined not to be rushed into manufacturing "just an old puppet" for NBC's new kiddie show. And certainly not a former Buffalo disc jockey, Bob Smith, who a week before Christmas was asked if he could throw together a children's show to premiere in seven days.

The show was called *Puppet Playhouse*, and it went into the program logs for five o'clock, Saturday, December 27. The day before, a rehearsal was scheduled for the WNBC technicians. The run-through consisted of a check on the film chain of the old silent movie to be run. Then Smith charted out music with organist Edward Kean and effects with the sound man. Then a lot of time was spent making up funny names for characters on the show. Since Smith was from Buffalo, he became "Buffalo Bob," Vic Campbell became "Buffalo Vic." Eventually there would be half a dozen characters named "Buffalo."

The rehearsal went as smoothly as could be expected, given that the scripted star of the show, the puppet Howdy Doody, had not yet been delivered. Actually "scripted" is the wrong word since Smith and two others would rely on studio assistant Bob Keeshan to write down ideas for bits on cue cards. Only Howdy had a formal script since his lines had to be prerecorded, Smith having no skills as a ventriloquist.

The cast went home Thursday evening with a plan to squeeze in one more rehearsal the next afternoon. Then Murphy's Law took over: whatever could go wrong, did go wrong.

Friday afternoon it started to snow . . . and snow . . . and snow. A record twenty-five-inch snowfall blanketed the Northeast and crippled New York City. By Saturday morning, Manhattan theaters—Broadway and movie houses alike—decided to cancel all shows. The twenty thousand people who owned TV sets could stay in the snowbound comfort of their homes and watch a new NBC children's show, misadvertised in the *New York Times* as "Puppet Theater."

Bob Keeshan was in Forest Hills, Queens, looking out his window. He had been eagerly looking forward to his TV debut, carrying props and passing out prizes. "They told me they couldn't pay anything but I'd get to be on TV," said Keeshan. "I agreed, but with twenty-five inches of snow, I had no way to get to the studio."

Worse was the news that Frank Paris would not be able to deliver the puppet, Howdy Doody. Paris had made Howdy's face ugly—really ugly—with big jug ears and a hideous grin. He was fashioned after the already established bumpkin voice. Smith would later describe the design "as feeble minded as a puppet can look without drooling."

Paris refused to be rushed. While he snipped at his block of wood, he snapped at those who wanted him to meet the air date. When Buffalo Bob finally got the news that Howdy Doody was to be a "no show," he thought there was no possible worse news. That's when producer Roger Muir quietly spread the rumor that NBC was considering this week's show a "test"—that the backup star for the next week was ventriloquist Paul Winchell and the following week it would be the jolly voice of Kraft cheese, Ed Herlihy. This was no paranoid fear. NBC had already printed a brochure for advertisers in which Herlihy was scheduled to alternate with Smith.

Just before five o'clock, Eddie Kean, the writer of the show, frantically whispered an idea to Bob Smith while he waited for the stage manager's cue to begin the broadcast. He then went over to one of the two cameramen and added something to the shot list taped to a bulky RCA camera. In the control room the sound man, Jack Petry, was told to put away the prerecorded tape of Howdy's voice.

Bob Smith was not anticipating a long career in video. The eight kids who were seated in folding chairs in a section then called the "Fun House" had never seen a TV broadcast, and several had never seen a TV set.

Suddenly the red "ON THE AIR" light flashed, and Smith picked up his ukelele to sing words that would soon become an American institution:

> It's Howdy Doody time.
> It's Howdy Doody time.
> Bob Smith and Howdy too,
> Say Howdy do you do.
>
> Let's give a rousing cheer
> 'Cause Howdy Doody's here.
> It's time to start show
> So, Kids, let's go![1]

The next fifty-eight minutes contained the longest buildup ever seen on a television hour in which the subject of the buildup never appeared.

Those eight on-camera kids could barely wait for Howdy's debut. It's not completely clear what they were expecting to see. Many had been listening since 1945 to a Saturday morning radio show called *Triple B Ranch*. "Triple B" stood for "Big Brother Bob"—and that was Bob Smith himself, who wore a cowboy suit even though he was broadcasting on radio with listeners who couldn't see him. For that show, Big Brother Bob was encouraged to "create" another star for the show—to "do another voice."

The voice he selected he called his "Western voice," that of a country bumpkin character named Elmer who greeted the kids in a drawl not unlike Edgar Bergen's Mortimer Snerd: "Well, uh, howdy doody." Kids under the age of nine screamed with laughter at Elmer's voice and the toilet humor associated with the word "doody."

When kids in the audience of the radio studio asked Big Brother Bob to produce "Howdy Doody," he tried to explain that this was a voice that he did for "Elmer." There was no "Howdy Doody." But the younger kids weren't buying this explanation.

Then a light bulb went on in Bob Smith's head. Since children were referring to him not as "Elmer" but as "Howdy," he changed Elmer's name to Howdy Doody and pitched the idea of a TV show to NBC-TV executives. It took almost two years.

One of the NBC executives, Martin Stone takes some credit for the creation of *Howdy Doody*. He had taken his six-year-old daughter Judy to visit Smith's radio show. She shrieked with laughter, joining the pandemonium of all the other kids in the studio audience as they heard: "Hyuh Hyuh Hyuh. Well, Hooowwwdy Dooooody boys and girls." Thanks to Judy, it was inevitable that Howdy would get his own TV show.

Once the *Howdy Doody* show became the first big success of the 1948 television year, Judy, of course, got no mention. First an announcer from Buffalo, Vic Campbell, took credit for suggesting the Howdy voice. Then NBC executive Warren Wade said that he'd met producer Roger Muir in the army and that they both discovered "Howdy" on the *Triple B Ranch*. Success has many fathers . . .

The unvarnished truth is that Buffalo Bob Smith "invented" Howdy Doody as surely as he invented himself. From when he was eleven, he self-promoted his way upward in radio beginning with Buffalo's *Boy's Club of the Air*, through his work with a singing group on *Simon Supper Club*, which led to a great spot on *The Kate Smith Show* in New York. The new singing group including Foster Brooks (later the incurable drunk on the *Dean Martin* TV show), called itself "The Four Cheers," and performed on *The Cheer Up Gang*. All this led to a morning Buffalo radio show, and in turn to a morning New York show, with a bonus of a Saturday morning's kid's show, which would lead inevitably to *Puppet Playhouse* on December 27, 1947.

On that historic day, Judy Stone and seven other young fans some-how got through the snowstorm to Rockefeller Center. As the show progressed, these "pioneers" were getting restless. Where was Howdy Doody? Instead, the opening act was the performing dogs of the Guadschmidt Brothers, French poodles that were trained to knock down their trainers at regular intervals. In his biography, Buffalo Bob gives full credit to the Guadschmidt poodles' "nonstop hilarity" but makes no mention of a sketch artist named Nino or Prince Mandez the Magician.

At 5:52 there were only a few minutes left, and still no Howdy Doody. Eddie Kean, the show's writer, feared a kiddie mutiny. Bob Smith knew he had to deal with it. Head on.

"Well, kids, have we got a surprise for you! As an extra special treat tonight, I brought my friend Howdy Doody along."

Cheers from the kids.

"You know, Howdy does the 'Triple B Ranch' show with me here in New York, and a lot of you kids have asked to see what he looks like."

"Yheyyy!" followed by a small chant: "We want Howdy Doody, we want Howdy Doody." Bob silenced the crowd as Camera Two slowly pushed in for a closer shot.

"Well, kids, I asked Howdy to come on the show today, but he says he's too shy to come out of his drawer in my desk here and say 'Hello.'"

Then Bob leaned over and shouted to the desk, "Hey, Howdy boy, are you still in there?"

Camera Two showed a tight shot of the drawer, and while Smith was off-camera and out of the kids' view, he did his Elmer voice, covering his mouth with a hand.

"Yuhhho. Gorsh, Mr. Smith, Ah'm in here, but Ah'm too darned bashful to come out! Kyuk ho ho ho ho."

"Come on, Howdy boy!" said Smith in his own voice. "The kids want to see you!"

Of course, Howdy never came out. How could he? He was still in Frank Paris's workshop. But amazingly, the kids believed Buffalo Bob's alibi. Maybe the stunt worked because kids had been brought up on radio, practiced in using their imaginations. Maybe it was because TV was so new that no one knew what to expect, so that anything that happened was acceptable. Sure enough, the next day *Variety* raved, and thanks to the storm-stranded viewers, the ratings were huge.

There was some kind of magic about that first program and the promise of more to come. Maybe the snowstorm had something to do with it. It stranded these TV pioneers inside their TV studio, where they had to create special television magic: a puppet show without a puppet.

EPILOGUE: "WHO'S ON FIRST?"

An Afterword

Several years ago Walter Matthau shared the dias at an awards banquet with Laurence Olivier. When the conversation turned to television, Matthau found the occasion to drop the fact that he had appeared as Iago in the "*first televised Shakespeare*" in 1948. "No, dear boy" interrupted Lord Olivier, "*I* was in the first televised Shakespeare, *As You Like It* for the BBC, August 26, 1936."

So who was indeed first? This book has described a lot of firsts. The first TV set. The first TV broadcast. The first country with television. The first city. The first commercial. The first drama. The list goes on and on. And so would footnotes if this were a doctoral thesis, because every fact about the prehistory of television is debatable. For example, by television do we mean a moving image on a screen, simultaneously performed somewhere else, or do we mean the kind of picture tube we've known from the dawn of regular television history (1948). This book described the early attempts of the mechanical system which failed, and then awarded the blue ribbon to Philo Farnsworth's dissector tube. But the real reason for this choice was simple: Farnsworth's story was the most interesting.

Today 98 percent of all American households have at least one TV set. But the age of television is about to be overthrown by the age of computer. The analog system of TV will give way to digital, but the change will not come easily. Back in 1966, ads for American-made Zenith TVs proudly boasted that they had "no plastic printed circuit boards. . . . Every connection is carefully handwired."

The TV set of tomorrow will dictate the TV programming of tomorrow. Each set will become something like a personal computer, creating, storing, and transmitting signals all on its own. It will have its own instant replays. A multi-camera sporting event could be received with all of its camera images intact and unedited.

The fighting for channel allocations, which we saw in the mid-1940s, has already given way to hundreds of channels. TV, as we know it now—and saw it in 1945 —will still have its old menu of game shows, cop shows, talk shows, etc. But eventually they will give way to interactive, individualized programming.

If Moss Hart's fellow writers in the 1940s were left wondering why mankind had to have "so much entertainment," imagine what they would make of the programming possibilities in the years ahead.

A

THE
PLEASE
STAND
BY
LIST OF FIRSTS

1923: Vladimir Zworykin plans an early iconoscope tube test on the dirigible *Akron*. Before the test can be carried out the *Akron* crashes.

1926: The second all-electronic TV image is broadcast by Philo Farnsworth: a dollar sign.

1927: The first American government leader to appear on TV, Herbert Hoover, is followed by an Irish vaudevillian, A. Dolan, in black face.

1928: Baird performs his second major TV experiment, in which a television image is passed through a human eye that was removed in surgery thirty minutes earlier. Baird himself describes it as "gruesome and a waste of time."

1928: TV's first dance team: "Jacqueline does athletic dances with her clever partner, Master Fremont."

1929: Television debuts: Claudette Colbert, Walter Huston, Babe Ruth, Jimmy Durante, Al Jolson, Milton Berle.

1930: The first commercial. Boston's W1XAV is fined by the Federal Radio Commission for a spot promoting the fur industry.

1931: Grayce Jones and Frank DuVall become the first couple legally married on live television.

1931: The first tap dancer on TV to simultaneously dance and play the violin—Jack Fisher. The picture is on W2XAB—the sound on W2XE radio.

1931: CBS does the first *Million Dollar Television Broadcast*. Natalie Towers goes *Waltzing Through the Air* wearing rare gems from Cartier's vaults, valued at a million dollars.

1931: TV debuts George Jessel, Mae Murray, Sophie Tucker, Ted Healy.

1936: Charles Laughton and Paul Robeson stage a remote broadcast from a Dutch airplane for the BBC, which calls it a "first." It's actually a "second." NBC's "first" in 1939 is a late "third."

1936: The BBC's Leslie Mitchell is the first announcer to be televised without his trousers.

1937: George Bernard Shaw becomes the first man to be televised by the BBC without any makeup at all. Two months later Dolores Ray is the first woman.

1937: The first "Sherlock Holmes" production *The Three Gerridebs*. The *New York Times* calls it, "no serious challenge to the contemporary stage or screen."

1937: John Cameron Swayze does the first regular newscast, in Kansas City, where the studio lights were so hot he paints his eyebrows to protect them from burning.

1938: TV's first rave review for Gertrude Lawrence who performs twenty-two minutes of a Broadway play, *Susan and God*.

1938: Joan Collier on the BBC is the first performer to collapse unconscious while on the air. She falls over backwards in the middle of her song.

1938: Russian TV cameras, blind to shades of red, make gymnast Olga Vysotskaya appear nude.

1938: The longest chord ever sustained by a TV orchestra occurs when Margot Fonteyn races fifty yards between two BBC studios during a live ballet.

1939: The first baseball game on TV. Announcer Bill Stern forgets his toupee and almost misses the broadcast.

1939: The first solo whistlers—The Novel Brothers—debut on a program that includes "Ray Post and his Lie Detector."

1940: Video signals from New York jam video signals from Philadelphia. Some are convinced this is proof that the earth is flat.

1940: The first quiz show - WRGB's *Spelling Bee*. Film slides reveal the correct spelling to the home audience.

1941: WGRB recreates the Japanese attack on Pearl Harbor, but the marionette strings directing the miniature planes get hopelessly tangled.

1942: "The Dancing O'Haras," two sisters and a brother, perform the first TV dance routine with their feet chained together. But no one tells the cameraman, and the entire routine is confusingly photographed in a tight waist shot.

1943: The first TV beauty contest, "The Electronics Queen," is a feature on the *All-Polish Show* from WRGB in Schenectady.

1943: TV's first magician, Hal Vine, fails to convince home audiences that he is actually using his tongue to thread together a dozen razor blades.

1946: The BBC presents wrestling on TV; then quietly drops it with an announcement that it is "too undignified for television."

1946: Frank Dane, the unmanageable star of soap opera *Hawkins Falls* is written out of the show—the first TV actor to be killed over a contract dispute.

1946: Chef James Beard's TV show *I Love to Eat* is the first to use indelible ink to bring out the mold in Roquefort cheese.

1946: The first "happy talk" newsanchors appear in Chicago—Cubberly and Campbell.

1947: The FCC cancels a hearing for applicants for licenses for San Francisco TV channels. With six channels available, only six applications are received; all get their stations without having to argue their cases.

1947: Bob Hope inaugurates commercial TV in Los Angeles but flubs the station's call letters.

1947: The Trade Company of Albany Park, New Jersey, introduces a new coin-operated TV receiver, which it intends to distribute to homes for free.

1957: *I've Got a Secret* panelists cannot guess that Philo Farnsworth invented television.

B

A FEW
SELECTED
EPILOGUES

Eddie Albert scored on Broadway in *Brother Rat* and in movies like *Roman Holiday*, among many. His 1960s TV series *Green Acres* is destined to be rerun forever.

Red Barber, who retired to Florida, broadcast sports news for NPR until his recent death at the age of eighty-three.

Tony Bundsmann (Anthony Mann) went to Hollywood and directed thirty-nine feature films. He died in 1967 of a heart attack while directing *A Dandy in Aspic*. He did only one more piece for TV, an episode of *It's a Big Country*, which was never released.

Fred Coe produced the *Philco Television Playhouse* and was executive producer on *Mr. Peepers*. Then he directed *The Miracle Worker* on Broadway and *A Thousand Clowns* on film. He died in 1979.

Harry Coyle is retired on his farm in Lawrence, Kansas. He likes to pose for still photos in the tall cornfields.

Hugh Downs is a fixture on ABC television, appearing weekly on the *20-20* news magazine.

Allen DuMont's fourth network went dark in the early 1950s, not with a whimper but with a bang. It was the only network to telecast the complete Senate hearings between the U.S. Army and Joseph McCarthy.

Betty Furness became a widely recognized female spokesperson on TV in the 1950s, most famous for her struggle with a Westinghouse refrigerator door that refused to open as scripted. In the 1960s she became a political leader of the consumer movement, later returning to television as a consumer commentator. In 1991, the *Today* show retired her involuntarily at the age of seventy-six. When she died in 1994, the *New York Times* characteristically listed the date of her TV debut as 1948.

Jon Gnagy continued his art instruction program on CBS into the early '50's only to run afoul of the Committee on Art Education which decreed that "television programs of the Jon Gnagy type are distructive to the creative and material growth of children."

Dennis James went on to co-star with the Old Gold dancing cigarette pack, and then appeared on almost every major game show and a few minor ones like *Haggis Bagis*. He currently appears on telethons and celebrity golf shows. Dennis still has a great tan.

David P. Lewis, writer-producer of *Faraway Hill*, returned to advertising saying, "I've never been a fan of soap operas." He died in 1992.

Norman Lloyd is perhaps best known as the Nazi spy who clings to the Statue of Liberty in Hitchcock's *Saboteur* or as the headmaster who fires Robin Williams in *Dead Poet's Society*. Like many of the artists interviewed for this book, he dipped his toe in TV waters in the 1930s but didn't return to it for over ten years, making his mark as the producer-director of many of *Alfred Hitchcock Presents* shows. In the 1980s, he starred in *St. Elsewhere*.

Florence Monroe stayed in television after all. Not with DuMont but with the CBS station in New York City, where she produced educational shows, primarily for schools. For her long service in this field, she was awarded an Emmy.

Paul Nipkow died on August 24, 1940. The inventor of the Nipkow disc that made early TV possible, he didn't have enough money to renew his patents and ended up taking a job as a railway signal engineer.

William S. Paley died in 1990. After reading the manuscript for the ghostwritten autobiography of his entire life, he paid the writer more than $100,000 to have it killed.[1]

Bob Paris, Howdy Doody's puppet designer, continued to be a thorn in NBC's side. Later in his first broadcast year, Howdy's head was completely bandaged and kids were told it was for an election contest. In actual fact, the show was about to unveil a totally new face by a totally new puppet designer - one who allowed Smith and NBC to stop paying royalties.

Edmundo Ros continued to be a top BBC personality. London's *Coconut Grove* on Regent Street was renamed the "Edmundo Ros Club." In 1952, on a children's program, he sang a song about a parrot he'd lost and invited children to let him know just what they thought this parrot might look like, with a prize for the best answer. The BBC was unprepared and shocked by the results. Expecting kids' artwork, British post offices were inundated with parrots: live ones, dead ones, and stuffed ones.

David Sarnoff fulfilled his dreams of empire. A year before Sarnoff's death, at a star studded salute, Frank Sinatra (who had refused to sing on NBC television in 1937 for five dollars) sang for free. Special lyrics to "The Lady is a Tramp," written for Sarnoff, ended "That's Why the General Is a Champ."

Dinah Shore. By 1948 the two kids who had been invited by NBC to sing on television for five dollars, Dinah and Frank Sinatra were the most popular vocalists in America. Her *Dinah Shore TV Show* was a Sunday night staple on NBC for another decade. She died in 1994. Her biography lists the *Ed Wynn Show* in 1948 as "her first time on TV."

Ed Wynn's nerves about live television never went away. His problems on Rod Serling's *Requiem for a Heavyweight* led to an auto-biographical *The Man in the Funny Suit*.

Buffalo Bob Smith lives in Florida and still makes public appearances for the legions of *Howdy Doody* fans.

John Cameron Swayze went on to such popularity that a tie manufacturer turned out "Swayze" ties and Milton-Bradley marketed an educational board game called "Swayze."

Burr Tillstrom died in 1985 at the age of sixty-eight. Never for a single day of his performing life did he ever consider merchandising his puppet creations for toys, dolls, or theme parks.

C
LADIES
BE
SEATED

The complete script of the February 25, 1945 ABC broadcast over General Electric's Schenectady station WRGB.

VIDEO		AUDIO
#1 LS [longshot] of audience standing and singing.	FADE IN #1	MUSICAL SIGNATURE SUNG BY AUDIENCE— "You Are My Sunshine"[1]
TITLE 1.	LAP DISS Over #1	

The Blue Network of the American Broadcasting Company [2]

---

1. The American Federation of Musicians was on strike over the rate schedule for live music. *Ladies Be Seated* had no band, so the audience of standing ladies sang to old records.

2. The show was local, not network, and the American Braodcasting Company had only one "network" —radio. It was no longer "blue."

VIDEO	AUDIO

TITLE 2. LAP DISS
Over #1

presents Johnny Olsen in

TITLE 3. LAP DISS

"LADIES BE SEATED"

#2 TIGHT SHOT TAKE #2
of audience.

PAN audience as they sing.

#3 MCU announcer TAKE #3 **ANNOUNCER**
(as they finish chorus) Ladies, be seated!

#1 LS of audience TAKE #1 AUDIENCE (sitting)
as they sit.

#3 MCU announcer TAKE #3 **ANNOUNCER**
Welcome to the first television presentation of the popular radio show, heard every weekday over the Blue Network at two-thirty-Ladies Be Seated.[3] The show where anything can happen, and usually does. The show where you get money for being funny. . . . And now, here's your master of mirth, that minstrel of merriment—Johnny Olsen!

Announcer turns and gestures upstage. APPLAUSE UP FULL AND SUSTAINED. FANFARE BRINGS HIM ON.

3. This of course was the true "Blue Network"—ABC radio.

VIDEO	AUDIO
#1 MS of upstage TAKE #1 entrance, taking in some audience. Catch Olsen as he enters and hugs one of the contestants. Olsen gives another hug . . . then goes to announcer and her.	**OLSEN** (He ad libs) **ANNOUNCER** (off) Hey, Johnny! **OLSEN** (making a take) Huh? . . . Oo ooooh!
#3 med. two-shot TAKE #3 Olsen & announcer.	**ANNOUNCER** Wait a minute, Johnny . . . Wait a minute! **OLSEN** Hah? . . . when I see those eyes, those lips, those nose? . . . **ANNOUNCER** But those audience! **OLSEN** (indicating studio audience) You mean all these people here? **ANNOUNCER** (indicating camera) I mean all those people there. **OLSEN** (peering into camera) I can't see 'em, Helen.[4] **ANNOUNCER** No, but they can see you, and I think it might be a good idea to say hello to them and start the show . . . Well, it's all yours, Johnny. (going off) See you later.

4. The announcer, Helen, was a rare instance of a female emcee. There had been a few in radio particularly during the war, but now TV was replacing them. "Penny," the girl whose last name was never revealed was, in fact, *Mrs.* Johnny Olsen.

VIDEO	AUDIO
Olsen comes in tighter.	**OLSEN** (Olsen ad libs opening. Gets in plug and introduces Penny.)
#1 MS of Penny TAKE #1 and first contestants. PAN with Penny and contestants.	APPLAUSE AS PENNY TAKES BOW. **OLSEN & PENNY** (Asks Penny if she has two service men for the first stunt. She brings them up.)
#3 tight-three shot. TAKE #3	**OLSEN & CONTESTANTS** (Olsen interviews them.)
READY #1 for MS of stunt.	1. DOUGHNUT ROUTINE: (Two men—six doughnuts hanging on strings. Contest to eat around holes without biting through.)
#1 MS of stunt. TAKE #1	MUSIC-Cancan from "Gaite Parisienne." START MUSIC ON OLSEN'S CUE - "Go."
#3 catch BCU's. READY #2 for pay-off.	MUSIC OUT ON OLSEN'S CUE—"The Winnah."
#2 PAN with contestants. TAKE #2	**OLSEN** (Pays off contestants. Calls for applause.) CHASER MUSIC AS THEY RETURN TO SEATS.

. . . . TIME (   ) . . . .

VIDEO	AUDIO
#1 MCU of Johnny. TAKE #1 Penny brings two women in.	**OLSEN & PENNY** (Olsen interviews two housewives brought up by Penny.)

VIDEO		AUDIO
#3 three-shot	TAKE #3	OLSEN & CONTESTANTS (He describes what they are to do. Calls for raincoats. The women put them on.)
READY #1 for stunt.		
READY #2 for audience reaction.		NO MUSIC DURING THIS STUNT.
#1 MS of stunt.	TAKE #1	2. BOAT ROUTINE: (Housewives get in canvas boat. Pans are tied to their heads and a little water poured in. They are given brooms and told to paddle as they sing "Row, Row, Row Your Boat." They are not supposed to spill the water as Johnny makes them go faster and faster. Olsen yells while an assistant is swinging a big bucket . . . he lets them have it. It turns out to be puffed rice. Pays off contestants. Calls for applause.)
#2 PAN with contestants	TAKE #2	CHASER MUSIC AS THEY RE-TURN TO SEATS.

. . . . TIME (   ) . . . .

VIDEO		AUDIO
#1 MS of Penny as she brings up lady.	TAKE #1	PENNY & LADY Johnny, I want you to meet a very lovely lady, etc. NO MUSIC DURING HEART-THROB.
#3 tight two-shot	TAKE #3	OLSEN & LADY 3. HEART-THROB: Olsen interviews mother with four sons in service. At the end she is given a bouquet of flowers.

VIDEO	AUDIO
Olsen comes in tighter.	**OLSEN** (Gets in short plug for next week and invites studio audience.)

. . . . TIME (   ) . . . .

#1 tight three-shot	TAKE #1	**OLSEN, PENNY & A WIFE** Gag interview with wife. The wife is asked if she will unveil a statue. MUSIC, "Pomp and Circumstance." START ON OLSEN'S CUE, "Bring on the Statue." **4. STATUE ROUTINE:** (Penny blindfolds wife and leads her upstage. The husband has been previously taken to dressing room and fixed up. Johnny comes to camera and tips off audience that the statue will be her husband. "Statue" is brought in swathed in sheets and pillowcase. Wife unveils "Statue" revealing husband in red flannels. Pay-off comes when blindfold is removed and she find it is her husband.)
#3 med. three-shot	TAKE #3	**OLSEN, PENNY & WIFE** (Pays off contestants. Calls for applause.)
#2 PAN with wife as she sits.	TAKE #2	CHASER MUSIC AS SHE RETURNS TO SEAT.

. . . . TIME (   ) . . . .

VIDEO		AUDIO
#3 tight four-shot	TAKE #3	**OLSEN** (Interviews three servicemen. Tells them they are to have privilege of dancing with the famous danseuse, Madame Lazonga.)

MUSIC - 1. WALTZ; 2. CONGA; 3. JITTERBUG.

DOLLY BACK #1
to catch dance.

<u>5. MADAME LAZONGA</u>:
(They are taken offstage and the "madame" is brought on. She is a life-size rubber dummy. The first serviceman dances a waltz with her; the second a conga; the third a jitter-bug number, during which the air escapes and Madame Lazonga collapses.)

<u>OLSEN</u>
(Pays off contestants. Calls for applause and says it is time for the finale by "the entire company.")

AUDIENCE STANDS AND SINGS
"You Are My Sunshine."

#3 MCU   TAKE #3
announcer.

ANNOUNCER
(after one chorus) SINGING IN BG.

READY #1 for CU of Olsen.

Well, time's up for tonight. Don't forget to sit down with us again next week at this same time for another program of LADIES BE SEATED. But, before signing off, a final word from Johnny Olsen.

#1 CU of Olsen.   TAKE #1

OLSEN (over singing)
(He gives closing commercial and concludes with) . . .

"And remember, you get money for being funny on LADIES BE SEATED."

VIDEO	AUDIO
DOLLY BACK #1 to take in audience.	MUSIC SIGNATURE UP FULL - (Third Chorus)
TITLE 4. LAP DISS This has been a presentation of the American Broadcasting Company.	
FADE OUT	FADE OUT MUSIC ON APPLAUSE.

NOTES

PROLOGUE

1. Max Wilk, *The Golden Age of Television*, (Mount Kisco, NY: Moyer Bell, 1989), p. 2, 3.

INTRODUCTION

1. Gilbert Seldes, *The Great Audience*, (New York: Viking Press, 1951), p. 105.
2. Hugh Downs interview.
3. Orrin E. Dunlap, Jr., *The Outlook for Television*, (New York: Harper Brothers, 1932), p. 212.

CHAPTER 1

1. George Everson, *The Story of Television*, (New York: W. W. Norton, 1949), p. 38, 39.
2. *Television*, TV documentary, 1988.
3. George Everson, *The Story of Television*, (New York: W. W. Norton, 1949), p. 63, 65.

4. ibid, p. 92.
5. ibid, p. 123.
6. ibid, p. 246.
7. ibid, p. 165.
8. ibid, p. 208.
9. ibid, p. 240.
10. ibid, p. 248.

CHAPTER 2

1. Joseph H. Udelson, *The Great Television Race*, (University, Alabama: University of Alabama Press, 1982), p. 26, 27.

2. C. Francis Jenkins, *Vision by Radio, Photographs and Photograms*, (Washington: Jenkins Laboratories, 1925), p. 25, 118.

3. Orrin E. Dunlap, Jr., *The Outlook for Television*, (New York: Harper Brothers, 1932), p. 68, 69, 70.

4. Quarterly Report for W3XK, September 30, 1930. Edited by G. E. Sterling.

5. ibid

6. *The Queen's Messenger* is reported in *New York Times*, (12 September, 1928), p. 1, 10; Radio News 10, no. 6 (December, 1928) and Television News 1, no. 4 (September-October, 1931), p. 315. Also Dunlap, ibid, p. 88, 89.

7. Gordon Ross, *Television Jubilee*, (London: W. H. Allen, 1961), p. 21.

8. Script *CBS Television Inaugural Broadcast*, 21 July, 1931.

9. Sally Bedell Smith, *In All His Glory*, (New York: Simon and Schuster, 1990), p. 186.

10. Gordon Ross, *Television Jubilee*, (London: W. H. Allen, 1961), p. 14.

11. Orrin E. Dunlap, Jr., *The Outlook for Television*, (New York: Harper Brothers, 1932), p. 81.

12. Orrin E. Dunlap, Jr., *The Outlook for Television*, (New York: Harper Brothers, 1932), p. 82.

13. Gordon Ross, *Television Jubilee*, (London: W. H. Allen, 1961), p. 26.

14. ibid, p. 28.

15. ibid, p. 36.

16. *The Billboard*, 3 December, 1932, p. 15.

17. "20th Anniversary of CBS Television," CBS Press Information, 10 July, 1951, p. 5.

CHAPTER 3

1. "The Museum of Television and Radio." April, 1991 pamphlet, p. 22.

2. Tom Lewis, *Empire of the Air*, (New York: HarperCollins, 1991), p. 326.

CHAPTER 4

1. Dinah Shore interview.

2. ibid

3. ibid

4. ibid

5. ibid

6. ibid

7. Arthur Hungerford interview.

8. Eddie Albert interview. Also: *The Billboard*, 14 November, 1936, p. 6.

9. Arthur Hungerford interview.

10. ibid

11. ibid

12. ibid

13. *The New York Times*, 8 June, 1938, p. 29.

14. "Susan and God" audio tape of telecast, W2XBS, 3 June, 1938, Museum of Broadcasting, New York City.

15. Arthur Hungerford interview.

16. ibid

17. ibid

CHAPTER 5

1. Cohen, Heller, Chwast, *Trylon and Perisphere*, (New York: Harry N. Abrams, 1989).

2. Tom Lewis, *Empire of the Air*, (New York: HarperCollins, 1991), p. 275.

3. *The New Yorker*, May 27, 1939, "The Talk of the Town."

4. Hugh Downs interview.

5. Dinah Shore interview.

6. Betty Furness interview.

7. Burke Crotty interview.

CHAPTER 6

1. Dennis James interview.

2. Thomas A. DeLong, *Quiz Craze*, (New York: Praeger, 1991), p. 52.

3. Mike Stokey interview.

CHAPTER 7

1. Gordon Ross, *Television Jubilee*, (London: W. H. Allen, 1961), p. 31, 32.

2. Richard Hubbell, *Television, Programming and Production*, (New York: Holt, Rinehart & Co., 1945), p. 185, 186.

3. Richard Hubbell, ibid, p. 199.

4. Richard Hubbell, ibid, p. 194.

5. Gordon Ross, ibid, p. 58, 59.

CHAPTER 8

1. William Hawes, *American Television Drama*, (Alabama: University of Alabama Press, 1986), p. 124, 125.

2. Mike Stokey interview.

3. William Hawes, ibid, p. 126, 127.

4. Franklin Lacey interview.

5. Hawes, ibid, p. 128, 129.

6. "KTLA 40th Anniversary Show," 1987.

7. Mike Stokey interview.

8. "KTTV 35th Anniversary Show," 1992.

CHAPTER 9

1. Joseph H. Udelson, *The Great Television Race*, (University, Alabama: University of Alabama Press, 1982), p. 74.

2. ibid, p. 67, 68.

3. William Parker, oral history, Broadcast Pioneers Museum.

4. Max Wilk, *The Golden Age of Television*, (New York: Moyer Bell, 1989), p. 230.

5. Hugh Downs interview.

6. ibid

7. ibid

8. ibid

9. ibid

CHAPTER 10

1. Thomas Lyne Riley, "The Television Director" in Porterfield and Reynolds, eds., *We Present Television*, (New York: W. W. Norton, 1940), p. 169-172.

2. Norman Lloyd interview.

3. ibid

4. ibid

CHAPTER 11

1. Noran Kersta interview.

2. ibid

3. Arthur Hungerford interview.

4. Judy Dupuy, *Television Show Business*, (Schenectady: General Electric), 1944.

CHAPTER 12

1. Richard Hubbell, *Television, Programming and Production*, (New York: Holt, Rinehart & Co., 1945), p. 130, 131.

2. Judy Dupuy, ibid.

3. David Schoenbrun, *On and Off the Air*, (New York: E. P. Dutton, 1989), p. 45.

4. ibid, p. 48, 49.

5. ibid

6. Stanley Kaufman interview.

7. David Schoenbrun ibid, p. 49.

8. David Schoenbrun ibid, p. 55.

9. Stan Chambers interview.

CHAPTER 13

1. *The New Yorker*, May 27, 1939.

2. ibid

3. Harry Coyle interview.

4. Florence Monroe interview.

5. Harry Coyle interview.

6. ibid

7. Dennis James interview.

8. Harry Coyle interview.

9. ibid

CHAPTER 14

1. Lee De Forest, *Television Today and Tomorrow*, (New York: Dial Press, 1942), p. 293, 294.

2. *New York Times*, 26 May, 1946, p. 7:1.

3. Televiser 4, (January-February 1947) :34.

4. Dennis James interview.

5. Betty Furness interview.

6. Florence Monroe interview.

CHAPTER 15

Most of the material in this chapter is adapted from General Electric's own publicity pamphlet by Judy Dupuy, published in 1949.

The other source is *Televiser 2*, (Summer, 1945) with an article "2-Year Log of Outstanding WRGB Programs."

CHAPTER 16

1. *Television 3*, October, 1946: 12.

2. Stephen Davis, *Say Kids! What Time is It?*, (Boston: Little Brown, 1987), p. 25

3. Noran Kersta interview.

4. ibid

CHAPTER 17

1. The material for this chapter is adapted from Worthington D. Miner's "A Report for the Columbia Broadcasting System on Twelve Years of Television," (1942) and *Worthington Miner Interviewed by J. Schaffner*, (Metuchan, NJ: Scarecrow Press, 1985).

2. Sally Bedell Smith, *In All His Glory*, (New York, Simon and Schuster, 1990), p. 269.

3. ibid

CHAPTER 18

1. The material for this chapter is adapted from original French sources:

Pierre Sabbagh, *Histoire de la Television Francaise*, (Paris: Editions Fernand-Nathan, 1982).

Pierre Miguel, *Histoire de la Radio et de la Television*, (Paris: Librairie Academique Perrin, 1972).

Henri Spade, *Histoire d'Armour de la Television Francaise*, (Paris: Editions France-Empire, 1968).

The author is indebted to Chip Kaplan for his editorial assistance on this chapter.

CHAPTER 19

1. The source material for this chapter was a biography of James C. Petrillo, *The Musicians and Petrillo*, (Leiter, Robert D., New York: Octagon Books, 1974).

CHAPTER 20

1. The source material for this chapter was an interview with Florence Monroe.

CHAPTER 21

1. *Worthington Miner Interviewed by J. Schaffner*, (Metuchan, NJ: Scarecrow Press, 1985).

2. William C. Eddy, *Television, the Eyes of Tomorrow*, (New York: Prentice Hall, 1945), p. 305.

3. William C. Eddy ibid, p. 306.

4. Florence Monroe interview.

CHAPTER 22

1. Eddie Kean, "It's Howdy Doody Time," written by Eddie Kean. Stephen Davis, *Say Kids! What Time is It?*, (Boston: Little Brown, 1987), p. 37.

EPILOGUE

1. Sally Bedell Smith, ibid, p. 605

BIBLIOGRAPHY

ABRAMSON, ALBERT. *The History of Television: 1880-1941*. North Carolina and London: McFarland & Co., 1987.

ALLAN, DOUG. *How to Write for Television*. New York: E. P. Dutton, 1946.

BARNOW, ERIK. *The Golden Web*. New York: Oxford University Press, 1968.

BETTINGER, HOYLAND. *Television Techniques*. New York & London: Harper Brothers, 1947.

DAVIS, STEPHEN. *Say Kids! What Time Is It?* Boston: Little, Brown & Co., 1987.

DE FOREST, LEE. *Television Today and Tomorrow*. New York: Dial Press, 1942.

DELONG, THOMAS A. *Quiz Craze*. New York, Westport, CT, London: Praeger, 1991.

DOWNS, HUGH. *Yours Truly . . . Hugh Downs*. New York: Holt, Rinehart & Wilson, 1960.

DUNLAP, ORRIN E., JR. *The Future of Television*. New York & London: Harper Brothers, 1942, 1947.

———. *Outlook for Television*. New York & London: Harper & Brothers, 1932.

DUPUY, JUDY. *Television Show Business*, General Electric, 1944.

EDDY, WILLIAM C. *Television: The Eyes of Tomorrow*. New York: Prentice-Hall, 1945.

EVERSON, GEORGE. *The Story of Television: The Life of Philo T. Farnsworth*. New York: W. W. Norton, 1949.

GLUT, DONALD F. and JIM HARMON. *The Great Television Heroes*. New York: Doubleday, 1975.

GREENFIELD, JEFF. *Television: The First Fifty Years*. New York: Harry N. Abrams, 1977.

HAWES, WILLIAM. *American Television Drama*. Alabama: University of Alabama Press, 1986.

HAY, PETER. *Canned Laughter*. New York & Oxford: Oxford University Press, 1992.

HUBBELL, RICHARD W. *4000 Years of Television - The Story of Seeing at a Distance*. New York: Putnam's, 1942.

———. *Television Programming and Production - Third Edition*. New York & Toronto: Rinehart & Co., Inc., 1945.

HUTCHINSON, THOMAS H. *Here Is Television, Your Window to the World*. New York: Hastings House, 1950, revised edition.

JOHNSON, WILLIAM O., JR. *Super Spectator and the Electric Lilliputians*. New York: Wallace Literary Agency, 1976.

JONES, EVAN. *Epicurean Delight: The Life and Times of James Beard*. New York: Alfred A. Knopf, 1990.

KEMPNER, STANLEY. *History of Television: Scientific Background*. Atlanta, GA: Television Encyclopedia Press, 1965.

LEE, ROBERT E. *Television: The Revolution*. New York: Essential Books, 1944.

LEITER, ROBERT D. *The Musicians And Petrillo*. New York: Octagon Books, 1974.

LEWIS, TOM. *Empire Of The Air: The Men Who Made Radio*. New York: HarperCollins Publishers, 1991.

MACGOWAN, KENNETH. *Behind The Screen: The History and Techniques of the Motion Picture*. New York: Delacorte, 1965.

MIGUEL, PIERRE. *Histoire de la Radio et de la Television*. Paris: Librairie Academique Perrin, 1972.

1946 American Television Directory. New York: American Television Society, Inc., 1946.

PARKER, FRANCINE. *Stages: Norman Lloyd*. Metuchen, N.J. & London: The Director's Guild of America and The Scarecrow Press, 1990.

PORTERFIELD, JOHN and KAY REYNOLDS. *We Present Television*. New York: W. W. Norton, 1940.

ROSS, GORDON. *Television Jubilee - The Story of 25 Years of BBC Television*. London: W. H. Allen, 1961.

SABBAGH, PIERRE. *Histoire de la Television Francaise*. Paris: Editions Fernand-Nathan, 1982.

SANDERS, MARLENE and MARCIA ROCK. *Waiting for Prime-Time*. New York: Harper & Row, 1990, revised edition.

SCHAFFNER, FRANKLIN J. *Worthington Miner*. Metuchen, N.J. & London: The Director's Guild of America and The Scarecrow Press, 1985.

SMITH, BUFFALO BOB and DONNA MCCROHAN. *Howdy and Me*. New York: Penguin Books, 1990.

SPOSA, LOUIS A. *Television Primer of Production and Direction*. New York & London: McGraw-Hill Book Co., Inc., 1947.

STERLING, CHRISTOPHER H. and JOHN M. KITTROS. *Stay Tuned: A Concise History of American Broadcasting*. California: Wadsworth, 1978.

Television Volume III (1938-1941). Princeton, NJ: 1947.

UDELSON, JOSEPH H. *The Great Television Race*. Alabama: University of Alabama Press, 1982.

WILK, MAX. *The Golden Age of Television*. New York: Moyer Bell Limited, 1989.

WINSHIP, MICHAEL. *Television*. New York & Canada: Random House, 1988.

ACKNOWLEDGMENTS

This book would not have been possible without dozens of broadcast pioneers who agreed to be interviewed, including Betty Furness, Hugh Downs, Dinah Shore, Eddie Albert, Nick Kersta, Harry Coyle, Art Hungerford, Florence Monroe, Dennis James, Mike Stokey, Stanley Kauffman, Ted Bergman, Norman Lloyd, Gary Simpson, and Stan Chambers.

Oral histories and memoirs were a big help particularly those of Red Barber, Ted Husing, Bob Kesshan, Worthington Miner, Lenox Lohr, William Paley, Lee De Forest, Richard Hubbell, David Schoenbrun, Doug Allan, Marla Lewis, Gilbert Seldes, William Fineshriber, and Ernst Alexanderson.

Contemporary articles and books by the pioneers themselves were invaluable and are listed in the bibliography. These include works by David Sarnoff, Philo Farnsworth, Lee De Forest, William Eddy, and Lou Sposa.

In addition, I received great help from the University of California - Los Angeles library, the Broadcast Pioneers Association (Catherine Heinz, director), the David Sarnoff Research Center, as well as the photo collections of NBC, BBC, the Hall of History, and KTLA, Los Angeles.

For primary source material covering the big moments of the first decade of television, I am indebted to the *New York Times*, *Chicago Daily News*, *Los Angeles Times*, *The New Yorker*, *Billboard*, and *Variety*.

For smoothing down the path of research, thanks to authors William Hawes, William Eddy, Judy Dupuy, Eugene Lyons, Joseph Udelson, George Everson, Erik Barnow, Ira Flaton, Thomas A. Delong, Asa Briggs, and especially Pilar Viladas.

I could never have even started writing this book if it hadn't been for the encouragement of Ed Victor, as well as my wife, Jimmie. I would never have finished it without the tireless assistance of Kathleen Callahan. Finally, I would never have developed an interest in the subject if it hadn't been for my first employer, Robert Saudek, producer of *Omnibus*, himself a great broadcasting pioneer.

INDEX

About The Author

Michael Ritchie is a film director whose work
includes *The Candidate, Downhill Racer, Fletch,
The Bad News Bears, Semi-Tough, The Positively True
Adventures of the Alleged Texas Cheerleader-Murdering
Mom* for HBO, and *The Fantasticks*.
He is a member of the Creative Counsel of the
Museum of Television and Radio.